SACRAMENTO PUBLIC LIBRARY

D0469448

THE
FIRE SMART
HOME HANDBOOK

WITHDRAWN
FROM COLLECTION

ALSO BY CLYDE SOLES

Climbing: Training for Peak Performance
Climbing: Expedition Planning
Rock & Ice Gear: Equipment for the Vertical World
The Outdoor Knots Book
Land Navigation Handbook
Backpacking Basics
Outdoor Knots
Knots for Climbers
A Positive Occurrence in the Countryside

THE
FIRE SMART
HOME HANDBOOK

Preparing for and Surviving the Threat of Wildfire

CLYDE SOLES

Foreword by Molly Mowery

LYONS PRESS
Guilford, Connecticut
An imprint of Globe Pequot Press

For Cindy.

This book exists because of my lovely, adventurous wife, Cindy. In the past three years, we have gone through two major natural disasters: eight days of evacuation for fire and five days of entrapment by flood. Together we have learned a lot about dealing with the stress of situations beyond our control and the frustration that comes with recovery.

To buy books in quantity for corporate use or incentives, call **(800) 962-0973** or e-mail **premiums@GlobePequot.com.**

Copyright © 2014 by Clyde Soles

All rights reserved. No part of this book may be reproduced or transmitted in any form by any means, electronic or mechanical, including photocopying and recording, or by any information storage and retrieval system, except as may be expressly permitted in writing from the publisher. Requests for permission should be addressed to Globe Pequot Press, Attn: Rights and Permissions Department, PO Box 480, Guilford, CT 06437.

Lyons Press is an imprint of Globe Pequot Press.

All photos by the author unless otherwise indicated.
Illustration on p. 42 by Robert L. Prince.

Project Editor: Lauren Brancato
Layout Artist: Melissa Evarts
Text Design: Sheryl P. Kober

Library of Congress Cataloging-in-Publication data is available on file.

ISBN 978-0-7627-9690-8

Printed in the United States of America

10 9 8 7 6 5 4 3 2 1

The author and Globe Pequot Press assume no liability for accidents happening to, or injuries sustained by, readers who engage in the activities described in this book. Wildfire mitigation requires using dangerous tools in difficult terrain. You can get seriously injured or killed. Approach each task with extreme caution. We recommend that, with any piece of machinery, you read all manuals and instructions carefully and completely before attempting to operate it.

AUTHOR'S NOTE

Since 1910, when seventy-two firefighters died in the Big Burn, ten other wildfires have taken place in which ten or more perished. Most recently fourteen died on Storm King in 1994, and nineteen at Yarnell in 2013. Every year, around a dozen other wildland firefighters are killed in the United States.

These men and women who are literally on the fire line, as well as the cadre behind them, deserve our support. We can do that by making our properties safer. We can also pressure the local, state, and federal governments for increased funding for our firefighters, and we can contribute to the fallen through the Wildland Firefighters Association (wffoundation.org).

CONTENTS

FOREWORD

The wildfire profession is full of what I call "insider baseball" terms: ladder fuels, defensible space, crown fire, home ignition zone, fire-resistant, fuel management, initial attack, fire adapted, spotting, and firestorms. Not only that, but we have mastered using this jargon to tell people what to do to reduce wildfire risk to themselves, their families, their property, and their communities. We've created an abundance of toolkits, PSAs, videos, and other awareness campaigns to help solve the ever-growing threat of wildfire hazard to communities around the country.

So when Clyde Soles asked me to review *The Fire Smart Home Handbook*, I was curious to see how his book might offer something not already covered by other publications—and I was more than pleasantly surprised!

This book offers far more than the average pamphlet or brochure. Clyde expertly takes his personal experiences as a homeowner living through multiple wildfire events and combines them with his background as a professional gear reviewer. The result is a tremendously useful and successful guide that offers more than you ever thought you could know about preparing your family and property for the next wildfire.

The biggest game changer with this handbook is that it provides a detailed and comprehensive approach on how to get the wildfire mitigation done. We all know what people should do, yet we rarely focus efforts on explaining to homeowners the different considerations and decisions they will encounter when confronted with efficiently and safely preparing for the next wildfire.

The 2012 Flagstaff Fire, west of Boulder, Colorado

This book takes it to that next level of understanding and practical advice, embracing the "do-it-yourself" spirit of the West with a clear sense of stewardship and responsibility. Topics range from providing an exhaustive list of tools that the homeowner can choose from to do proper tree trimming and landscaping, sharing insights on the importance of evacuation lists and who should be involved in writing them, rethinking the false sense of security with a fire safe, and handling worst-case scenarios—which should provide all the more incentive to prepare!

Taking ownership of the problem also has many rewards for the homeowner: developing a sense of connection to one's land and property, increasing the natural aesthetics, improving habitat and forest health, reducing unwanted critters near the home, building a sense of community with neighbors, and having peace of mind the next time smoke appears on the horizon.

Not only is this book helpful to homeowners living in the wildland-urban interface, but practitioners would also do well to read its contents. Clyde has sprinkled in interesting tidbits (for instance, do you know the difference between hot and cold lightning?), and he offers that rare perspective of how homeowners think, act, and prepare. As each step is broken down throughout the book, we are reminded it's far more effective to keep actions simple, including repeating the mantra, "Fire doesn't care."

My experience working with communities throughout the United States and internationally tells me that, regardless of the terms we use, the emphasis has always been and should always be focused on taking action to reduce risk. Whether risk reduction is through an established program, a behavior-changing model, rigorous codes, or plans, it is essential to provide a hands-on approach such as that offered in *The Fire Smart Home Handbook*. Hopefully the first action you'll be inspired to take after reading this book is a trip to the local hardware store or dusting off some tools in the shed.

Molly Mowery
president and owner, Wildfire Planning International

former program manager, Fire Adapted Communities & International Outreach, Wildland Fire Operations Division, National Fire Protection Association

INTRODUCTION

The Fire Smart Home Handbook is a practical guide for homeowners in the Red Zone—the mix of ecosystems and housing where there is a high risk of wildfire. If you live in the Wildland Urban Interface (WUI, pronounced woo-ee), sooner or later fire will happen. Given this reality, it is wise to prepare for the inevitable.

In the past two decades, fires have become much bigger. In the Lower 48 states, the average total number of acres burned has increased well over threefold—from about 2 million acres in 1992 to nearly 7 million in 2012—and 2012 ranks third for most land burned with a total of 9.1 million acres, closely trailing 2006 with 9.9 million and 2007 with 9.3 million.

Although the amount of land burned annually has been increasing, the average number of fires has actually decreased slightly, from about 78,000 fires in 1992 to about 76,000 in 2012. But during that same time period, the average size of each fire grew from about 20 acres to about 95. The year 2012 set a record with an average of 165 acres burned per fire.

We can't blame all of those intense fires entirely on global warming, though it does constitute a factor. During the past two decades, the federal budget for fire suppression has been slashed severely. Ironically, the cost of putting out huge fires gobbles up the funds once dedicated for mitigation projects. The number of (antiquated) air tankers decreased from forty-four in 2002 to ten in 2013, making fast attack on fledgling fires even more difficult.

As the fires become larger and more people move into areas susceptible to them, the number of homes destroyed will also increase. A 2012 study showed that California has almost 300,000 homes worth a total of $60 billion at either high or very high risk of wildfire. In those same two categories, Texas has over 200,000 homes valued at $30 billion, and Colorado has roughly 100,000 homes worth the same amount.

Fortunately, there are many simple steps that we as homeowners and communities can take to increase the odds of surviving a catastrophic wildfire. Fire mitigation doesn't have to cost a fortune if we're willing to do the work, and it can both enhance the scenery and potentially increase the value of your home.

This book derives from my experience caring for 35 acres of forest in the Colorado Front Range. Having worked on the land for the past seven years, I have learned a great deal about what to do—and what not to do—when preparing for wildfire. Our home above Boulder, Colorado, is situated in a mix of ponderosa pine, Douglas fir, and grasslands. I've felled hundreds of trees from tiny saplings to one giant that towered over 150 feet tall.

I have also had two too-close-for-comfort encounters with wildfire. Until you've felt the initial gut-wrenching moment of realization, followed by a frantic what-do-we-do-now sensation, it's hard to comprehend the frustration and helplessness that a major fire can arouse.

My first experience came on June 27, 1990, while attending graduate school in Santa Barbara, California. After days of brutal heat and during one of the region's powerful Santa Ana windstorms, an arsonist started the Painted Cave Fire. In just over four hours, 5,000 acres went up in flames as the fire roared down the mountain and jumped eight lanes of highway. The smoke blew so thick that I couldn't see the other side of our street. One woman died, and 440 houses and 28 apartment buildings were destroyed. The arsonist didn't go to jail due to a lack of evidence, but a jury ordered him to pay $2.75 million for his stupidity.

Two decades later, on September 6, 2010, my wife and I boarded a plane on the East Coast to return home to Colorado. On Facebook, a friend posted a photo of a smoke plume behind our house and described high winds. At the same time, my wife's phone rang as one of her friends called to warn us of what became known as the Fourmile Canyon Fire. As the flight attendant was closing the cabin door and giving us the evil eye about using our phones, my wife had just enough time to call another friend to rescue our cats.

It was a long and worrisome flight home. Halfway across Kansas, we spotted the smoke plume. As we were driving back from the airport, it loomed ominously overhead. We talked our way through the first roadblock and got to the base of a hill, just 2 miles from our house, when a fire truck coming toward us blocked our way. "Get out *now!*" the driver yelled. We could hear the fear in his voice and didn't argue.

Six days passed before we could return. On two occasions, we had reason to believe that we'd never see our house again. As it turns out, the fire roared within half a mile of our home, which suffered extensive smoke damage. But we got off easy compared to the 169 families who lost their homes. At the time, Fourmile was the worst fire in Colorado history, but recent years have proved even worse, with the 2012 Waldo Canyon Fire consuming 346 homes and the 2013 Black Forest Fire claiming 486 homes.

The goal of this book is to help you prepare for wildfire and to save you time and money along the way. No one can guarantee that your house or land will escape unscathed if a major conflagration erupts— but you can greatly improve your odds with a little preparation.

THE
FIRE SMART
HOME HANDBOOK

WILDFIRE

The number of homes built in Red Zones, regions at high risk of wildfire, has skyrocketed. Fire prevention has suppressed these areas from the natural cycle of burn and return for over a century, allowing latent fuels to increase. At the same time, we face a warming climate, which means bigger, more intense fires. We're already seeing the results of these combined causes. Almost like a switch was flipped in the mid-1980s, the frequency of fires in the West has jumped more than 300 percent and the average number of acres burned has increased by 500 percent.

To prepare for fire, it helps to have a good understanding of how wildlands burn. Despite media hysteria about "walls of flames consuming houses" or "houses bursting into flames," that is rarely what happens. Learning about the true nature of fire is the first step in protecting your home.

BASICS OF WILDLAND FIRE

For a fire to start and continue, three components are required: heat, fuel, and oxygen. Fires move fastest in the direction of the most abundant supply of all those elements, known as the "fire triangle." Remove or significantly reduce any one of those components, and the triangle collapses and the fire will go out. Wildland firefighters must manage heat and fuel.

Heat
A heat source is needed to spark a fire. Nationwide, humans cause the vast majority of wildfires; most arise from accidents such as

unattended campfires, sparks from equipment, discarded cigarettes, and power line arcs. But in some regions, lightning can start around half of the number of wildfires.

For lightning to start a fire, something called continuing current—found in all positive discharges (5 percent of all strikes) and 20 percent of negative strikes—must be present. This "hot lightning" lasts only a tenth of a second longer than "cold lightning" (the temperature is actually the same, around 50,000°F), but it's the duration of heat that sets things ablaze.

In the western United States, "dry lightning" is common—that is, all the energy transference without the rain. Sometimes the rain evaporates before it hits the ground, known as virga or high-base moisture; other times the lightning reaches out from a storm into an area not getting drenched. Either one presents a bad scenario because each has a nasty spark but no moisture to dampen things down.

In many cases, the true catalyst of the fire occurred long before the wildfire erupted. For example, the third and fourth most destructive fires in Colorado history smoldered for days before winds got them started. The Fourmile Canyon Fire resulted from an improperly doused fire pit used four days earlier, and the High Park Fire began with a lightning strike on Wednesday evening that smoldered until winds kicked up on Saturday.

Once the initial heat source ignites the fuel, wildfire spreads in two phases. At first, convection from surface fuels carries the fire upward to aerial fuels such as tree branches. As the size and intensity of the burn grows, radiation preheats surrounding fuels, and the fire spreads laterally. In some cases, the fire gets so hot that the radiant heat can ignite fuels before the core flame even reaches them.

Hot weather exacerbates fire because fuels prove easier to ignite and burn. This is why fires often rage in the afternoon—the hottest and driest part of the day. Fires tend to die down at night when the atmosphere cools and humidity increases.

The Fourmile Canyon Fire looms above Boulder, Colorado.

As you know from standing around a campfire, increasing your distance from the flames will decrease the heat. This is why it's so important to remove big flammable objects from near your home. Doing so decreases the chance for radiant heat to ignite the structure. Firefighters cool a fire with water, but spraying your yard or home in advance of a fire has only a minimal effect due to the drying force of the radiant heat.

Fuel

The type, quantity, vertical arrangement, and moisture content of fuel present major factors as to how quickly a fire will spread. This is where you, the homeowner, can alter the course of a fire.

Small, flashy fuels—dry grass, pine needles, twigs, etc.—are the tinder you use to start a campfire because they ignite easily and burn fast. Medium-size fuels—branches, small trees, and bushes—are the kindling that turns a low-intensity fire into a major event. Heavy fuels—thick branches, logs, tree trunks—have a lower ratio of surface area to volume, so they need more time to heat up before they will burn.

It may not be possible to remove all the small fuels, often called fine or light fuels, around your house, and it may not be practical to remove the heavy or coarse fuels. But removing the kindling in the area around you can greatly improve your situation.

The more fuel available, the hotter a fire will burn, which in turn helps it spread faster. In forests, the fuel load is measured by tons per acre of flammable material. Decades of fire suppression can allow the fuel load to increase to 50-plus tons/acre. After mitigation, that fuel load should measure less than 10 tons/acre. Many communities in fire-prone areas have collection areas where homeowners can drop off wood and brush collected from their property.

In housing developments built in the Red Zone, however, the fuel load unfortunately includes all the houses and cars next to yours. When entire neighborhoods burn, nearby trees often remain unscathed because houses set other houses on fire. While you can't change that situation, you can take steps to increase your own home's chance of survival.

A surface fire on a forest floor usually has flames only 3 or 4 feet high (though their length may reach several times that measurement) and reaches temperatures around 1,500°F. When a forest contains a lot of mixed-age trees, saplings are often growing next to giants. These small trees act as ladders and allow a surface fire to climb into the canopy, creating a dreaded active crown fire. Once the fire reaches the treetops, flames can exceed 165 feet and temperatures may peak at around 2,400°F.

These dramatic differences between a surface fire and a crown fire are why it's so important to eliminate ladder fuels when doing your mitigation. When you look at the land around your house with the dispassionate eye of forest fire, you'll start to see it differently.

As you survey the firescape, keep in mind that dead fuels include all the lifeless twigs and branches still on the trees. Also keep in mind that because they're elevated, they dry out even faster than surface fuels. Cleaning out the canopy can help reduce the intensity of a crown fire.

Oxygen

Limiting the supply of oxygen is impossible on a large scale. However, a shovel of dirt proves quite effective at smothering embers. In a confined space, CO_2 fire extinguishers can displace oxygen long enough to suppress small fires.

WILDFIRE CAUSES

The more people that live in a region, the more arson or accidents will start forest fires. Nearly all fires started by humans occur in relatively accessible areas, which also makes them somewhat easier to extinguish, whereas lightning can strike far from any road.

When lightning strikes a dead tree, it often explodes and can send a shower of embers; without rain, embers from an exploded tree often turn into a fire right away. However, the water in a live tree conducts the electricity to the ground, and the roots may smolder for days until wind stokes a fire.

From 2001 through 2010, lightning caused an average of only 15 percent of the forest fires in the United States; the rest were manmade. But over that same time period, lightning-caused fires burned an average of 61 percent of acreage consumed. In other words, humans started 85 percent of the fires, but those fires burned only 40 percent of the land affected by fires.

Power lines start fires when a tree branch comes in contact with the wires or a falling tree lands on them. Four of the twenty largest fires in California resulted from power lines and burned over 600,000 acres. Power lines also sparked the second-largest fire in New Mexico and the most destructive fire in Texas, both in 2011. These fires often result in huge settlements from power companies and their contractors, but that doesn't help you as a homeowner much.

Animals start a surprising number of fires as well. Instigators include birds landing on power lines, birds dropping fish on transformers, beavers felling trees onto power lines, bears and bobcats climbing power poles, a bull pushing over a power pole while scratching an itch, mice chewing on electrical cables, and in one remarkable instance, a squirrel storing food inside the engine of a truck.

Back in the human column, though, many fires result from carelessness like escaped agricultural burns, poorly extinguished campfires, and car mufflers or power tools igniting grass. When this happens, frequently only a few acres burn because somebody calls the fire department right away and they suppress the blaze fairly quickly. Unmitigated stupidity causes an alarming number of fires, however. This ever-growing category includes wedding parties that send candle lanterns aloft into the sky—pretty, yes, until they set something on fire. The third-largest fire in California history, the 2013 Rim Fire near Yosemite, was started by a hunter's illegal campfire that spread out of control, consuming 400 square miles.

Some imbeciles go target shooting using exploding targets, which looks great on TV shows but is really dumb in dry grassland or forest. The 2012 Sunflower Fire in Arizona burned 18,000 acres after a man fired an incendiary shotgun shell into brush. Shooting at exploding targets has caused at least sixteen fires in the Rocky Mountain West, including the 2012 Springer Fire in Colorado that burned 1,100 acres.

Occasionally, a prescribed fire escapes its boundaries and erupts into a major conflagration. The 2000 Cerro Grande Fire, which burned 48,000 acres and 235 homes in Los Alamos, New Mexico, started as a controlled burn in Bandolier National Monument. The 2010 Davis Fire grew from a 537-acre prescribed fire in Montana's Helena National Forest into a 2,000-acre fire. The 2012 Lower North Fork Fire, which burned over 4,000 acres, destroyed twenty-three homes, and killed three people, was started by "slop over" from a Colorado State Forest Service controlled burn.

While these escaped fires are tragic, they are the rare exceptions. In 2012 more than 16,600 prescribed fires across the country burned almost 2 million acres of land, yet only 14 fires in 11 states escaped their boundaries, burning between 3.5 and 21,000 additional acres. That Lower North Fork Fire could have been prevented with better weather forecasting and monitoring. Yet a controlled burn in Utah escaped nearly three weeks after the initial fire.

Sadly, arson has caused some of the biggest fires in recent years. Some firefighters or their family members have started fires to generate work ("job fires") or were overly fascinated by fire. In California, roughly 10 percent of wildfires start as arson.

Raymond Oyler, the arsonist behind the 2006 Esperanza Fire in Southern California, which killed five firefighters, became the first person in the United States to receive the death penalty for a wildfire. The 2003 Old Fire, also in Southern California, scorched 90,000 acres and destroyed 1,000 buildings, and five people died of heart attacks. After a lengthy trial in 2012, a jury found the arsonist guilty and sentenced him to death.

FIRE BEHAVIOR

There are three basic types of wildland fire: ground, surface, and crown. Ground fires creep along in the duff (ground litter of dead needles) and roots, consuming all the organic matter. Most common in extreme drought, ground fires may even kill large trees because of the long period of high temperature. They can also sterilize soil and increase water runoff, raising the chances of flash flooding.

Surface fires are the most common and, for our purposes, desirable. These burn leaves, downed branches, and low vegetation without penetrating the soil because they tend to move fast. Even a very hot fire won't raise soil temperature significantly if it passes through quickly. Small trees may burn, but large trees often survive as the fire rushes through. Occasionally a tree or clump of trees burns, called a passive crown fire, but these are isolated incidents.

When the entire canopy of a forest blazes, you have an active crown fire—and a real problem. These fires leave little behind because the intense heat burns down to mineral soil like a ground fire.

To a certain degree, surface fires behave in fairly predictable ways. Experts can often calculate where the fire will burn and how fast it will travel. With this data, firefighters can anticipate what will happen in the next hours and days.

In general, fires spread out along the surface as broad ovals with different rates of growth. The heading fire moves fastest and with the greatest intensity as it burns downwind or up a slope. The backing fire moves slowest with much less intensity as it goes upwind or downslope. Flanking fires form the long sides of the oval and travel at intermediate speeds. Often fingers will shoot out, and islands inside a fire will remain that don't burn right away.

A firefighter mops up after a surface fire.

Of particular concern, a wind-driven fire can produce a shower of millions of firebrands, glowing embers lifted into the air that create countless spot fires. It's these firebrands that destroy most homes, not the wall of flames.

An analysis of the 2012 Waldo Canyon Fire in Colorado Springs showed that 54 percent of the homes lost were due to firebrands, and direct contact with flames destroyed only 8 percent. Another 22 percent of the homes were lost due to trees and bushes next to the homes igniting, usually because of firebrands, and then setting the building on fire. The remaining 16 percent of houses were lost when the home next door caught fire first and the radiant heat set the neighboring building ablaze.

Wind

Anyone living in Southern California or the Front Range of Colorado is familiar with heinous downslope winds. These routinely reach speeds of 60 mph and on occasion gust to well over 100 mph.

If a fire ignites during one of these wind events, it sends out firebrands hundreds of yards in advance of the flames. Those firebrands create countless spot fires that then merge with the main fire and form a new fire front. In extreme cases, like the 2007 Guejito Fire outside San Diego and the 2011 Wallow Fire in Arizona, embers ignited fires 3 miles ahead of the flames. Reports from Australia tell of firebrands traveling over 10 miles.

After the devastating 2011 Bastrop Fire in Texas that burned nearly 1,700 homes, a researcher collected trampolines that survived. On just one trampoline, he counted 250 burn holes in 1 square meter of fabric. When thousands of firebrands are pelting your property, it needs strong defenses to survive.

If you live in an area where downslope winds are routine, you have a pretty good idea of where the fire will be coming from. If you sense even a hint of smoke during one of those windstorms, pack your bags and get out!

But you also need to anticipate upslope winds on clear days. As the sun heats the ground, warm air rises. This natural phenomena means that, excepting a major weather system, fires often burn upward. Upslope winds usually range from 5 to 10 mph, though the longer and steeper a slope, the stronger the wind.

This diurnal wind effect works in reverse at night. As shade covers a slope, the ground temperature drops quickly, and a slight downslope wind results. Though typically only about 2 to 3 mph, that's still strong enough to push smoke down and out. The downslope wind is why, if you're near a mountainous wildfire, it's common to get strong whiffs of smoke in the middle of the night even if the fire is burning far in the distance.

Drought

If you've ever tried to start a campfire with green wood, you know it's no small task. The moisture content of living plants is normally around 125 percent to 200 percent of their desiccated mass, but in prolonged drought that can drop below 100 percent, making them much easier to ignite.

A rainstorm has little immediate effect on the moisture content of living plants. However, dead fuels do respond to changes in humidity based on their size. Small-diameter fuels, like brown grasses and pine needles, absorb moisture very quickly but also lose it fast when everything dries out. These are called 1-hour fuels because they respond quickly to changes in moisture conditions.

Small branches and woody stems between ¼ and 1 inch in diameter are called 10-hour fuels. Because of their size, they take more time to absorb moisture after rainfall, but they also burn hot when dry. Dead branches and trees between 1 and 3 inches in diameter are 100-hour fuels, which take longer to ignite but can burn for hours. Larger-diameter logs and stumps are called 1,000-hour fuels; these seldom burn, but when they do they can smolder for days.

In damp weather, dead fuels may have 30 percent moisture content, but after a prolonged session of hot, dry weather, that can drop to 3 percent or less in small-diameter fuels. Even larger trees that normally would have 10 to 12 percent moisture in the summer can drop to 5 percent in extreme drought. By comparison, kiln-dried wood from a lumberyard usually has around 8 percent. Below about

20 percent moisture, the organisms that decay wood decline, so deadfall basically just lies on the ground waiting to burn.

Professionals use several indexes to rate the severity of drought—KBDI, Haines, Palmer, etc.—but these don't matter on the local level. As you walk around, just look, listen, and feel. If all the grass is brown, pine needles crunch loudly underfoot, and leaves crumble in your hand, then conditions are very bad, and you need to prepare to evacuate.

Topography

The lay of the land also presents a major consideration in your mitigation efforts. Normally fire travels uphill much faster than downhill because the flames preheat the fuel, often aided by updrafts created by the fire as well as diurnal winds.

You've likely already experienced the effect of slope on fire. If you light a match and hold it upright, it burns slowly downward. If you hold it horizontally, it burns toward your fingers a bit faster. But tilt the head of the match downward, and it will quickly burn your fingers if you're not careful.

The steeper the slope, the faster a fire will advance. For the homeowner, this principle translates as follows: The steeper the slope below your house, the more space you need between combustibles. Chapter 2 will give you more specific recommendations.

The aspect of a slope—that is, the direction it faces—also has a big influence on wildfires. Sunbaked slopes that face south to southwest will be hotter and drier than shady north-facing slopes. Thus, plant life often differs and fire burns more intensely where the sun shines most often.

The contours of the land can also worsen fire severity. In narrow ravines and gullies, heat dries both sides of a slope, and winds are funneled up while drawing air from below as in a chimney. Saddles and gaps along a ridge also act as fire magnets because of the way wind flows through them, often becoming very turbulent at these spots. Most dangerous of all are box canyons, which channel and trap heat.

On the other hand, terrain can be your friend in a wildfire. Roads, trails, and ponds act as firebreaks. Ridges block the horizontal movement of wind, so if a fire races up one side, upslope winds on the other side can push it back.

While lying outside the standard definition of topography, the proximity of homes around you plays a major role during firestorms. Neighboring homes pose a direct threat to yours because they essentially serve as giant piles of fuel. The closer houses huddle together, the greater the likelihood of the entire street going up in smoke. Modern developments sit so tightly that making each unit 1 foot narrower allows for an extra dwelling every fifty houses. But when one burns, they all burn.

Both the 2000 Cerro Grande Fire in Los Alamos and the Waldo Canyon Fire offer classic examples of houses setting other houses on fire. Many of the trees surrounding the houses survived, singed only on the side facing the buildings. This anomaly emphasizes the need for community-wide efforts at fire mitigation. All your efforts may be for naught if the neighbors do nothing.

Extreme Fire Conditions

All bets are off when conditions turn extreme. If the relative humidity drops below 20 percent and the moisture content of small fuels falls under 5 percent, you're sitting on a powder keg. Add wind speeds above 20 mph, and conditions are ripe for catastrophe. Once a fire becomes a conflagration, it cannot be controlled until it enters an area of reduced fuel or the weather changes.

A less obvious situation leading to extreme fire behavior involves a large decrease in air temperature in the atmosphere with relatively little wind. In this scenario, heated air rises faster and pulls in more air from all over, so inrushing winds become erratic.

A small fire becomes a large one when the convection column of rising heat overpowers local winds. Often this occurs when the fire is crowning. If you see a huge column of smoke rising 20,000 feet in the air, you know there's a *major* problem. Such mega fires can even spawn true clouds, called pyrocummulus, which can generate their own weather (lightning and rain).

If the large fire generates rotating winds, it becomes a firestorm— and the situation quickly goes from bad to worse. In October 1871 the Peshtigo Fire burned nearly 4 million acres and killed over 2,000 people in Michigan and Wisconsin. Writing about this deadliest fire in American history, Denise Gess described a firestorm as "nature's nuclear explosion. Here's a wall of flame a mile high, five miles wide, traveling 90 to 100 miles per hour, hotter than a crematorium, turning sand into glass."

More recently, the 1991 Oakland Firestorm in the hills of the eastern San Francisco Bay Area burned only 1,500 acres. But it moved so quickly that in about 10 hours the fire claimed 25 lives and destroyed more than 3,000 homes, causing $1.5 billion in damage.

These firestorms can create intense vertical vortexes of flame, called fire whirls, that can rip standing trees from the ground. Fire whirls can also loft embers high into the air, and strong winds can carry them for miles. Fire whirls aren't tornadoes—because they are anchored to the ground—but one documented case of a true fire tornado occurred in Australia when the 2003 McIntyres Hut Fire generated a thunderstorm from which the tornado sprang.

At times, particularly frightening horizontal roll vortices can form—essentially sideways fire whirls that move across the landscape. The Waldo Canyon Fire, the second most destructive to property in Colorado history, and the 2011 Las Conchas Fire, the second-largest fire in New Mexico history, both experienced such horizontal whirls, hundreds of acres across, that lasted for minutes.

A nearby thunderstorm can also cause a complete reversal in wind direction as the cold air from the storm sinks, sending powerful outflows of air. This is what happened in the 2013 Yarnell Fire in Arizona, causing the largest wildland firefighter fatality in eight decades when nineteen Hotshots were overrun and died.

Another nightmarish scenario can occur when a convection column suddenly collapses either from its own weight or from a nearby thunderstorm pushing the column away from the heat source supporting it. When the column collapses, it sends a powerful downdraft pushing out from the center of the fire in all directions, causing flames to erupt unpredictably. A column collapse resulted in the death of six firefighters in the 1990 Dude Fire in Arizona. Another collapse contributed to the death of two firefighters in the 2009 Station Fire in California.

DANGER RATINGS

If you live in a fire-prone region of the United States, you've seen the road signs featuring either Smokey the Bear or the movable arrow that indicates the fire danger rating as: Low, Moderate, High, Very High, or Extreme. These ratings derive from the past few weeks' weather, the type of area fuels, and the moisture content of both live and dead plants.

Around the world, slightly different rating indexes are used. For example, Canada and Europe use Very Low, Low, Medium, High, and Very High. South Africa prefers the terms Safe, Moderate, Dangerous, Very Dangerous, and Extremely Dangerous. Australia has a rating system with six levels: Low–Moderate, High, Very High, Severe, Extreme, and Catastrophic.

While most people have a vague idea about what the terms mean, it's helpful to have a more precise definition. Skeptics claim that officials keep the danger ratings falsely high to scare people and create bans on fun activities. However, each adjective level also corresponds to a level of staffing required at fire departments, so there is a financial disincentive to "cry wolf" with inflated ratings.

When the rating is Low (Green), it's hard—but not impossible—for a fire to start and even harder for it to spread. Most likely there is deep snow cover or so much rain has fallen that you should be worried about flooding. This is an ideal time to burn slash if you have the necessary permits, but it may prove a challenge to get the fire started.

A good portion of the year, hopefully, puts you in the Moderate (Blue) area. This is typically when the grasses are green and a decent amount of moisture has fallen from the sky. If a fire starts, it's easily contained and stays on the ground. Burning of slash is possible, but you must take a lot of precautions.

Through much of the late summer in a typical year, the danger rating is likely High (Yellow). Grasses have gone brown, and it doesn't take much effort for a serious fire to get going. That said, it can probably be stopped relatively easily, so fast response to smoke is critical. A Stage 1 fire ban is probably in effect, meaning no outdoor smoking or fireworks, and campfires in designated sites only. At this time of the year, you should be relaxed but alert. If a fire arises in the vicinity, you have some time to prepare.

Worry when the rating hits Very High (Orange). The weather has been hot and dry for so long that all of the small fuels can ignite from even a spark. When you walk outside, grasses and fallen debris crunch ominously underfoot. A Stage 2 fire ban has likely prohibited all open fires, the use of chain saws and similar tools, and motor vehicle use off developed roads. If even a tiny fire starts, it can turn into a riproarer in mere minutes. Have your evacuation kit ready, and go over evacuation procedures with everyone.

If the danger rating is Extreme (Red), your escape

A sign you *don't* want to see!

vehicle(s) should be packed, fueled, and pointed in the right direction. At this point the fire departments, on full alert, are preparing for the worst. Stage 3 fire bans have closed specific areas of forests, and Stage 4 bans have closed practically everything. The professionals are scared, and you should be, too. Do *not* count on the county sending out an automated Reverse 911 call as a warning. The moment you see or smell smoke, get out! In these conditions, a fire can consume thousands of acres before anyone has a real handle on the situation.

In addition to fire danger ratings from the Forest Service, the National Weather Service also issues alerts. A Red Flag Warning means that very high to extreme weather conditions will exist within the next twenty-four hours. It is typically associated with winds greater than 25 mph, high temperatures, and low humidity, but there can be other factors as well, such as dry lightning. A Fire Weather Watch is issued up to seventy-two hours in advance and is generally a heads-up that a Red Flag Warning may be coming.

These weather warnings tell fire departments and local governments to go on high alert and possibly bring in more staff. For homeowners, a Red Flag Warning means to be extremely careful when working outdoors, especially with power tools. It's also a strong hint to make sure you are ready to evacuate and have prepared your home to survive.

In the 1960s, Australia developed a Grassland Fire Danger Index that quantifies the potential severity of a wildfire. The National Weather Service has adopted this index, which factors in the weather and dryness of grasses, to issue a warning when the potential for explosive fire is very high or extreme.

WILDLAND TYPES

The plant life around your home determines the nature and frequency of wildfires. If you live in a fire-dependent ecosystem, the trees and shrubs have adapted to fires at more or less regular inter-vals. If fire is suppressed for too long, either the ecosystem will change as different species move in, or a massive fire will eventually balance the deficit.

If you learn about the historical fire patterns in your area, you can do a better job at managing your property. It's important to under-stand that ecosystems are dynamic, which means they grow, mature, reproduce, and die. You can perpetuate a healthy, resilient landscape by ensuring a diversity of species, age classes, and spatial arrange-ments on your property.

Some regions, such as the tallgrass prairies of the Midwest, can survive only with the help of fires every five to ten years. If fire is excluded for too long, shrubs and trees overtake the grasslands. Grazing offers no substitute either because livestock are selective in what they eat, and mowing doesn't reduce biomass or enhance soil chemistry. However, many ecosystems in the Wildland Urban Interface must be managed without prescribed burns or natural fire. In many cases, houses and other structures would be endangered. In other forests, fire simply cannot be managed.

Beetle-Killed Forests

The media has paid a lot attention to forests killed by the mountain pine beetle, often with dire warnings of impending apocalypse. As usual, the situation is far more complex and the answers not as cut-and-dried as they'd have you believe.

In Colorado the most recent epidemic has affected 3.3 million acres since the outbreak began over a decade ago, and spruce beetles have killed another million acres of trees. While lodgepole pine was the first victim of the attack, roughly one-third of the trees killed in the past year were ponderosa pine.

The fears about epic wildfires fueled by all the dead trees are only partially founded. During the first three to four years after attack, the red needles can ignite up to three times faster than green needles.

In hot, dry conditions, a surface fire can quickly become a crown fire even without the aid of wind. Two recent studies indicate that severe drought plays a bigger role in killing trees than pine beetles.

But at least with lodgepole pine, once the needles fall off, they decompose relatively quickly. After trees enter this "gray stage," the risk of crown fire decreases. The dead wood still acts as a huge fuel source, but fires are more likely to remain on the surface. Eventually these dead trees fall to the ground and decompose as a new forest replaces them . . . assuming a fire doesn't intervene.

Mountain pine beetles are remarkably hardy. During midwinter the larvae contain enough glycol—a chemical compound you'll recognize from antifreeze—to protect them against extreme cold. The temperature at the bark of the trees must reach -30°F to cause significant mortality. Even a few days of -20°F can't make a real dent in their numbers. Given recent weather trends, don't count on Mother Nature to help out with this forest pest.

Logging the dead trees often isn't a viable solution because many are too small or too remote to be of commercial value. Large sawmills operate on high volume and want trees with only minimal flaws that have died recently, because they contain the most valuable wood for lumber. To get the heavily blue-stained wood desirable for flooring and furniture requires harvesting old-growth trees that have been dead a long time. This artisanal lumbering (sustainablelumberco.com) is more expensive and gets only the leftovers from larger logging operations.

Other uses for beetle-killed trees include pellets for heating homes and wood straw for erosion control. The pellet market tanked, however, when the price of oil dropped dramatically in 2009, so there was less demand for woodstoves. Pellets are now used mostly for soaking up oil spills (as a better alternative to kitty litter). Wood straw is making inroads as a superior product to hay for protecting soil after fires because it doesn't blow away and is weed free. It's too early to tell whether these products, while intriguing, will remain commercially viable.

Even when pine beetles kill 80 percent of a forest, the remaining forest recovers relatively quickly. Surviving trees and seedlings have more water, light, and nutrients, so they grow faster.

Ponderosa Pine / Douglas Fir

Throughout much of the mountainous West, ponderosa pine grows in the zone between grasslands at lower elevations and alpine forests at higher elevations. In many areas, particularly on north-facing slopes, which have more moisture and shade, ponderosa pine mixes with Douglas fir (unrelated to fir trees). Other regions have nearly pure stands of ponderosa.

At lower elevations, ponderosa pines usually grow in grasslands that routinely catch on fire. In a low-intensity fire, young trees (less than six years old) die, but more mature trees survive because they have thick bark, deep roots, and tend to shed their lower branches quickly. However, at higher elevations, fire occurs less frequently and overcrowding tends to result in tall, spindly trees with thinner bark. These stands are more susceptible to crown fires that can wipe out large sections of forest.

When mature, at around forty years, Douglas fir also proves quite resistant to wildfire due to its thick bark. However, the younger trees have thin bark and many narrow dead branches that drape down onto the ground, making them great fire ladders. When a forest is fire suppressed, over time the Douglas fir tends to crowd out the ponderosa pine.

When fire wipes out a stand of ponderosa pine or Douglas fir, there's a good chance aspen trees will replace it. These deciduous

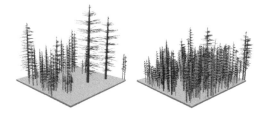

A natural pine forest prior to fire suppression (left) and the forest after 70 years of mismanagement (right)
US FOREST SERVICE

trees are relatively resistant to crown fires and normally burn only in the late fall after they have lost their leaves.

Thinning a dense ponderosa stand has two advantages: It reduces the fire hazard, and it makes the trees more resistant to mountain pine beetle. By significantly opening the stand so that roughly 20 feet separates trees a foot in diameter, you minimize the chance of crown fires and give the trees more of the light and water they need for vigor. Where possible, leave a mix of ages and keep other species such as Douglas fir or western larch. This gives the forest greater protection from beetle attack and makes good habitats for animals.

Lodgepole Pine

Lodgepoles differ from ponderosas, yet they also have adapted to fire and are very common throughout the western United States and Canada. In areas that have experienced large fires, lodgepole pines form pure, dense stands. Where fire hasn't occurred in several centuries, mixed forests more commonly occur as other tree species move in. Lodgepoles grow tall and straight, but they have thin bark and shallow roots, which make them unlikely to survive a fire.

While ponderosas have evolved to resist burning, lodgepoles have adapted to burn completely every couple hundred years. A waxy resin seals their cones, melting and releasing the seeds when temperatures reach around 120°F. Without fire, the trees reproduce very slowly because few seeds reach the soil. Because the cones remain viable for decades, fire releases a huge number of seeds at once. It's possible for 20,000 trees to grow on an acre (called a dog-hair stand).

The age of the stand also affects its flammability. For the first 50 years after a fire, the new forest has little fuel that can burn readily. Between 50 and 150 years, the trees reach a height of about 50 feet and grow so dense that little light reaches the forest floor. As a result, few ladder fuels can carry a fire into the crowns. The trees most at risk of major fire are 150 to 350 years old. At this stage, some trees have died due to overcrowding and others due to age, so light spurs the growth of plants and fallen trees increase the fuel load.

For the homeowner in a lodgepole pine forest, fire mitigation is entirely different than for those living in a ponderosa forest. The shallow lodgepole root system makes them susceptible to blowing down in strong winds (called windthrow). If the trees already have reached pole size, limit thinning to 25 percent of the stand—even if pine beetles have killed them. For small saplings, thin more extensively, and the trees will resist windthrow as they mature.

Unfortunately, this thinning won't effectively reduce the risk of crown fire. You also need to remove downed logs and other fuel from the forest floor. Consider cutting out some sections and planting aspen or leaving open areas as meadow.

Subalpine Conifers

Forests at higher elevations tend to experience fewer fires because of the cooler temperatures and moister conditions. For spruce and true fir stands in Colorado, the interval between fires may last as long as 700 years. However, if a fire does get going, it's likely to burn big.

Homeowners at these higher altitudes generally cannot use thinning to reduce the potential for devastating fires. Instead, consider cutting out patches, creating meadows, and converting some of the forest to aspen. In addition, haul away as much of the excess fuel on the forest floor as possible.

Pinyon-Juniper Woodland

A mix of various species of pinyon pine and juniper covers much of the Four Corners region of the Southwest. At higher elevations, pinyons tend to dominate, often forming tight forests intermixed with shrubs such as Gambel oak. At lower elevations, the more drought-tolerant junipers abound along with sagebrush.

Prior to the suppression of wildfire and overgrazing by livestock, most of this land consisted of open savannah with an abundance of grasses and non-woody flowering plants. The pinyons and junipers were spaced widely and seldom had a closed canopy.

Without frequent, low-intensity fire to burn through the grass, the trees have taken over. Both pinyon and juniper are extremely combustible, with branches that reach to the ground, making them very easy to ignite. When they burn, flames often reach 16 feet, making for hot, fast-moving fires.

As the trees crowd out the grasslands, the diversity of plants and animals decreases. In many areas, erosion has increased because declining understory can't hold soil in place. The trees also consume more water than the grasslands they replace, so stream flows also decline. Neither livestock nor mule deer will eat pinyon or juniper unless the animals are starving, so grazing lands have also been reduced.

Both pinyon and juniper resist drought. However, stressed pinyons are susceptible to attack by the Ips beetle, which burrows under the bark and cuts the flow of sap from the roots. Large populations of pinyon have died in recent years from beetle attacks.

Because the pests are attracted to the scent, landowners in an area with an Ips beetle invasion should cut trees between November and early March. If that isn't possible, spray high-value trees with permethrin soon after cutting. Because the beetles breed several times per year, spray important pinyon trees three times per season.

When thinning pinyon-juniper woodland, keep a mix of ages. Trees fewer than 8 inches at the base need about a 10-foot radius cleared around them for adequate light and water. Trees between 8 and 16 inches need about a 30- to 40-foot circle, and larger trees should have about 50 feet of space.

You should mitigate Gambel oak on your property, too. When the leaves of this brush dry out, they become extremely volatile. This was the fuel for the blaze that killed fourteen firefighters on Colorado's Storm King Mountain in 1994.

Grass and Desert Shrub

Wildfires in grasslands move fast and furious. Fanned by powerful winds during a drought, a grass fire can be difficult to contain because of distant spotting in the one-hour fuel. Often occurring on relatively flat terrain, these fires—in areas such as Texas and Oklahoma all the way up to Alberta, as well as much of eastern Australia—consume tens of thousands of acres in a hurry. The grasslands of the desert Southwest and Hawaii are becoming more dangerous because of invasive species. Buffelgrass, fountaingrass, molassesgrass, and natalgrass all hail from Africa, while cheatgrass (downy brome) invaded from Europe. All of them burn very hot and fast when they dry out, increasing the intensity of fires.

Hawaii faces a unique situation due to the invasion of fountaingrass and molassesgrass, which have replaced much of the native forests. Unlike other regions, Hawaiian ecosystems are not adapted to fire, so when an area burns it doesn't recover; instead it converts to invasive grasslands, thus compounding the problem. The 2005 Waikoloa Fire burned 25,000 acres and forced the evacuation of an entire village, which was saved by a fire break built just one month earlier. When the invasive grasses are still green, you can kill them with an herbicide such as glyphosate (Roundup). Once the plants are half dried out, the only way to eliminate them is by pulling them up with a digging bar; mowing is ineffective.

Both creosote bushes and desert sage hold a lot of dead, woody, flammable material that sends out a lot of sparks. They are popular decorative plants, but you don't want them within 50 feet of your house.

Chaparral and Woodlands

Among the most fearsome of all wildland fires are those that occur in chaparral, a mixture of tall shrubs. These plants create the intense, fast-moving fires that have claimed thousands of homes in California, Arizona, and New Mexico. Other regions of the world with wet winter months and hot, dry summers have similar plant communities. These include the northern Mediterranean countries, central Chile, the Cape region of South Africa, and western and southern Australia.

Contrary to popular belief, frequent small fires are not the norm in chaparral, nor do the resins produced by some chaparral plants increase flammability. It's the drying out of leaves in hot weather that matters. Also, old-growth chaparral doesn't need fire to rejuvenate the stand.

However, massive yet infrequent fires historically happen in periods of extreme drought. Many of these plants come back quickly after fire. Some sprout from stumps, and others produce seeds that lie dormant until activated by heat. These characteristics give the young plants a head start over the competition in a blackened landscape. After a fire, chaparral needs fifteen to twenty years to regenerate. If fires occur more frequently than that, or if the fire happened during the wet season, the chaparral may convert to a grass- and shrubland where fires travel even faster.

For homeowners surrounded by chaparral, keep it—don't clear it because the benefits outweigh the risks. Even eucalyptus trees are fine as long as they are adequately spaced. As with mitigation in other regions, remove all the flammable material within 30 feet of your home. In particular, eliminate fire-prone ornamentals like Mexican fan palms.

In the next 70 feet—more if you live at the top of a slope—thin the chaparral, prune the lower limbs, and remove all the dead material. Leave enough canopy, though, so that half the ground is shaded to reduce the growth of weeds. If you clear too much land, weedy grasses will infest the land and actually increase the risk of fire. Of particular concern are invasive species, like fountaingrass, that crowd out native plants and are extremely fire-prone.

Woodlands adjacent to chaparral are themselves susceptible to massive fires as well. As with other woodlands, thinning and reducing the fuel load on your property is important.

Riparian Zones

It may seem counterintuitive that the wetlands next to streams and ponds pose a high fire danger. Indeed, in wet years the increased humidity and high moisture content of the plants in these regions act as firebreaks. But problems arise in severe drought.

Because of the moisture, riparian zones tend to have heavy brush and an accumulation of dry fine fuels. By definition, streambeds lie at the bottom of valleys, so when conditions dry out you have a lot of fuel in natural conduits. Fires in these areas can burn quickly and intensely. During the 2007 Angora Fire in South Lake Tahoe, California, overgrown watersheds channeled flames and 254 homes were destroyed.

After a low- to medium-intensity fire, riparian zones tend to recover quickly, because many of the plants there will send up new shoots from roots. However, high-severity fires can disrupt the environment so much that invasive species move in. The changes can be permanent, which also alters the animal life of the stream area.

Eastern Forests

Though the East Coast has a lot more rainfall than much of the West, it's not immune to fire either. During droughts, massive fires have occurred in the southern pine forests of Florida, Georgia, and the Carolinas. The Atlantic Coastal Pine Barrens, such as in New Jersey, is notorious for difficult-to-fight fires. If the climate warms, much of the eastern half of the country could become a Red Zone.

The major difference with eastern forests is that many receive their moisture year-round as rain. In the West, most forests get the bulk of their moisture in the winter as snow. Once all that melts by the end of summer—or even the end of spring in a lean year— western forests have gone bone dry. As Easterners frequently attest, hot summers also tend to be uncomfortably muggy. All that humidity helps keep dead fuels moist. In the West, people start complaining when humidity levels crest 30 percent, but that number can drop to near zero in the worst heat waves. While the fire season in the western mountains tends to wind down in late fall as snow begins to fly, it often flares up in the southern and eastern United States as the leaves drop from trees.

In addition, Florida leads the nation in the number of lightning strikes, with roughly 1.5 million per year, because sea breezes on both coasts push ground air up to create thunderstorms. In times of drought, this makes for a dangerous combination. In June 1998 over 300,000 acres across six counties burned in northeast Florida, forcing the evacuation of nearly 40,000 people.

Lest New Englanders get too complacent, consider that the third-largest fire on record in North America occurred in New Brunswick, Canada, and Maine. The 1825 Miramichi Fire burned nearly 4 million acres and claimed 160 lives after a particularly hot and dry summer. No region of the country is immune to wildfire.

Carbon Cycle and Wildfires

Wildfires release a lot of carbon dioxide into the atmosphere. For the United States, it's an estimated 290 million metric tons annually, which is about 6 percent of the emissions from fossil fuels. This naturally leads to concerns about increasing global warming. The good news is that the vast majority of the carbon from fires will be reabsorbed as vegetation recovers in about a century. The particles released also tend to have a cooling effect in the atmosphere.

Overall, research indicates that even if wildfires increase in size and frequency, there will be no net increase in global warming as a result. The carbon from cars and coal burning power plants is another matter since that doesn't get recovered.

SURVIVABLE SPACE

In 2008 California adopted a new building code that, among other points, required homeowners in the Red Zone to perform fire mitigation within 100 feet of their homes. Other states like Colorado have, so far, left such mandates to the discretion of county governments. In all likelihood, if you have a mortgage, your insurance company has the final word on how much mitigation is required.

Regardless of laws and financial pressures, preparing your property for wildfire is the smart thing to do. In addition to protecting your home, you can also increase its value and enhance the surrounding habitat.

You may have heard the term "defensible space." It was coined in 1980 in the *Fire Safe Guide for Residential Development in California*. At the time, it was a great concept, but times have changed. From the late 1960s to the early 1990s, fires in the western United States consumed around 3 million acres every year. Since the mid-1990s, fires are now consuming roughly 7.5 million acres per year.

Based on core samples from sediments in mountain lakes combined with other climate data, scientists now have a wildfire history of the West going back 3,000 years, and a strong correlation exists between the amount of ash in the atmosphere and global temperature. You can argue the reasons until you're blue in the face, but nearly everybody without an underlying agenda agrees that the planet is warming, and there's little expectation that things will cool down any time soon. That likely means more and bigger fires and longer fire seasons, which in turn means that resources for fighting fires will be stretched thinner and thinner.

A harsh reality remains: In this new age of fire, you probably can't count on anyone to defend your house. The modern paradigm for wildland firefighters is to prepare houses for a fire if possible, then retreat to a safety zone. Only after a fire passes through will they jump back into action and try and save houses not already too involved. The logistics of that protocol mean that your house needs to survive, unaided, for at least an hour as the fire passes. You need to create survivable space, not defensible space.

RULES OF SURVIVABLE SPACE

The first rule of creating survivable space is: **Start at home and work outward.** Thinning trees does little good if you haven't protected your home from the onslaught of firebrands. Simple tasks like cleaning gutters and under your deck yield the biggest payoffs.

The second rule is: **Pay attention to details.** Wildfire will find the weakest link in your defense. Pack rats make nests of grasses and twigs that are perfect bowl-shaped starters for a fire and are often located along outside walls of houses. One of the homes consumed in the Fourmile Canyon Fire benefited from all the mitigation work normally recommended and then some. But in the panic of evacuation, somebody left a broom on the deck. Outcome? A total loss.

The third rule of survivable space is: **Fire doesn't care about property lines or HOA rules.** If you've done everything by the book but your neighbors haven't lifted a finger, your house could still be in trouble. Homeowners' associations (HOAs) frequently have ridiculous requirements that put everyone in danger, such as mandating cedar shake roofs or insisting on pretty landscaping over survivable space.

KNOW YOUR PROPERTY

Fire may not care, but the law does. **Know your property boundaries.** Unless you have explicit permission from a neighbor, mitigating his or her land by mistake can lead to a lawsuit and a world of financial hurt. You need to know what's yours and what isn't, particularly if you have fences that were put up before the advent of modern surveying techniques. Before the age of GPS, fences often provided rough estimates to property boundaries. Sometimes they were installed in a hurry to control livestock before a developer turned the land into your home.

Establish an accurate boundary line for your property. Doing so may require a careful reading of your deed. You may need to visit your county assessor's website or even go to your city's archives for good maps. As a last resort, you can hire a licensed surveyor, which also gives you a good defense in case of a legal dispute.

Once you know what's yours, politely ask your neighbors if they would like a little help with mitigation on their property. They may not mind you cutting down a 20-foot pine tree if you ask first. But you'll be shocked to find out what it costs to replace one if you did it by mistake. In this case, it's smarter to ask permission than to ask forgiveness.

EVALUATING YOUR PROPERTY

Perhaps, when you look out your windows, you see a serene setting of trees and meadows with neighbors not too close. Leading to your home might be a winding road, paved or not. Life's great . . . until it isn't. One of the hardest parts of preparing your survivable space is letting go of emotional attachment. When you look at the devastation of other people's neighborhoods after a wildfire, it might be difficult to make the connection—"This could happen to me"—but you have to do it.

As you walk around your property, repeat the mantra: Fire doesn't care. Look at the kid's wooden playhouse: *Fire doesn't care*. That cedar fence looks great: *Fire doesn't care*. That nice shade tree: *Fire doesn't care*. Property lines: *Fire doesn't care*.

It's tough, but you have to make some hard decisions. Sometimes you'll have to convince your family and neighbors. You have to do it, but don't do anything rash without discussing it first with your spouse or you could end up sleeping on the couch.

How you look at your property also depends on where you live. If your house lies in the mountains, up in the hills, or in the boonies, you probably live in true wildland. However, if you look out your window and can see your neighbor brushing her teeth, you're likely living on the urban edge. Either way, you could still be in the Red Zone.

How the government classifies your property affects building permit requirements and, likely, insurance rates. Check with your county to find the exact definitions, but remember that you'll pay a hefty premium for not mitigating your property.

In Boulder County, a "High Hazard Wildfire Site" describes a location on a steep slope (over 60 percent) surrounded by grass and brush; or a site on a moderate slope (over 40 percent) with a thinned forest nearby (medium fuel); or any site surrounded by dense forest (heavy fuel). An "Extreme Hazard Wildfire Site" describes a moderate slope with medium fuel and more than eight days of critical fire weather per year, or any site on a moderate slope with a heavy fuel load.

In states where wildfires pose a significant problem, the state forest service likely has created fire hazard maps for the entire state. For example, coloradowildfirerisk.com says the following about our home:

Large Flames, up to 30 feet in length; short-range spotting common; medium range spotting possible. Direct attack by trained firefighters, engines, and dozers is generally ineffective, indirect attack may be effective.

Significant potential for harm or damage to life and property.

Increased to extensive preparedness measures may be needed to better protect your home and property. This is an important consideration in a scenario where sufficient fire-fighting resources are not available to protect your home or property. Be firewise and take the necessary steps to protect your home and property today.

This generic information applies to most homes in the Red Zone, so it isn't very helpful. The technology and data behind websites like this will improve, and such sites can offer a good wake-up call to homeowners, but don't base mitigation decisions on them alone.

New Home Considerations

If you're considering purchasing or building a home, investigate the wildfire risk. In addition to evaluating the house or land, check the fire history of the region, response times for the fire department, and whether the area has adequate water (fire hydrants with sufficient emergency pressure, a nearby lake, or a community cistern).

Your insurance agent likely will have many related questions that will affect your premium. Constructing a new home requires meeting all the building codes. But if you need to do extensive remodeling of an existing house, you might have to bring all of it up to the latest codes, which is going to cost you.

Given the choice between buying or leasing, it's better to purchase your own propane tank and have it buried. A leased tank usually can't be buried, and it locks you into a single propane supplier, preventing you from shopping around for the best price.

Walk the power lines on the property to make sure the electric company has been trimming the trees as required. If any limbs are at risk of touching the wires in a windstorm, call the service number and request a crew to fix the problem. Working around live wires has a high risk of fatality unless you know exactly what you're doing and have the right gear.

Another consideration is ease of access to the roof and gutters for cleaning. This may not seem important when you're shopping or designing, but it can become a real hassle for decades to come. If you can, opt for a home that has a simple roof with fewer angles to collect debris. If you're buying a preexisting home, gutter screens are widely available at home improvement stores and relatively easy to install.

Look into the rules of your HOA to confirm that you can create a survivable space around your home and outbuildings. Find out if the HOA supports the local fire department and whether it has a documented fire mitigation plan.

Urban Edge

When more than one house occupies half an acre, it is considered an urban area. Back that same area up against a vast expanse of greenbelt, and it becomes an interface community. This makes for a tough situation because many people don't realize they're living in a high-risk area. It seems so city-like: There are paved streets, small yards, and municipal water and sewage, yet all this wonderful open space nearby. It's easy to get lulled into complacency. But even if your home sits several blocks from parkland, it may be at high risk of burning. All those houses between you and a potential wildfire act as better fuel than if you were living next to a stand of trees.

When you hear about hundreds or even thousands of homes being consumed by fire, it's often houses on the urban edge where people thought they were safe in "the city." Recent examples include the 2011 Slave Lake Fire in Alberta, Canada, that forced the evacuation of an entire town of 7,000 people and burned 433 homes to the ground. The 2012 Waldo Canyon Fire outside Colorado Springs destroyed 346 homes after 32,000 residents evacuated.

Preparing for fire in this situation requires community-wide education and action. Ideally, homeowners will work with local fire department, city, county, and even state officials to create a buffer zone up to 1,600 feet wide. This doesn't have to be a clear-cut area— just a strip of well-mitigated land between the tree canopy and houses, which also serves as a great playground for kids.

That's only one step, though. Every homeowner needs to take all the little steps to protect his or her home from firebrands. Add a stone or metal buffer between your house and a wooden fence. Consider replacing that spruce tree next to the house with an aspen or oak. By all means get rid of the juniper.

Intermix Living

For subdivisions relatively close to cities, homes often have lot sizes of 0.5 to 5 acres, called "intermix." This area packs a lot of fuel (buildings) into a relatively small space with fire-prone vegetation in between. Homeowners frequently resist thinning their trees because they want to maintain a sense of privacy.

These vulnerable communities often have a couple of main roads with moderate grades. If there is municipal water, it often has minimal pressure and flow with few fire hydrants. During a major fire, the water system will be overwhelmed, and outside water will have to be brought in . . . if there's time.

Compounding the problems, intermix areas usually lie near cities, and many of the residents bring with them city attitudes about living. These newcomers are often vociferously opposed to doing what is necessary for protecting their property. They seldom understand the ecology of the area and remain headstrong in defying common sense.

If you own a home in an area like this, it's important to talk with your neighbors about fire mitigation. Legally you can't do work on other people's property without their permission. But remember that firebrands can easily travel a mile, so your neighbors' lack of action puts your home at risk. Lead by example, and show your neighbors how great properly mitigated land looks.

Rural Living

With homes farther from the city, lot sizes tend to increase. An area is considered rural when lots range from 5 to 40 acres.

In Colorado, a 1972 law requires that lots be 35 acres to get a domestic well permit that allows outside watering. Smaller lots can get a household-use well permit that doesn't allow for washing cars or watering gardens; water must be hauled in for anything outside the house. In 1986, Boulder County took it a step further to slow development and downzoned unincorporated areas to a minimum lot size of 35 acres.

Larger lot sizes like these also come with drawbacks. Frequently, roads are steeper than 12 percent and narrower than 12 feet, which makes it difficult for fire vehicles to enter while residents are evacuating. Many roads dead-end, so escape may be cut off. Driveways are often long and may not have a turnaround suitable for trucks. There are no fire hydrants and possibly no surface water, like swimming pools or lakes. All these factors combine to make these communities extremely vulnerable to fire.

On the positive side, homeowners with large lots may be more willing to conduct extensive fire mitigation on their land because privacy usually isn't a problem. In some cases, there's room for a circular driveway or a large parking pad that can allow fire trucks to turn around easily.

Area homeowners may also show more flexibility in working together on community-wide projects like creating firebreaks that cross property lines. A do-nothing neighbor with an untreated cedar shake roof and unmitigated property may also pose less of a danger farther away.

Wildland Living

True wildland has less than one house per 40 acres. Many of these homes and cabins are off the grid, so either they have no electricity or they make their own. Sometimes only a boat or plane provides access. From a firefighter's perspective, these homes are so isolated that essentially they're on their own in a major fire. When resources are scarce, in a triage situation, remote homes fall low on the priority list.

These homeowners probably see an idyllic house in the mountains. Fire sees fuel.

A big ranch, particularly one with many structures and livestock, essentially needs to become its own fire department. This means ensuring a large water supply and all the pumps and hoses needed to deliver it to the fire. That level of preparation and technology lies beyond the scope of this book, though all the same concepts of mitigation apply.

FIRESCAPE

From your roof or a nearby hill, look around—not just at your own property or even that of your immediate neighbors, but the entire area from the mountains above your home to the valleys below. This is your firescape. It's the land that likely will burn when the excrement hits the fan. Understanding your firescape will help you prioritize mitigation efforts, and it will give you a better idea of where the fire will come from and its intensity when it reaches your home.

At the most basic level, pinpoint your house on a map, and draw a circle roughly a mile in radius around it. Look at the contours of the terrain, taking into consideration the factors discussed in the previous chapter. The circle now becomes a big oval that extends downhill, with your home near the top. In some cases, like at the crest of a ridge or top of a knoll, a couple of ovals may overlap at your house.

In addition to looking around your home from a high point, you can learn a lot about the firescape on your computer. Find your house in Google Earth (free) or a good topographic map program with 3D capability like Maptech Terrain Navigator Pro ($300, expensive but superb) to examine the area really well. These satellite imaging services allow you to change both viewing altitude and position as though you were flying overhead in a helicopter.

After you evaluate the landscape, factor in prevailing wind conditions. Sometimes the branches on trees will give you a hint. Powerful downslope winds from the west fan most of the brutal fires in the Colorado Front Range. In Southern California, the Santa Anas come from the east. (Winds are described by the direction from which they originate, so an easterly wind blows from east to west.) Extend the oval of your firescape further into the direction of the prevailing winds.

The firescape surrounding your home may have changed from a pure circle into an amoeba-like form that could have arms extending for miles. It's on those long areas of fast-burning fuels that you will need to concentrate your efforts.

Our home stands on the crest of a ridge with a seasonal stream on one side, about 200 feet below, and with another drainage nearly 500 feet below on the other side. A fire rushing uphill from either or both directions is possible. These slopes run mostly to the east, while the worst winds come from the west. Even though it's downhill to our house on the western side, we must anticipate an onslaught of fire from that direction as well.

DESIGNATING ZONES

When looking over your property, draw imaginary lines dividing it into zones of defense that receive different levels of treatment. As mentioned earlier, the key to successful fire mitigation is to start from your home and work outward.

The combined area of Zones 1 and 2 is known as the Home Ignition Zone. This is your survivable space and your primary defense against wildfire. A myth persists that this entire area must be clear-cut to keep your home safe—complete hogwash. You can still have lots of trees and plants as long as you're smart about it.

The following sections offer *minimum* suggestions for zone sizes. If you have the space, make Zones 1 and 2 larger to give your home even more protection. However, there's also a point of diminishing return, so you'll have to weigh aesthetics in the balance as well.

Zone 1

Imagine a massive wall of flames and firebrands racing toward your home. The area extending roughly 30 feet from your home is Zone 1 and can make the difference between survival and total destruction. Pay special attention to this critical area of defense. Zone 1 requires the most modification and upkeep of the landscape, but your diligence will pay off with greater safety for what you cherish.

The immediate 3 to 5 feet surrounding your home (Zone 1A or the Fire-Free Five) are the most critical. If the outer walls of your home consist primarily of wood, this inner region needs to be practically noncombustible, such as closely trimmed grass, ground plants, or a bed of crushed rock. One drawback to rock and gravel is that they can be a nuisance to clear of pine needles and cones: Raking can prove difficult, and a blower throws stones around, too.

If you have stucco, stone, or similar flame-resistant outer walls, you have a bit more flexibility in landscaping because you can plant low-growing bushes and flowering plants. The key in this case is to plant isolated clusters rather than dense groups. Keep all plants away from windows and vents. There is no such thing as fireproof vegetation.

Regardless of wall or deck material, remove anything that burns from next to the house. That includes stacks of firewood, piles of lumber, spare tires, plastic toys, and even plastic hose reels. A cedar fence attached to your house is an invitation for fire, so consider an

Firewood stacked against the house is just dumb.

A wooden fence will bring the fire right to this house.

This wooden lattice won't keep embers out, but it will carry fire up to the deck and those stored tires, which make great fuel.

alternative such as metal, brick, or stone. If you have an arbor or pergola, make sure it's made from fire-resistant materials, and clean out dead leaves regularly.

Measured from the outer edge of your house (or deck or shed), Zone 1B should extend for at least 30 feet. The goal here is to remove most of the fuel that can directly set your house on fire. Doing so will reduce the radiant heat that reaches your home and helps break up a fire front. Again, that *doesn't* mean clear-cutting the land.

Inside this perimeter, you can have trees and bushes, but they need to have plenty of spacing between their outer edges. Where possible, opt for deciduous trees like aspen and oak—but absolutely no juniper or pinyon trees! Remove all limbs, no matter the species, to a height of about 15 feet, or as high as you can get on younger trees while leaving the upper two-thirds of the canopy.

A shed near a house extends the Zone 1 perimeter, and stainless steel mesh around the base helps keep out firebrands.

Prune any and all branches at least 10 feet back from the house and 15 feet from a chimney. Allowing limbs too close to the house is one of the most common mistakes that homeowners make in the Wildland Urban Interface. Remember, no matter how much you like that branch where it is: *Fire doesn't care.*

With municipal water, you have the option of maintaining a green lawn that also serves as a pseudo-firebreak. But if you live on the urban edge, it's smarter to save water by xeriscaping with fire-resistant ground cover and plants. During drought, watering restrictions mean that lawns barely stay green. Under the withering heat of a fire, they can bring the flames to your doorstep.

If you live in an intermix or rural part of the Red Zone, water is in short-enough supply that you're probably not irrigating a lawn of

Kentucky bluegrass. Therefore, you need to trim all natural grass in Zone 1 to a height of no more than 6 inches.

It's important to avoid "zone creep." This happens when you lean a few scraps of lumber against the house or you take the winter tires off the car and just can't resist that convenient storage space under the porch. Perhaps you built a wooden play set for your children that's a bit too close to the house.

In the mountains, where many people use their fireplaces in winter, woodpiles can easily creep closer and closer to the house. In late fall and early winter, when no snow covers the ground, conditions are often dry, and wildfire once again becomes a real threat. At the very least, cover your woodpile with a heavy-duty canvas tarp (10- to 12-ounce cotton duck) to reduce the chance of firebrands igniting the pile. Better yet, keep your close-in pile of wood in the garage or a metal shed and your main piles far out in Zone 3.

Zone 2

The next area of defense consists of moderate fuel reduction. Topography and the dominant plants around you should influence the size of Zone 2. The steeper the slope and the longer the potential flames from burning vegetation, the more space you need. Unless you live on a large expanse of flat ground, Zone 2 is rarely a perfect circle.

On the uphill side and the sides of your house, if you live among trees, you can allow the outer edge of Zone 2 to come in a bit closer (see Table 1). But below your house, particularly if the slopes are steep, you need to push that edge back considerably. When the trees are particularly tall or the slope very steep, you need to increase the estimate in Table 2 even more.

If you have tall chaparral, give much more space on slopes around you because these plants are so combustible in a drought. This also includes streamside vegetation—alder, ash, cottonwood, mesquite, saltcedar (aka tamarisk), sycamore, and willow—because these areas can generate high-intensity fires. Riparian areas grow quickly

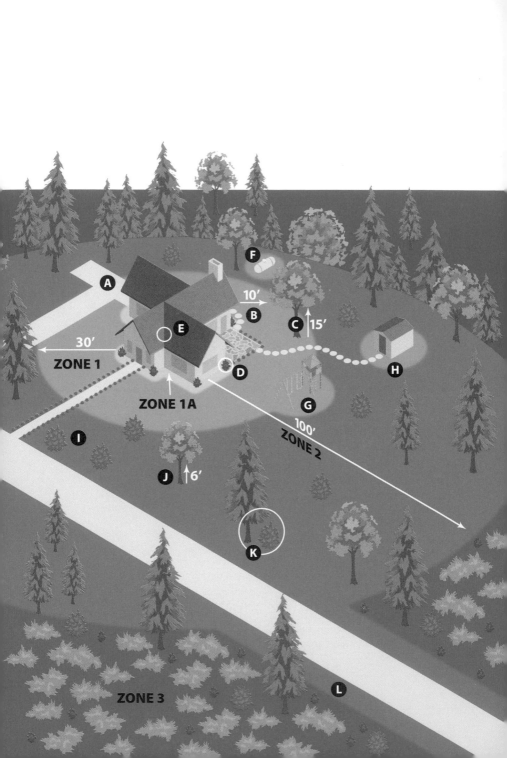

A) The T-shape of this driveway allows large fire trucks to turn around. Without an easy escape path, the fire department won't position a truck nearby.

ZONE 1 is the critical 30 feet surrounding your house. Remove all combustible items and keep plants low to the ground.

ZONE 1A is the 3 to 5 feet next to the walls and decks of your home. Any plants here need to be fire resistant and well watered. Homes with wood siding should have noncombustible mulch.

B) Prune tree branches to maintain at least a 10-foot gap from the roof.

C) Remove all branches on mature trees to a height of 15 feet. Ideally, you should have only deciduous trees in Zone 1.

D) Locate any bushes next to the house away from windows. Use drip irrigation and a timer to keep them hydrated.

E) Roof valleys and gutters are prone to filling with leaves, pine needles, and other highly flammable litter. Clean these out at least once a year.

F) Place the propane tank at least 30 feet from the house. Keep grasses trimmed low to the ground, and remove nearby branches from trees.

G) Anything flammable, such as wooden play set or a pile of firewood, requires extending the perimeter of Zone 1.

ZONE 2 extends roughly 100 feet from the house, somewhat less on the uphill side and significantly more on the downhill side.

H) Locate large combustibles, such as a shed or woodpile, well away from your home. A stone walkway can slow a surface fire.

I) Small bushes in Zone 2 are fine as long as they are spaced out to about three times the height of the bush.

J) Prune branches of smaller trees to about 6 feet, large trees to about 10 feet.

K) Eliminate all ladder fuels that can carry flames into the tree canopy.

ZONE 3 is managed wildland where ladder fuels are removed and trees are thinned for forest health.

L) Trim grasses on both sides of driveways and roads and prune trees to permit easy passage of fire trucks.

because of all the available water, but in times of drought they also create a lot of tall, fine fuel with very long flames.

While trees and shrubs can be more abundant here than in Zone 1, they are spaced more widely than in Zone 3. This too depends on slope angle, as shown in Table 3. Calculate tree spacing from the outer edge of the crowns so, depending on size, the stems on a 30 percent slope will be around 30 to 40 feet apart. On that same slope, the clumps of 5-foot shrubs should have about 20 feet of space among them.

Table 1: Minimum Zone 2 Distance to Uphill and Sides of House				
Percent Slope	Slope Angle	Tall Grass	Tall Chaparral/ Riparian	Trees
0–20%	0–11°	30'	100'	60'
21–40%	12–22°	50'	200'	90'
> 40%	> 22°	70'	200'	110'

Table 2: Minimum Zone 2 Distance to Downhill Side of House				
Percent Slope	Slope Angle	Tall Grass	Tall Chaparral/ Riparian	Trees
0–20%	0–11°	30'	100'	80'
21–40%	12–22°	50'	200'	100'
> 40%	> 22°	70'	200'	170'

Table 3: Minimum Zone 2 Tree Crown and Shrub Clump Spacing			
Percent Slope	Slope Angle	Tree Crown Spacing*	Brush and Shrub Spacing
0–10%	0–6°	10'	2.5 x shrub height
11–20%	7–11°	15'	3 x shrub height
21–40%	12–22°	20'	4 x shrub height
> 40%	> 22°	30'	6 x shrub height

*For deep-rooted trees only

When deciding on which trees to keep, give preference to hardwoods (alder, maple, oak) and aspen because they resist fire more than conifers. Particularly scraggly, bent, or diseased trees should go. But some cool-looking trees with character are worth keeping even if they are malformed.

In Zone 2, instead of limbing to 15 feet, as in Zone 1, here large trees should be limbed to around 10 feet. Smaller trees can have limbs lower to the ground, but the bottom limb should be at least twice the height of the tallest grass in summer. These little trees may not survive a surface fire, but you'll reduce ladder fuel, so it's worth the gamble to maintain age diversity.

In addition to thinning and limbing bottom branches, also remove dead branches in the crown. With self-pruning trees, like ponderosa and lodgepole pine, this fuel will eventually fall to the ground on its own, but speeding the process with a pole saw can help reduce intensity if a crown fire does happen.

One of your goals is to reduce fuel load, so most of the branches and small trees you cut down, called slash, need to be either hauled away or chipped. This organic material breaks down very slowly in dry climates, so leaving it intact only partially solves the problem.

Zone 2 also serves as a firebrand trap. If you clear it down to bare ground, glowing embers can roll along, unimpeded, until they reach your house and pile up.

While you don't usually closely trim grasses in most of this zone, some exceptions apply. Both woodpiles and propane tanks (or similar massively combustible objects) should have grasses and any other flammable material cut to 3 inches for a distance of 10 feet. On both sides of your driveway, trim grasses and shrubs for a couple of feet all the way to the main road. Prune any branches that overhang the driveway to allow at least 15 feet of vertical clearance.

If your property boundary lies within 100 feet of the house, Zone 2 mitigation is your only option. Hopefully you can convince your neighbors to continue your work on their land.

On our property, we created an additional buffer between Zones 2 and 3, essentially a ring of open space about 30 feet wide between tree canopies. When viewed head-on from the house, this outer perimeter isn't noticeable; the forest looks uninterrupted. The theory is that a crown fire in Zone 3 won't move into Zone 2 because of the gap between the crowns of the trees.

Zone 3

Including your house, all of Zone 1 and 2—your survivable space—probably consists of less than 1 acre. That may place a significant portion of your land in Zone 3 or even out to the hinterlands of Zone 4. If you own 5 acres or fewer, consider the entire outer perimeter as Zone 3.

Zone 3 is where you manage the wildland to make things better. Limb trees here to between 4 and 6 feet. Remove ladder fuels as well as thin, scraggly trees that will never have good vigor. Keep larger and healthier trees as well as a mix of younger ones for diversity. Consider culling a few larger trees to open the canopy and create gaps that would drop a crown fire to the ground.

A forest is considered mitigated when you can easily look through it as you walk around. If you can see only 20 feet into the woods, the trees need cleaning out. The goals for Zone 3 are maintaining forest health and reducing fire hazards. A more vigorous forest is better capable of fighting off insect attacks and surviving severe drought.

Use Table 4 to estimate spacing for trees with deep roots (ponderosa pine, Douglas fir, etc.). If two trees

Table 4: Minimum Zone 3 Tree Spacing*	
Tree Diameter	Average Stem Spacing between Trees
4"	11'
8"	15'
12"	21'
16"	28'
20"	35'
24"	42'

*For deep-rooted trees only

are roughly the same diameter, go off the chart. If you have a 4-inch and a 16-inch next to each other, average the distance for a spacing of about 20 feet.

As mentioned in Chapter 1, high winds can easily knock down trees with shallow roots (lodgepole pine, Engelmann spruce, etc.). Therefore, those trees require tighter spacing than Table 4. Your best bet may be to create clumps of trees or simply remove as much of the understory fuel load as possible. When vegetation is clumped with adequate spacing, a crown fire is more likely to fall to the ground.

If possible, remove or chip the slash generated from Zone 3 to reduce the fuel load; we'll go over this in detail in Chapter 4. If you get a major infestation of beetles or mistletoe, clear out the badness. Leave a couple of snags (dead trees) per acre for cavity-nesting birds; just make sure they won't eventually fall across a road or onto a power line.

Our Zone 3 includes a seasonal stream that flows about three months of the year (until it turned into a raging torrent during the storm where we got 17 inches of rain in one week), so we have a riparian habitat in addition to our forest. Down in this valley thrive mountain maples, which are more of a big shrub than a tree. I call them "kindling bushes" because the older ones have dozens of dead stems—about 12 to 20 feet long and 2 inches in diameter—that droop to the ground. These make for perfect fire-starter material and then a big fireball if not cleared out.

Zone 4

If you own more than 5 acres of land, the outer areas fall into Zone 4. This is the "everything else" part of your property. It's lower priority than the other zones, but don't totally ignore it. This wildland should be managed, not abandoned.

The main objectives here are culling diseased trees and adding fuelbreaks. Realistically, you likely won't have the time or resources to mitigate this zone aggressively, but if you spot a pine tree that has turned red, it's worth your time to find out what caused the problem. You might nip a beetle infestation in the bud.

Zone 4 is also called the Community Ignition Zone because it often consists of a mix of public and private lands on the urban edge. This mixture of ownership creates problems that require creative thinking to bring everyone together for the common good. Working together to create a Community Wildfire Protection Plan (CWPP) can make you eligible for grants from county, state, and federal resources to help with thinning projects and the creation of fuelbreaks, firebreaks, and safety zones. Speak with the appropriate government officials to find out more.

Shaded Fuelbreaks

If you have roads or trails running through Zone 3 on your property, you can turn them into shaded fuelbreaks without too much effort. You can also take advantage of streams or rock outcroppings to create fuelbreaks.

Creating a shaded fuelbreak basically means following the Zone 2 recommendations for thinning. The idea is to limit the ability of a fire to spread by slowing its speed and reducing intensity. Shaded fuelbreaks also give firefighters a good line of defense. By leaving this

Table 5: Minimum Fuelbreak Distance above and below a Road				
Percent Slope	Slope Angle	Uphill	Downhill	Total
0	0°	100'	100'	220'
10	6°	90'	115'	225'
20	11°	80'	130'	230'
30	17°	70'	145'	235'
40	23°	60'	160'	240'
50	27°	50'	175'	245'
60	31°	40'	190'	250'

area shaded, you reduce the growth of weeds, so the area will require less maintenance as well.

The width of a fuelbreak will vary with both terrain and predominant species. Around 200 feet wide is a good average, but areas with very tall trees or really steep slopes may need 300 feet or more to slow a fire effectively.

Firebreaks

The terms "fuelbreak" and "firebreak" are often used interchangeably, but they're not the same thing. Creating a firebreak means removing everything that can burn, all the way down to mineral soil, to stop a surface fire. The width of a firebreak reaches around two to three times the height of the nearest grasses and shrubs, so it's typically 5 to 15 feet wide.

Firebreaks can also serve as access roads for four-wheel-drive fire trucks, which makes them invaluable for reaching a remote lightning strike quickly. However, firebreaks require annual maintenance to remove weeds, and they can suffer from soil erosion.

A superb application of a firebreak is a 3- to 5-foot perimeter of gravel or crushed rock around your house. It will keep flames from creeping right up to the structure and also tends to hold embers away from the building.

Safety Zone

During a large fire, especially if it's crowning, firefighters will pull back to a location in which everyone is safe until the fire front passes. Then they rush back in and try to douse any fires on houses that are salvageable. The farther the safety zone is from your house, the longer it will take them to get back to save it.

If you or your community has a lot of land, consider creating a dedicated safety zone for firefighters. This is a large open area or meadow located below a potential fire where they can retreat. It must meet quite a few criteria to be deemed safe, so not any old

Table 6: Safety Zone Guidelines		
Flame Height	Distance from Center to Flames	Area
10'	40'	$\frac{1}{10}$ acre
20'	80'	$\frac{1}{2}$ acre
50'	200'	3 acres
75'	300'	7 acres
100'	400'	12 acres
200'	800'	50 acres

location will suffice. The safety zone requires enough space to pro-tect the crew from radiant heat, which means the separation dis-tance must be four times the height of the flames on all sides. Table 6 provides estimates for a single truck with a three-person crew on flat ground with no wind. If more personnel and equipment are involved, the terrain slopes, or the wind is blowing, double these numbers.

Because 1 acre roughly equals the size of a football field, it takes a considerable amount of space to protect firefighters in big fire events. Thinning the area around the safety zone will reduce flame height and the need for as much acreage.

Beyond adequate size, the safety zone needs to lie where fire-fighters can reach it quickly via two different escape routes. It can't sit at the top of a steep hill because it will take too long for humans to climb, yet very little time for a fire. Likewise, it can't lie in a saddle or narrow canyon that would funnel winds. If you identify an area that might make a suitable safety zone, consult with your local fire department to ensure the firefighters agree. Assuming it meets all the necessary criteria, they will mark the area on their maps and share its location with other firefighters in the event of a fire.

TOOLS OF THE TRADE

Knowing what to do and actually doing it are different matters. As a homeowner interested in doing the right thing, I've heard ad nauseam to do this or do that, but no one ever says how. I'm pretty sure that most fire mitigation articles are written by city dwellers who have never actually walked the walk.

Having worked as a professional gear reviewer in the outdoor industry for two decades, I take considerable interest in the performance of all the tools that I use. I recommend the following, but do your research and perhaps you'll find something better for your needs.

HAND TOOLS

Before starting with more expensive and often more dangerous power tools, see if you can get by with hand tools. Small projects often go faster if you go manual, and there's something to be said for the physical exertion and lack of noise.

Pruning Saw

A basic folding pruning saw is the single most valuable purchase for fire mitigation. Carry it with you when walking your property so you can use it to clean things up as you go. You never know when you're going to come across a sapling or errant limb that needs trimming, so it's great to have a pruning saw available.

The Fiskar 10-inch folding saw with a wood handle is cheap, but it's flimsy and bulky, adequate if you have only a few limbs to prune. The 7-inch Corona Clipper ($20) is more compact and has wicked teeth but has a mediocre locking design. My favorite is the Silky Pocket Boy 170 ($40) with large teeth and a red handle, making it harder to lose. (The version with medium teeth comes with a black handle.) This fits easily in a pocket, so it's always handy; it feels great in the hand; and it cuts tree limbs like butter. The blade is made of thin, hard steel that stays sharp for a long time, but it can snap if you aren't careful.

Silky Pocket Boy 170 pruning saw

Hatchet and Ax

When you're running a chain saw, you might also want to carry a Fiskar X7 hatchet ($25). This is useful for limbing or cutting out bark to check for signs of beetle attack. More frequently, you can use it as a hammer for pounding wedges when felling a tree to change the direction of fall or to free a pinched saw blade. (The X7 is a great little hatchet, but it comes with a shoddy holster that won't attach to a belt. Buy a leather holster for it and trim a bit of the pinky guard from the handle.)

A Fiskar X15 chopping ax ($35) offers an alternative to the chain saw if you have only one or two trees to cut. With a 24-inch handle, this ax has a nicer swing and better control than the hatchet, while the sharp blade makes for great efficiency. It's no Gränsfors Bruks Scandinavian forest ax, but it also doesn't cost $130.

Fiskar X7 hatchet and X15 ax

A chopping ax is also very useful for limbing trees because it's nearly as fast as a chain saw; one good stroke can take out a branch an inch in diameter. Always be aware of your feet placement, though, and what the ax will do when it makes the final cut.

For splitting wood, the handle of a chopping ax is too short for safety, and the head is too narrow for efficiency. If you plan to make a lot of firewood, get a proper splitting ax like the Fiskar X27 ($55) with a 36-inch handle and wedge-shaped head.

Brush Tool

If you have a lot of bushes to hack through, it's hard to beat a good machete. There are many blade styles, but the bush machete is the one you want. The best come from Central or South America—not China. An 18-inch Imacasa Pata de Cuche machete with a plastic handle and a sheath costs only $30, delivery included (machete specialists.com).

A proper bush machete has a thin, high-carbon steel blade with a wide belly so it swings easily with little fatigue. Many knockoffs have thicker steel blades that make them heavy and poorly balanced. For clearing a lot of brush, longer blades are better; consider a 26- or 28-inch machete.

Most people tend to use a death grip on a machete, but the proper technique involves a more relaxed grip and a flick of the wrist at the end of the swing. Try to cut at a 45° angle to the stem and hit with the sweet spot of the blade (the wide belly near the tip). Be careful, though, about a glancing blow deflecting the blade into your leg! The pros use a 3-foot stick with a hook

Imacasa Pata de Cuche machete

at the end in their other hand to improve cutting efficiency. You can pull the brush aside with the hook and hold it taut to get at the stem. The hook also increases safety by keeping your free hand out of the blade's way.

Machetes usually come from the factory only partially sharpened, so you'll need to finish the job when it arrives. That's OK because they receive a lot of abuse in the field; you'll need a sharpening stone anyhow. The Lansky Puck ($8) and some 3-In-One oil make quick work of sharpening all kinds of garden tools.

An alternative to a bush machete is a brush ax (cuma machete) with a downward curving blade (e.g., the Gerber Gator Brush Trimmer, $35). These cut vines better because the hook gathers the vegetation and concentrates the cutting edge. They're more difficult to sharpen, however, and they have a much shorter blade (9-inch), so you may prefer the regular machete.

When you put a brush ax on the end of a long pole and sharpen the back edge, you get a ditch blade. The Council 640C ($50) has a 16-inch blade on a 40-inch hickory handle and is ideal for attacking blackberry vines and zombies. Yet another variation on the theme is the Swedish brush ax ($45), which concentrates a significant amount of mass into a 5-inch blade at the end of a 27-inch handle. While a machete or regular brush ax is a one-handed tool, the Swedish brush ax is a two-handed tool so you can deliver a lot of power in one swoop.

Swing Blades

There are three common styles of swing blades: grass whip, weed cutter, and scythe. For cutting dry grass, the lightweight L-shaped grass whip (roughly $20) does a decent job. But when the grass is wet or the weeds are thick, the more massive triangular frame weed cutter (around $25) gives extra power. For mowing large areas the old-fashioned way, a scythe with a 26- to 32-inch blade (upward of $150) is the way to go.

My True Tempergrass whip came with a dull serrated blade made worse by a thick coat of paint, so I had to do a fair bit of sharpening. The wood handle was a bit slick, so I added a few wraps of bicycle handlebar tape for a more secure, comfortable grip. The bend of the shaft was intended for a shorter person, so I put it in a vise and lessened the angle to level the blade to the ground. After all that, it's a handy tool to whack down a little bit of grass.

The grass whip is a one-handed tool that works well with a long pendulum swing. Beefier weed cutters tend to work better with a two-handed swing that goes up only a little bit—not a full golf swing—relying more on mass than speed.

I have no personal experience with a scythe. Blades can be either serrated (bevel up) or smooth (bevel down); the latter require more frequent and careful honing. For either type, maintain the factory 25° bevel. If the blade is detachable, check the screws often or replace them with locknuts.

Winch and Pulleys

If you have to cut a tree leaning in the wrong direction, a come-along winch can be a useful tool. For this situation, I have a Maasdam Pow'R Pull 2-ton winch ($40, excellent quality) as well as a 30-foot tow strap with hooks ($20) for extra length and a 6-foot tree-saver strap without hooks ($15) for anchoring. You can also use this system for pulling a vehicle out of a ditch, tightening a wire fence, or pulling out stumps.

Another option is the Maasdam Rope Puller ($50) used with $1/2$-inch three-strand rope. This gives you the option of using a 200-foot length of rope (about $100) for longer pulls, but it will be a slow haul. You may also want a pulley like the CMI 2-inch with bearings ($30) to increase pulling power. Place the pulley high up in a tree to redirect the rope and help lift the end of the log off the ground for easier dragging.

All sorts of Z-rig and other configurations can be rigged with various combinations of pulleys and rope grabs (ascender, slings with Prusik knots, etc.). We use these in the climbing and whitewater

Maasdam Pow'R Pull come-along

worlds because of portability. The systems can certainly cross over to hauling timber.

If you have a lot of logs that need dragging, a skidding cone ($160) could make your life a lot easier. This is a heavy-duty plastic cone that goes over the front of a log to prevent snagging. A less expensive alternative is to buy the plastic tray for a wheelbarrow ($40) and rig it as a drag bed.

Carry your come-along and gear in a small duffel bag. The bag also doubles as an important safety device. If something breaks free while a steel cable is under high tension, it can fly back and hit you or a bystander with tremendous velocity. Prevent this by putting some rocks in the duffle bag and draping it over the cable to act as a damper.

Lopper

Loppers are basically overgrown scissors made for cutting small branches. When I was starting out on our mitigation project, I bought a pair of Corona loppers. They are well built and cost only

$25, but loppers are now my least used tool. They're too bulky to carry around and aren't much faster than a folding pruning saw. Loppers also don't give as much reach as you'd think because the handles have to be opened so wide to get around a branch, and sometimes you have to get into an awkward position to make the snip. Ultimately, I used them more as a long hammer to break off dead limbs. However, they do come in handy for reaching into small, prickly bushes to prune.

Better loppers have a compound action or gear mechanism to increase cutting power over the models that have just a simple pivot. These require opening them wider, however, so that reduces their reach. When using the loppers, don't twist the handles when biting tough branches. Sharpen them as you would the head on a pruning pole.

Pole Saw

While you can get by without loppers, a pole saw is one of the most valuable tools for fire mitigation—and in this case longer is abso-lutely better. Since you need to stand back a bit to saw effectively (vertical is both difficult and dangerous), even a 6-foot-tall person will be able to cut only about as high as the pole is long.

The longer the pole, the more dead branches you can clear from the canopy to reduce crown fire danger. You may also need to prune larger branches to increase spacing between trees or to your house. A long pole saw is also invaluable for cutting out branches infected with mistletoe; this can save a tree that would otherwise die prematurely.

Silky Hayauchi pole saw and Fiskars Pruning Stik

The 12-foot Fiskars Pruning Stik ($80) comes with a saw attachment, but the saw is a piece of junk. The saw blade is only mediocre at cutting, in part because the pole flexes so much when extended. The plastic bracket that holds the blade snapped off twice with minimal pressure. The telescoping 21-foot Silky Hayauchi with hook attachment ($300) has been worth every penny. This fantastic pole saw has an incredible blade that cuts with minimal effort. The oval shaft has minimal flex even when fully extended, and the handle wrap provides good grip. Everything about this tool says quality.

If you need more reach, American Tree Service Supply offers a 30-foot aluminum sectional pole. With the recommended accessories (case, scabbard, and handle), it will run about $250. You can buy more 6-foot sections if needed.

If those are too expensive, the Gilmour 20-18 pole saw ($65) might be worth considering. This three-section fiberglass pole extends to 18 feet when assembled. It has a reputation for being wobbly at the connections, though, so you may want to epoxy them together.

Fiberglass doesn't conduct electricity easily, so this type of pole is safer when working around power lines. That said, you need to be *extremely careful* with any pole around electricity. The line running from the pole to your house is only 220 volts, but the lines between poles can transmit many times that. It's best to call the power company and have them maintain their lines.

The only accessory for a pole saw that I recommend is a hook for pulling branches to the ground. Pruning attachments add a lot of weight, and you generally don't need to prune so high. For easiest cutting, it helps to remove sap from the blade occasionally using a solvent. Otherwise, pole saws are largely maintenance free.

Pruning Pole

With a pole saw, you can only cut smaller branches next to the trunk or larger branches partway out. If you want to trim flexible branches high off the ground, the pruning pole is a better option.

There are two types of heads used on pruning poles and loppers. An anvil pruner has a straight blade that crushes the branch against a flat block; these are better for thick branches and deadfall. A bypass pruner slices the branch between two curved blades, much like a pair of scissors, so it does less damage to green branches. For that reason, I prefer the latter style.

The conventional pole has a rope dangling off to the side that likes to get caught on branches. That's why the Fiskar Pruning Stik is such a great tool; the webbing is internal. You close the bypass head by pulling either the orange handle (most of the time) or the orange ball at the end when you need maximum reach. While it will fit over $1^{1}/_{4}$-inch-thick branches, the practical limit is about 1 inch, and that requires a hard pull; $^{3}/_{4}$ inch or less is no problem. The head angle is easily adjusted, too, which can come in handy.

Do yourself a favor and touch up the bypass scissor blade with a diamond stone. To get it back to the best cutting performance, sharpen only the beveled edge of the blade; don't touch the flat backside or the hook on the other handle.

Stirrup Hoe

To keep weeds from growing around the propane tank, I use a True Temper stirrup hoe ($25), aka a scuffle, hula, action, or loop hoe. The sharp steel blade wiggles underneath the soil and cuts roots with ease while minimizing soil disturbance. This works on both a forward and backward stroke, so you can quickly weed a lot of ground.

True Temper stirrup hoe and swing blade

Tree Puller

If we had tamarisk (saltcedar) on our property, I would absolutely own one of these to rip the nasty plant from the ground. The Pullerbear Grip XL ($150, pullerbear.com) grabs the plant by the stem and rips the roots out of the ground. This tool is also great on manzanita, Russian olive, Scotch broom, and just about any other woody plant. The Pullerbear is available in several sizes. The Grip XL version has a 50-inch handle and weighs 13.5 pounds. This will rip out weeds with stems more than 2 inches thick with minimal effort due to the 18:1 gripping force and 6:1 lifting leverage. For soft ground, you can attach a scrap of wood to create a bigger base.

Rakes

Raking up leaves, pine needles, and pinecones in Zones 1 and 2 is a great start for keeping fire away. There are five basic types of rakes that all have specific purposes: leaf, shrub, bow, thatch, and fire. Depending on where you live, you may want two or three rakes. Fortunately, they cost only about $25 each.

If you have big yard with lots of deciduous trees, you probably want a leaf rake with a plastic head at least 24 inches wide; the Fiskar is arguably the best. However, these are not well suited to pine needles and cones. For those, a better choice is a leaf rake with steel tines because of their greater durability and stiffness.

Leaf and bow rakes

To get between bushes and around rocks, a shrub rake is a good choice. It's merely a leaf rake around 8 inches wide. Some companies offer adjustable heads that go from wide to narrow, but most look flimsy at best.

The bow rake has a level head with rigid tines. This is

good for spreading gravel, among other landscaping tasks, and raking up pinecones. A thatch rake breaks up and removes dead grass from a lawn, so it's most useful for suburbanites.

A fire rake typically has four tempered-steel triangular teeth that can be sharpened with a file. It is fairly light to carry and is useful for clearing small brush, grasses, and weeds. It isn't as versatile as a McLeod tool, though, which can do all of that and more.

McLeod Tool

A favorite tool of firefighters and trail builders, the McLeod combines a hoe, heavy-duty rake, and tamper. It loosens topsoil, cuts sod, and moves large amounts of material a short distance. Designed in 1905 by Malcom McLeod, a Sierra National Forest ranger, it's such a versatile tool that you may reach for it often if you have a lot of land to maintain. Mine has grubbed out duff from around the bases of trees, created a few trails, helped clear a mudslide, and done general yard work.

Standard McLeod tools have a bolted-on head (allowing for disassembly) that is 9 inches wide and 11 inches deep and a 48-inch handle. They cost between $50 and $70. While adequate—and the more expensive one with the ash handle meets US Forest Service specs—there are better options.

My favorite is the Lamberton rake (lambertonrake.com), which has a 14-by-6-inch head (other sizes available) and 54-inch handle and costs $80 delivered. The wider head and longer handle make for more efficient raking. The narrow sides of the head (equivalent to a grub hoe) get into tight spots for moving material and are sharpened for 2 inches, which is great for chopping roots. The head is welded

Lamberton rake

on, so the tool is flat on the bottom, which makes it better for tamping and checking the angle of a side-slope on a trail (just set it down and look at the handle).

Another popular McLeod variation, the Rogue Hoe 70HR54 (roguehoe.com) also has a 54-inch handle and costs $90 delivered. The heads have a slight curve (not flat like the others) because they are made from recycled agricultural disc blades. This is strong, high-grade tempered steel that holds an edge. The hoe side is 7 inches wide, and the rake side is 8 inches wide.

Pulaski Tool

Along with the McLeod, the Pulaski is considered a firefighter and trail builder essential. Ed Pulaski, hero of the Big Burn of 1910, created this combination of ax and adze. Aside from the obvious chopping part of the ax, this tool also cuts roots and digs up hard ground like a 3-inch grub hoe. You can often find it in

Pulaski tool, part ax part hoe

the garden section of hardware stores, though more likely it will be called a landscaping ax. The Ames version ($40) appears as good as the more official models ($60 to $70), but I haven't compared them in the field. A leather holster ($15) can transport the Pulaski safely.

Pickeroon

One of my all-time favorite back-saving tools, the Peavey pickeroon (peaveymfg.com) with a Hume head and 36-inch handle costs $50 delivered. This wicked-looking tool is great for dragging lumber and slash. It saves a lot of bending over

Peavey pickeroon

and reaching, and it's great for whacking off dead branches. (Watch your swing!) It even makes a nice walking stick when climbing a steep hill. Other versions have thick aluminum shafts. I prefer the Peavey because it has a traditional ax handle that allows a better grip for dragging really heavy loads.

My pickeroon receives a lot of abuse, so I wrap the handle near the head with tape to prevent splintering. Occasionally I have to take a file to the pick. I've also rounded the bottom of the handle a bit so it's more comfortable as a walking stick.

Slash Sling

This is a great tool for hauling slash piles to the road for chipping. It's a 20-foot automotive tow strap ($15) made of braided rope (not webbing) with hooks on both ends (remove any spring clips). Tie a slipknot at about the two-thirds point with the loop pointed toward the short end. Lay the long end of the sling perpendicular to your dragging direction. Pile a couple of bigger limbs with about 2 feet of branch past the sling. Heap smaller limbs onto the big ones until you have all you can handle. Then hook the sling around the stems so the harder you pull, the tighter it gets.

The slipknot provides a good handhold for pulling, while the short end of the sling can be passed over the shoulder and hooked into the loop for maximum pulling power. Add foam padding for greater comfort if desired.

A slash sling made from tow rope improves hauling efficiency.

Extension Ladder

You need a good extension ladder capable of reaching your highest gutters. Keep in mind, though, that according to the Consumer Product Safety Commission, 164,000 people visit the emergency room every year after falling off a ladder. While useful for other purposes, multifunction ladders (Little Giant and Werner MT series) pose a nuisance outdoors because you have to extend them on the ground and then position them. If you consider telescoping ladders that collapse inside themselves to save space, spend

Table 7: Ladder Selection (in feet)	
Highest Gutter	Ladder Length
< 9	16
9–13	20
13–17	24
17–21	28
21–25	32
25–28	36
28–31	40

the extra for a professional model (around $300 for a 15-foot ladder) that offers a higher safety factor than consumer models.

Your first decision will be length. To maintain the optimal 75.5° angle and extend past the gutter, your ladder needs to be taller than you may realize (see Table 7). All modern extension ladders have a decal on the side that shows the proper angle when erected; move the ladder in or out until the line parallels the wall. The base will stand roughly 1 foot out from the wall for every 4 feet of height.

Next comes the material choice. Although slightly heavier than aluminum (given the same duty rating), fiberglass ladders are best

Table 8: Some Type 1A Ladders				
Model	Material	Length	Weight	Price
Werner MT26	Aluminum	23'	63 lbs.	$300
Louisville FE3224	Fiberglass	24'	44 lbs.	$300
Werner D6224-2	Fiberglass	24'	52 lbs.	$300
Werner D1524-2	Aluminum	24'	45 lbs.	$280
Louisville FE3232	Fiberglass	32'	65 lbs.	$450
Werner D6232-2	Fiberglass	32'	88 lbs.	$420
Werner D1532-2	Aluminum	32'	81 lbs.	$400

Ladder leveler for greater safety

for gutter cleaning. They tend to be stiffer than aluminum, which makes them more reassuring when you're high up in the air. They're also stronger laterally; aluminum ladders can bend sideways when fully extended and stressed. Also, a fiberglass ladder won't send you to the hospital if you accidentally contact the power line running to your house.

The only real downside to fiberglass ladders is that they should be stored indoors to prevent UV degradation. Definitely get D-shaped rungs over round rungs for greater comfort. A 24-foot ladder will cost around $300, but consider it a lifetime investment.

Regarding the duty rating, if you're standing more than 15 feet off the ground, anything less than Type 1A (300 pounds) is foolish. You may weigh only half that amount, but the rating also reflects stiffness and strength in case of an accidental shift. If you weigh 200 pounds or more, a Type 1AA (350 pounds) is your only option.

In addition to the extension ladder, you should get a ladder stabilizer ($40 to $80). This is a set of wide arms that attach to the top of the ladder and rest against the roof so you don't crush your gutters. They're also useful for stability when painting, cleaning windows, and so forth.

If your house sits on a slope, you need levelers for your extension ladder ($60 to $90). These replace the feet on your ladder with extendable legs. You start with both collapsed, put the ladder in the desired position, then drop one of the legs down to contact the ground. This is much safer than trying to use boards or other nonsense to prop up the ladder on one side. The levelers also increase base width, even on flat ground, for more stability.

The actual chore of cleaning out your gutters can be made easier with a long pole that has a blade on the end. This will save you from having to reposition the ladder as often. You can make your own, but the Gutter Getter kit (workingproducts.com)—specifically designed for the task—is only $16. If you're a gadget freak, the iRobot Looj 330 ($300), a track-drive gizmo, flings leaves out of the gutter, but it makes a mess and you still have to climb up and down ladders.

Goats

It may sound silly, but these four-legged firefighters do a remarkable job of vegetation management. Goats selectively browse on brush and noxious weeds that are otherwise difficult to control. They prune trees to a height of about 6 feet, eliminating ladder fuels. They also work in rough terrain difficult to access with machinery.

The goat herders bring portable electric fencing to close off the area to be grazed. Companion dogs and herders watch over the herd. Each goat consumes about 8 pounds of plants per day—a herd of 400 can clear an acre in one day—and the goat herder will move them around to areas in need of grazing and to prevent overgrazing. Goats' split hooves help break up hard-packed soil for better aeration and water absorption, and goats also fertilize as they graze.

You can rent herds of goats all over the country; try rentagoat .com and goatfinder.com. For smaller projects, a trailer of about 50 goats usually can do the job in a couple of days. On large-scale projects, a herd might consist of 300 to 800 animals. One company in the San Francisco Bay Area, Ecosystem Concepts, Inc. (ecosystemconcepts .com), manages around 6,000 goats specifically for fire mitigation throughout the region.

POWER TOOLS

If, like me, you're a workforce of one, you need all the help you can get. Hand tools can do the same jobs eventually, but wouldn't you rather be hiking or riding a bike? I know I would, so bring on the power! Of course, these tools increase the odds of a trip to the emergency room or morgue, so bring on the extra caution, too.

Before entering the realm of power tools, prepare yourself for a lot of testosterone-fueled nonsense if you visit online forums. There is often a bias toward more horsepower and rpm's with little give for people with other needs. There are also loyalty wars between acolytes of Husqvarna ("Husky" in common parlance), Jonserd, Makita, Shindaiwa, Stihl (pronounced like "steel"), and other excellent brands. At that level, it's hard to go wrong.

Serious power tool users often revile products by Black & Decker, Homelite, McCulloch, Poulan, Remington, and Worx, among others. Some of these companies once had great reputations before they were bought out and the quality of their products declined precipitously. Each of these brands probably has a worthy product or two among a lot of mediocrity, but be skeptical of glowing reviews from people who use a product twice a year and have no basis for comparison.

My experience and that of countless others has been that entry-level power tools offer an exercise in frustration, especially if they run on a two-cycle engine. Even if you do everything right—fresh fuel, proper maintenance, and such—the "homeowner" level tools work great at first but quickly and literally become a pain in the elbow. (I blame a bout of tendinitis on countless pulls on the cord trying to start an inferior chain saw.)

You will save money in the long run, not to mention a lot of aggravation, by opting for professional-level power tools. These are more reliable, require less maintenance, and often get the job done quicker.

When choosing an outdoor power tool, you need to consider where to spend your money. The easy answer is a big-box store or online retailer, but those locations may not provide the best answer. Power tools get used hard and are going to need professional service. Tools that at first seemed like a great deal will lose their glamour when you discover parts are hard or maybe impossible to find locally. Paying for shipping both ways, as is standard practice, to send a tool to a warranty repair center will turn that seeming bargain into a money pit.

Even if up-front costs are a bit higher, shopping locally at a well-stocked specialty dealer that services its products will offer the best value in the long run. You're also likely to get a faster turnaround time on repairs when you need your tools most. The better brands are close enough in price that the level of service should be your deciding factor. If a great store nearby is big on Husqvarna but you were leaning toward Stihl, get the Husky, or vice versa.

Power Tool Safety

It's bad form to start a fire while you're working to prevent one. In California alone, improper use of power tools starts more than 1,600 fires every year. Fortunately, most of these are quickly extinguished, but each one carries with it the potential for major disaster.

Once the grass starts turning brown, you need to be extra careful when running your power tools. If possible, try to finish before noon (10:00 a.m. is better) so you aren't out in the heat of the day. If it's a very windy day—especially if a Red Flag Warning is declared—postpone your work entirely.

Your chain saw and other gas-powered tools should have spark arresters, and you should clean them occasionally. Some motorheads remove these metal grids for a slight power boost, so if purchasing a secondhand tool, make sure it's installed.

A steel lawn mower or bush cutter blade striking a rock can easily spark enough to start a fire. Don't use a lawn mower on tall grass or weeds; that's what string trimmers are for. Use a bush cutter with a grass blade only if you know *for certain* there are no exposed rocks in its path.

Never refuel a power tool while the motor is running! (You would think it would go without saying, but this mistake has sent people to the hospital.) Refill a chain saw's oil tank first so the engine has time to cool down; on other power tools without oil tanks, just give them a little extra time. No-Spill fuel containers really do help prevent overfilling, but if you make a mess, either wipe it up or let it evaporate before restarting the motor.

No-Spill fuel container

I shouldn't have to say this, but don't smoke when refueling either. If you hire contractors, make sure they understand that they will be fired immediately if they toss even one cigarette butt on the ground.

An automobile's hot muffler or catalytic converter can easily start a grass fire. Never park on tall grass unless you are sure the exhaust is cold. If you live in the Red Zone, keep a fire extinguisher in each vehicle you own.

Fuel

Balky engines on chain saws, weed trimmers, and lawn mowers aggravate countless people. If you have a problem starting or running a two-cycle motor, your first suspect is always the fuel supply. Closely related culprits include a clogged fuel filter or fouled spark plug.

Gasoline can degrade after only a few weeks of storage, particularly when exposed to oxygen and humidity (as in that half-empty jug or fuel tank in the garage). Big engines, like your car, seldom have issues with old fuel because they have computer-controlled injection. But small engines have tiny carburetors that easily clog with gum and rust; either they won't start at all or run poorly and frequently quit.

Ethanol is now added to nearly all gasoline sold at filling stations and compounds this old fuel problem. While not injurious to modern cars, ethanol can cause problems for small engines. It is known to degrade carburetor parts and fuel lines. In humid areas, the hygroscopic ethanol absorbs water, which can reduce lubrication and cause an engine to seize. While most gas now contains 10 percent ethanol (E10), the movement toward E15 will make the situation worse.

The best solution, if you go through only a gallon or two of gas each year, is purchasing canned fuel: Husqvarna Aspen, Stihl MotoMix, SEF (Small Engine Fuel), or TrueFuel. One-quart cans cost about $7 but contain high-quality gas with no ethanol; they come with the proper 50:1 oil mix; and they will never degrade until opened. Just open the can, pour it in, and get to work. Use only this in a new machine, and it will have a longer life with much lower maintenance costs.

At $34 per gallon, though, boutique fuel isn't a viable option if you have a lot of work to do. In that case, you'll want to buy from the pump and add a synthetic oil additive and a stabilizer (Sta-bil, Star Tron, or PRI-G), which puts your cost at around $7 per gallon. Spend the few extra pennies for the best two-cycle oil additive available; Stihl will double the warranty on new machines if you also buy a six-pack of Ultra.

Your best fueling option may be a two-container strategy: a round 5-gallon Type 1 steel storage can ($40) and a 1¼-gallon No-Spill plastic can ($18) that you bring for the day's work. High-density polyethylene (HDPE) cans are permeable to oxygen and water, so they're no good for long-term storage; plus they don't meet Department of Transportation requirements for transporting fuel.

When you fill your gas can, pick 89 octane E10 (likely mid-range) from a branded station (Conoco, Exxon, Shell, etc.). If they only have E15, go elsewhere. Sometimes premium gas (91 octane or higher) has less ethanol. Websites like pure-gas.org list stations nationwide that sell ethanol-free gas.

If the pump has a single hose for all types of gas instead of individual hoses, run some gas into your vehicle first to clear out the cheap stuff that the guy before you bought. Put the steel can on the ground to avoid a static discharge. Don't exceed the recommended fill limit either; gasoline expands when it leaves the cool ground and heats up in your garage. As soon as you get home, add the stabilizer. Add the oil mix when you transfer fuel to the smaller can.

In theory, if you use stabilizer when you buy fresh fuel and top off the tank, you don't need to run the engine dry at the end of the season. However, due to the ethanol content, it's a good idea to empty the tank and then run the engine until it quits. Before adding fuel to your power tool, give the gas can a good shake to ensure that any water that may have accumulated mixes in.

Even with a stabilizer, fuel over six months old may not give the best performance; I've used nine-month-old fuel without problems, but your mileage may vary. You can use old fuel in your car because the small oil content is negligible in a big engine.

If you live at a high altitude and mail-ordered your power tool, there's a good chance the carburetor will be set too lean. This is fairly easy to adjust yourself if you read the manual. If you don't feel up to it, have a local shop tune it up before you damage the engine.

Chain Saws

One of the most useful tools for fire mitigation is also one of the most dangerous. The moment you fail to respect your chain saw, it's going to bite you—*hard*. If you don't follow the rules when felling trees, you could end up in the hospital or the morgue.

Now, scary warnings out of the way, with a proper understanding of the gear, running a modern chain saw is probably safer than a lot of other things you do around the house all the time. The vast majority of injuries occur to casual homeowners who don't educate themselves beforehand—though seasoned pros get careless, too.

When picking a chain saw, the size of the blade, properly called the bar, will drive many other decisions. It determines not only the size of trees and branches you can cut, but also how much bending over you will do. Most manufacturers specify the cutting length of a bar. A few will try to fool you by stating overall length to make their cheap machines sound more impressive.

Chain saw bars in the 12- to 14-inch range are OK for light work but are too short if you have a lot of trees; you can still cut up an 18-inch tree with one of these, but it will take a long time. Most "homeowner" saws come with a 16-inch bar and a motor barely adequate to drive the chain.

The more powerful "ranch" and "professional" saws, best suited for mitigation work, can usually take 16-, 18-, or 20-inch bars. If you are over 6 feet tall, a 16-inch bar may feel a bit short when limbing downed trees. On the other hand, a 20-inch bar will feel notably heavier and harder to maneuver; it also puts more strain on the motor due to greater friction.

If you go beyond a 20-inch bar for felling large-diameter trees, you are dealing with a very heavy, very powerful piece of machinery. At this point, you're going to want a small, lightweight saw for limbing, too.

If you're wavering between a cheaper homeowner saw and a more serious chain saw, keep this in mind: When felling trees, speed is safety. When you drop a 40-foot tree to the ground, an enormous amount of kinetic energy releases. A wimpy little saw struggling to make the final back cut keeps you in the danger zone longer.

The other big consideration is the type of engine: AC (house current), DC (battery current), or gas. This option ties back to bar length because no battery-powered chain saw can drive a bar longer than 14 inches. All electric saws are limited to 16 inches, and even that might be bit of a reach.

While it might sound like a great feature, the tool-less chain tensioner on many chain saws often causes aggravation. These have a reputation for loosening and requiring frequent maintenance. This gizmo almost never appears on ranch or professional-level saws because their owners have little tolerance for poor performance.

We'll discuss kickback, a phenomenon related to improper use of a chain saw, in more detail in the next chapter. With proper training and experience, it's mostly a nonissue, but the average person with his or her first chain saw has neither, so companies offer a little help.

Most homeowner-grade chain saws come with an anti-kickback bar (narrow tip) and anti-kickback chain (extra humps); some even have a physical guard at the tip of the bar. These are safer for inexperienced users, but the trade-offs are slower cutting speed and reduced versatility. If you have fewer than 5 acres, use the anti-kickback bar and chain (packaged with a green label) because these do enhance safety. Replacing the cheap consumer chain with a quality version from Oregon or Stihl can boost performance considerably.

If you have more land to manage or many large-diameter trees, switching to a bar with a rounded tip and a regular chain (yellow label) will greatly speed your work. This combo also allows a more sophisticated plunge cutting technique that can be used on leaning trees to prevent a dangerous situation known as a "barber chair" where the tree splinters and falls unpredictably.

It's quite easy to put a chain on backward, which understandably can do all sorts of damage to your chain saw. Look at the sharp, angled cutting links on the chain. When installed correctly, they will point toward the tip of the bar on the top edge and toward the chain saw on the bottom edge. Do *not* gauge the direction by any writing on the bar because they're designed so you can flip them upside down to even the wear.

Electric
If you have a small lot (1 acre or less), your best option may be an electric chain saw and a long extension cord. These are lighter, quieter, and less of a hassle than gas-powered chain saws, but they limit your mobility radius. It would seriously ruin your day if you hit the cord with a running saw, so exercise extra care. A 14-inch bar is a better option for these saws because of that electrocution issue, and the shorter bar strains the motor less.

To run an electric chain saw 100 feet from an outlet requires a 12-gauge extension cord that you probably don't own because it's so heavy and expensive ($60). If you use a thinner cord (14-gauge is the most common) or go longer than the limit, there will be too much voltage drop on the chain saw under load. Voltage drop will cause the motor to turn more slowly and reduce cooling airflow, causing overheating and burnout. Using the wrong extension cord automatically voids your warranty, so you should toss the machine in the trash because it's too expensive to repair.

If you can live with a 100-foot limitation, the best value is the Makita UC3530A electric chain saw, which costs $200 and has a 14-inch bar. Other worthy contenders are the Husqvarna 316E ($300) with a 16-inch bar and the Stihl MSA 160C ($330) with a 14-inch bar. All weigh around 12 pounds and provide good power and durability.

Many cheap alternatives cost only $75 at big-box stores, but those typically have many internal plastic parts and light-duty construction. Consider these disposable chain saws with a short lifetime; repair is rarely practical. If this is all your budget allows, the motor should draw 13 amps at a minimum or you'll burn it out in no time. Replacing the 16-inch bar and chain with 14-inch can help longevity but defeats the budget constraint.

Much-hyped safety chain saws—Black & Decker Alligator ($80) and Worx JawSaw ($125)—can handle only 4-inch-diameter limbs, though the engines are so small that you can use 200 feet of extension cord. Because the bar is completely hidden, they do eliminate almost any chance of injury, but they aren't practical for more than light yard work.

Battery
If you want to be free of the leash without the hassle of gas, there are currently four battery-powered chain saws that warrant consideration. None of the 18-volt versions make the cut.

The Black & Decker LCS120 ($120) is a 20-volt model with an 8-inch bar that weighs just over 5 pounds; a spare battery costs $40. The Stihl MSE 140C ($350) has more power with a 36-volt motor and

12-inch bar; it weighs 11 pounds, but a spare battery will set you back $260. The Makita X2 LXT ($380 without batteries, $600 with two) with a 12-inch bar delivers 36 volts by using two battery packs. At present, the most powerful option is the Oregon CS250S ($410) with a 40-volt motor and a 14-inch bar; it weighs 10 pounds, and the spare battery costs $200.

While the Stihl and Oregon both cost around $600 with a spare battery, they do offer performance nearly equal to gas chain saws. That extra battery will let you keep working more than an hour at a time. (Actual run time is around twenty to thirty minutes, but you'll cut it off as you move limbs, etc.) The Makita only makes sense if you are already invested in their LXT system, of which I am a huge fan, and already have four of the 3-amp batteries (about $100 each). With any of these, you still need to stay within walking distance of the house for recharges, but overall they are good options.

Gas
If you have more than a couple acres of forest, a gas-powered saw with a 16- or 18-inch bar is the best choice for mitigation and cutting firewood. But selecting a chain saw from the plethora of offerings can be bewildering. Copious hype, not to mention countless bombastic opinions, will bombard you.

It's actually pretty easy to narrow down the options if you look at the overall project. Take a look around your property and estimate how many trees, 8-inch diameter or larger, that you'll be taking out in the next five years. Smaller trees come down so easy that you should count them more as branches.

If you have fewer than ten large trees to remove, you can get by with an entry-level consumer chain saw like a Homelite or Poulan/ Sears that costs $100 to $140. With good fuel and proper usage, they should last long enough to get the job done. If you have twenty to thirty trees to thin, it's worth spending more for a quality consumer model like a Husqvarna 240E or Stihl MS 181 in the $250 range that will offer better performance and reliability. These represent a good value and a nice feature set for the occasional user.

When you're looking at fifty to a hundred trees to cut, go for the extra power and ruggedness provided by the "prosumer" ranch chain saws. The Husky 455 Rancher and the Stihl MS 290 Farm Boss

The Stihl MS 261 pro chain saw delivers power and durability with minimal weight.

both cost $400 and have long track records. With 55cc engines delivering 3.5-plus horsepower, they make quick work of big trees. But at about 15 pounds, they'll also give you a workout.

It was the weight of the prosumer saws that finally drove me to purchase a professional saw, which has been a great upgrade. Both the Husqvarna 346XP ($510) and Stihl MS 261 ($550) weigh 2 pounds less than their prosumer models with about the same power output. If you are hefting a saw for hours on end and carrying it up and down steep, rocky slopes, that weight savings is worth the extra money. These pro saws also include other advanced features—such as a clog-resistant air intake, more durable piston rings, and a decompression valve—that make them more reliable and easier to use.

Maintenance

If you aren't willing to maintain a chain saw, don't buy one. It's not a tool that you can use and then ignore until next time. It isn't hard or even time-consuming, but some upkeep is mandatory.

First, keep the bar and chain oiled to prevent excess friction. Failure to refill the oil tank every time you refill the gas will result in the bar and chain overheating, which can result in a snapped chain and the ensuing torn flesh.

The best options for bar and chain oil are biodegradable products made from canola oil (Oregon Arborol, Stihl BioPlus). They cost around $22 per gallon compared to $15 per gallon for petroleum products but are less harmful to your lungs and plant life. Quart sizes are also available. If you want to save money, you can buy canola oil at the grocery store; don't try other vegetable or motor oils.

The chain will dull with regular use and even faster if you hit dirt or rocks. Do yourself a favor and purchase a spare chain when you get your saw. You can either learn to sharpen the chains yourself, or you can take them in and have them professionally sharpened.

You can hand-sharpen using a special file and jig sold by dealers. This is great for touch-ups in the field. I like to use a cordless Dremel tool with the chain saw sharpening attachment ($8) for fast touch-ups. If you go this route, order diamond-sharpening bits ($10 for four) because they don't decrease in diameter the way stones do as they wear. After two or three home sharpenings, it's worth having a professional sharpening with the expensive machinery.

Whenever you take the chain off, use a thin flat-head screwdriver to clean out the groove on the bar; this often fills with gunk that prevents proper oiling of the chain. Periodically flip the bar so the bottom edge is on top to even out the wear. Also clean the gunk out from the little hole where the oil comes out. For gas-powered saws, this is a good time to clean the air filter and possibly replace the fuel filter to keep your machine running smoothly.

Before you fire up your saw, make sure the chain is properly tensioned so it's snug against the bottom of the bar but not so tight that you can't move it by hand; it should be sharp, so wear gloves. New chains will stretch as they break in, so you may need to readjust during the work session, too. (Better chains are pre-stretched at the factory to reduce this issue.)

When working in very cold weather, you may need to re-tension the chain once it warms up. However, if you don't loosen it after you're done, the contraction of the chain can damage the crankshaft and bearings, giving you the unwanted opportunity to go shopping for a new chain saw.

All chain saws nowadays have a chain brake—that big plastic guard in front of the handle your left hand grips. This should stop the chain as soon as you pop it forward. Test it every now and then to make sure the clutch engages. If it doesn't, get it fixed . . . it's way cheaper than a hospital bill.

At least once a year, open the case and inspect the air filter to make sure it isn't clogged. You may want to replace the spark plug and fuel filter. Check the pull cord for fraying, too. If your saw is really cranky or running rough, it probably needs a visit to the maintenance shop for a carburetor tune-up.

Protective Gear

Like many homeowners with their first chain saw, I started out wearing no personal protective equipment (PPE) at all. I was hyperaware of the dangers, but I was still lucky not to get hurt. As my knowledge and experience have increased, so has my safety gear.

When you're thinning a forest, it's a given that large objects like branches and trees can crush you, which makes a helmet a really good idea. But a helmet works only if you wear it, and you won't wear a helmet that isn't comfortable. Modern forestry helmet systems integrate earmuffs for 25 decibels of sound protection and a face shield to protect you from flying objects. For me, a basic $45 system wasn't particularly comfortable, easy to use, or durable. After it pissed me off enough, I looked at several options and decided on the Rockman Premium Lumberjack System ($70), which has been superb, though I did add a welder's sweatband ($4) to keep sweat out of my eyes.

Good gloves are an absolute essential both for safety and comfort. Without gloves, your hands will get a lot of abuse from grabbing, dragging, and tossing tree limbs, not to mention blisters from using hand tools. My hands-down favorite are the Youngstown Kevlar gloves ($30) because they are rugged and offer full dexterity.

Leg injuries top the list of chain saw accidents. If you need convincing on the necessity of wearing protection, go to an Internet search engine and type in "chain saw accident photo." Warning: The results aren't

Essential chain saw gear

for the squeamish. Chain saw chaps sandwich a loose weave of tough aramid fibers in between rugged fabric on the outside. The fibers entangle in a chain and stop the saw cold before it gets to your leg; the more layers inside, the better the protection.

Chain saw chaps come in three styles: standard chaps, full-wrap chaps, and pants. Standard chaps offer the least protection but are better than nothing. Full-wrap chaps protect the front of your legs as well as calves and ankles, plus they stay in place when hiking in rugged terrain. Chain saw pants are good if you're cutting all day, but you'll probably want the option of removing chaps when your done. The better chain saw pants run nearly $300.

When sizing chaps, go longer rather than shorter; the leg covering should extend all the way to the top of your foot. The Labonville Full-Wrap Chaps ($75) are well built, offer better protection than most other brands, and come in different inseams for a good fit.

Chain saw safety boots to protect your feet also make sense—but decent ones cost nearly $200, and many are lousy for hiking on steep, rocky slopes. As with all boots, a good fit is the most important factor. The boots should have steel safety toes to prevent a chain saw from reaching your feet; Kevlar safety toes are ineffective.

Work Belt and Tools

While out in the field with your chain saw, it's helpful to carry a few tools with you. To make this easier, consider using a carpenter's tool belt rigged for your needs. The wide, padded waistband also offers a bit of lumbar support, because your back definitely will get a workout from all the cutting, hauling, bending, and lifting.

Your chain saw comes with a T-shaped bar wrench (called a scrench) for adjusting the chain tension and other basic maintenance, but it's awkward to carry and not particularly versatile. Instead, I carry the folding Top Saw Bar Wrench ($15), which includes many useful tools in a smaller package. It lets you make simple repairs in the field, so you can keep on working.

The Husqvarna 8-inch Timber Tongs ($35) are helpful for hauling slash. You can lay a large branch on the ground and then pile a bunch more on top of that. With the tongs, you then have a great handle for pulling the entire pile. If you don't have a pickeroon, you can use the tongs to drag a small tree to where you want to process it.

Both an 8-inch and a 10-inch plastic felling wedge ($8 to $10) come in handy often enough to carry or at least have nearby; the Black Bear Rifled wedges, my favorites, drive straight and stack well. These are used most often for changing the direction of fall for a tree with a moderate lean; you can stack two if you need more lean.

They can also help you free a stuck chain saw if you misjudge the tree's lean or the wind pushes it back. A wedge additionally lets you cut up large-diameter trees lying on the ground with less hassle: Simply insert it into the cut above the chain saw bar to keep the tree from pinching.

Work belt and helpful tools, plus a first-aid kit and whistle

To pound the felling wedges, use a hatchet that you carry on your tool belt. You can also use it for chopping off small branches, but a folding pruning saw is often faster to deploy. Sometimes my machete goes on the belt, too.

Black Bear felling wedges

Because I work alone in rather remote locations, I can't rely on having cell phone service, so I carry a safety whistle ($5). Even if I can get a cell signal and reach 911, help could be more than thirty minutes away. The whistle weighs nothing but carries much farther than a human voice, possibly alerting a neighbor.

Perhaps the most important tool-belt item is a first-aid kit. My kit is inexpensive ($30) and minimalist, but it can handle most injuries. It contains a Cederroth 4-in-1 Bloodstopper pack, some Band-Aids, two pairs of latex gloves, and a bottle of sterile eyewash. Add a QuikClot Sport sponge ($15), based on technology for battlefield dressings to stanch bleeding fast, and you're ready to go.

Felling Lever and Cant Hook

If you have many trees under 12 inches in diameter, a felling lever ($65) can be useful to direct the direction of fall. This is basically a crowbar designed for trees, so it has a wide foot and a thick wedge. On these smaller trees, plastic wedges don't have enough room to wedge, and even stacking can be tough.

The other valuable role of a felling lever is freeing trees that you've cut but are hung up in the branches

Felling lever with cant hook

of other trees. The cant hook grabs the bark and allows you to provide a lot of torque to twist the tree and encourage it to comply with
gravity.

In the land of big trees, cant hooks are usually single-purpose tools
with longer lever arms. These are used for rolling giant logs, mostly at
the lumber mill. When a foot is added to a cant hook to lift a log in
the air, it becomes a timberjack; this keeps your chain from hitting the
ground and saves some backache when bucking logs into firewood.

Timberjack and Log Holder

I wish I had discovered the Woodchuck Timber Tool ($150, woodchuck
tool.com) earlier because it would have made my life a lot easier. This
Swiss Army knife of lumber tools
is a serious cant hook for rolling
big logs and freeing hung trees.
It's a sturdy timberjack for lifting
logs off the ground to chop them
up without dulling your chain.
It's a burly carrier that allows
two people to drag a massive log
without too much strain. It can
even pull fence posts out of the
ground.

Woodchuck Timber Tool

Those features are all good, but my favorite is when I turn the
Woodchuck into a log holder. Either attached to the receiver hitch
on my truck or to a nearby tree trunk, this tool grabs one end of a
tree and holds the entire trunk almost at waist level. Then it's just a
simple matter of chopping the tree down to size . . . zip, zip, zip, and
done. This tool is a great back saver.

String Trimmer

Of all the fire mitigation tasks, cutting tall grass near your home
ranks in the top three. Depending on moisture levels, trim your

grass at least once and possibly two or three times per year. With a string trimmer, it takes only a couple hours, greatly increasing your safety.

Variously called a weed whacker, string trimmer, or line trimmer, the high-speed rotary "blade" is glorified fishing line. These tools are efficient on grass and weeds while doing minimal damage to heavy obstacles like walls, fences, and trees.

As with chain saws, you have a choice of electric, battery, or gas power. Pretty much all the same pros and cons apply to each power option. String trimmers can get by with much smaller motors, so electric and battery options are feasible for larger areas.

If all trimming is within 200 feet of the house, an electric trimmer is the best option because it offers decent power and less hassle. An inexpensive electric trimmer, like the Black & Decker ST1000 ($25), is lightweight but the 9-inch cutting swath makes for slow going, and it struggles with tall grass and weeds. A more powerful trimmer, such as the Stihl FSE 60 ($120), has a 14-inch swath and cuts as well as most gas trimmers.

Most of the battery-powered trimmers either struggle to get the job done on tall grass or they run out of juice before you can finish; most batteries last only fifteen to twenty minutes. Probably the best option in this category is the Toro 12-inch, 24-volt Cordless Trimmer ($150), which has enough power for a sizable yard.

If you have a big area to clear, such as a long stretch of road, a gas-powered trimmer is the only option. When choosing one of these, the first consideration should be whether the shaft is curved or straight. Light-duty homeowner models often have curved shafts, which are a little easier to keep flat. All heavy-duty consumer and pro string trimmers have a straight shaft because they deliver more power, durability, and reach with less vibration.

A decent straight-shaft trimmer will have at least a 21cc motor and will cost around $200; good brands include Echo, Hitachi, and Tanaka. The next step up is a 25cc engine on models such as the

Husqvarna 223L ($250) and Stihl FS RC-E ($260); the extra power helps with heavier weeds and tall grass.

Pro-level string trimmers have to run day after day, so they need to be reliable, efficient, and generate minimal vibration. These cost between $300 and $500, which makes them overkill for most home-owners. Some have a wide bicycle-style handle for more control and comfort. These use thicker line than the homeowner models, so they tend to last much longer, particularly when working around rocks.

Another option, if you have a lot of land, is a walk-behind string trimmer that has large wheels, such as the Husqvarna High Wheel Trimmer ($350) with a 22-inch cutting path. It looks like a mower with large wheels, but it's much more effective on weeds and dense grass.

An excellent alternative to a dedicated string trimmer is a power head with interchangeable attachments such as the Shindaiwa M254 ($330) and the Stihl KM110R Kombi ($340). The string trimmer attachment for the Stihl costs $100, making it an expensive tool if that's all you use. The big savings come when you get two or three

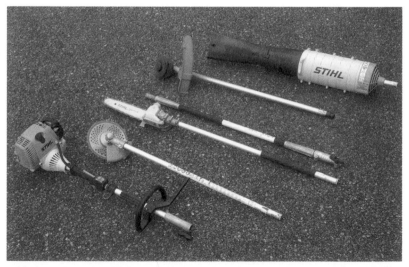

Stihl KM110R Kombi with brush cutter, pole saw plus extension, string trimmer, and blower

other attachments. These combination tools are compact when disassembled, so they're easy to transport and stow.

Gas-powered string trimmers are loud and powerful, so you do need protection. At a minimum, good ear protection is essential. I wear my chain saw helmet and have been thankful for the face guard many times after the trimmer whipped a rock at me.

These machines weigh around 10 to 14 pounds, which doesn't take long to cause fatigue. Many come with a padded shoulder strap to support the load, but it's a mediocre solution at best. A better alternative is a dual-strap shoulder harness such as the Husqvarna Brush Cutter Harness ($30), which distributes the weight evenly. Take the time to adjust the attachment point on the shaft for proper balance; the trimmer head should hang naturally just a few inches above the ground.

Bump-feed line systems can be another source of aggravation because they often have issues. Using higher-quality line can solve some problems because it tends to be more durable and less likely to melt together. Although square and other shapes may cut slightly better than round string, they're also more jam-prone and not worth the hassle.

The nylon used for trimmer line will dry out over time, making it brittle. To increase durability, keep your spare line moist by putting it in a ziplock bag with some water. After reloading the spool, you can spray the line with WD-40 or silicon to help it feed smoothly. Don't wait too long to bump for more string; if the stubs are too short, there is less centrifugal force to pull out extra.

If you're still having problems, switch the head to a fixed-line style, such as the Pivotrim Pro ($25), and cut your own line. Another alternative to the standard head that comes with the machine is the Oregon Speed-Feed ($30), which is a bump style that greatly simplifies reloading.

When using your string trimmer, the most effective technique is to swing it in an arc back and forth in front of you, using the tip of the string to clear a path through the grass. If you plunge too deeply into tall grass or weeds, the plants can wrap themselves around the hub. Trimming wet grass can lead to problems with the head clogging, and it may strain weaker engines to the point of damage.

Take care when working around the base of trees to avoid hitting the bark with the line. Too many whacks with the string on thin-barked species like Douglas fir can kill a tree. Do yourself a favor: If you're cutting out poison ivy or oak, wait until late fall when the leaves are gone.

Brush Cutter

A brush cutter is a string trimmer on steroids. Professional models are very powerful, with the bicycle handles for control and a full chest harness to carry the weight; these cost upwards of $800.

If you have a reasonably powerful string trimmer with a straight shaft, it can be converted to a brush cutter by swapping out the head, which will take a few minutes. At the most basic level, there are steel grass-cutting blades that have three to eight teeth. These don't work well on brush, and they require frequent sharpening. Another option is the Grass Gator Pro ($20), which has three pivoting steel blades that do an adequate job on small brush.

Because I went with the Stihl Kombi system, I have one attachment set up as a string trimmer and another set up as a brush cutter. This cost $140 with the blade and blade guard (limit stop) and takes about thirty seconds to swap out.

For really nasty brush and brambles and even small trees, the best option is a blade that resembles a table saw blade with eighty to a hundred carbide teeth ($20, carbidebrushcutterblades.com). These blades are incredibly effective on anything under 3 inches in diameter. As long as you don't hit rock or metal, the blades don't need sharpening.

Never use an actual table saw blade. Those are designed for a saw that spins at only 3,800 rpm, and they're made with hardened steel that will shatter if they so much as touch a rock. A brush cutter can reach 10,000 rpm or more, so the steel needs to be somewhat malleable to prevent a catastrophic accident.

Although they look aggressive, avoid brush cutter blades with chain saw teeth. They are heavy and cut a relatively wide kerf (thickness of the cutting blade). This puts more strain on the motor and leads to problems with the blade binding in the cut.

The blade on a brush cutter spins counterclockwise at incredible speed. This means that you can cut only with the left-hand edge. If you cut with the tip or the right edge, you'll experience violent kickback that can send that shaft and spinning blade off in an arc that can do serious damage to anyone in the area. Always wear a shoulder or chest harness to keep that blade from hitting you. It takes a long time for the blade to stop spinning.

It's best to spin the blade up to maximum speed before starting a cut into wood. If it begins to bog down, back off the pressure and allow the rpm's to rev up again. For thicker wood, change your angle of attack so the round blade cuts only a section at a time instead of trying to cut a U with lots of resistance.

Power Pole Saw

While a good manual pole saw is very effective, it's still too slow if you have a lot of land to mitigate. A battery- or gas-powered pole saw won't reach 20 feet up but makes fast work of branches less than 12 feet above the ground. The bar on these mini chain saws is only 8 to 10 inches long, but that's enough for branches up to about 4 inches in diameter.

The Black & Decker 20-volt Cordless Pole Saw ($140) will be adequate for small projects, but short battery life will be a problem for larger areas; a spare battery is $40. This also requires you to oil the chain manually.

The next step up from cordless is a gas power head, like the Toro two-cycle ($100), with a Ryobi Expand-It Pruner attachment ($100). For many property owners, this system will handle all of your needs.

It won't be as fast or as durable as higher-end equipment, but it should get the job done.

Dedicated gas-powered pole saws start at about $500 and have much more powerful engines with better-engineered components; the nicest models have telescoping poles. These are great for professionals but hard to justify for home use unless you get a combination tool.

For my Stihl Kombi, I went with their pole pruner attachment ($220) and an extension. At first, I tried to save some money and bought the steel shaft extension ($70), but quickly realized the system was poorly balanced and would be a lot of work to maneuver. So I ended up with the carbon fiber extension ($120), and the improvement was significant.

While you don't need chain saw chaps when using a power pole saw, you should wear a helmet and ear protection; the face guard isn't necessary, but safety glasses are a good idea. A chest harness or shoulder strap makes carrying the pole saw easier, but it limits your reach, so make sure there's a quick detach hook.

As with a manual pole saw, you need to stand a few feet back from the tree trunk to get a good angle. For large limbs, it's best to make the first cut a few feet out from the trunk, then make a second cut close in so the branch doesn't strip bark from the trunk.

Cordless Reciprocating Saw

If you've already invested in an 18-volt lithium-ion battery tool system (DeWalt, Makita, Ryobi), consider adding a cordless reciprocating saw to your collection. Sold without batteries, these cost only $100 and can be handy for a variety of house projects.

Makita cordless reciprocating saw

With a Bosch or Milwaukee five-teeth-per-inch pruning blade ($20 for a five-pack), a reciprocating saw cuts through limbs at about half the speed of a chain saw but faster than doing it by hand. The tool weighs around 8 pounds, so it's a bit lighter than a chain saw and tons heavier than a folding pruning saw.

Due to the cost of the charger and batteries, a reciprocating saw isn't a great choice if you don't have other tools in the cordless system. Also, it really isn't a replacement for a chain saw unless your needs are minimal.

Power Capstan

If you're working in hilly terrain and have a lot of trees to manage, a power winch could be useful. The options range from pathetic battery-powered toys to massive bumper-mounted hydraulic winches that could lift a truck and run all day. Vehicle-mounted winches have lots of power, but they can't reach many situations because they have only 100 feet of cable in most cases. Winches that use a chain saw as their power source are awkward and lack important features like a reverse setting.

For portability with serious pulling power, a good option is a gas-powered capstan like the Portable Winch PCW-5000 ($1,200) using low-stretch rope. This weighs 35 pounds but can pull 2,200 pounds at 40 feet per minute; using a snatch block, it pulls twice as much half as fast. By swapping the drum for a larger one, you can speed it up to 60 feet per minute, though it does reduce overall capacity to 1,800 pounds of pulling power.

Well known to sailors, a capstan is superior to a winch because you can use any length of rope and it's easy to take in or let out slack. Also, the pulling power remains the same. (It decreases by about 40 percent on a winch as the drum fills.) Most electric winches can run only for a short period of time before requiring a cooldown; a capstan can run as long as you have gas. Low-stretch rope doesn't have problems with kinking or vicious loose strands like steel cable.

Wood Chipper

If you live in a hardwood or aspen forest, consider a shredder (about $200 and almost all are electric), which is basically a string trimmer with a funnel on top. These are great for turning leaves into fine mulch ideal for composting. However, shredders can't handle pine needles, pinecones, or small branches well.

The next step up is a chipper/shredder with a big funnel for leaves and a small chute that accepts branches up to 3 inches thick. The better machines have at least a 5 hp gas-powered motor and are designed to be opened easily to clear clogs. These typically run about $700 to $1,400; anything less than that likely only accepts branches just over 1 inch in diameter, so it won't do you much good.

A strong candidate is the Patriot CSV-3065B (patriot-products-inc.com), which offers a good combination of power and performance. This is a direct-drive chipper that maximizes horsepower and durability, while most others use less efficient pulleys and belts. In addition, it has no screens to clog, it's easy to change the knives, and it comes with a three-year warranty.

A wood chipper is good for reducing pine needles—which have a waxy coating that slows decay—and pinecones into mulch that composts faster. But you have to cut branches down to straight pieces that will fit the small funnel. These machines are good for yard cleanup, but for reducing massive piles of slash, you need to rent or hire a commercial chipper. (See "Chipping" in Chapter 4.)

Rough Terrain Mower

Landowners with large lots of overgrown terrain may want to consider a lawnmower on steroids—the rough terrain mower (drpower .com and mackissic.com). Running between $2,000 and $3,800, these self-propelled machines can take out 3-inch-diameter saplings and weeds 8 feet tall. Like all mowers, the blades can create sparks if they hit a rock, so don't mow during the heat of the day and keep an extinguisher handy.

For most homeowners, a bush mower attachment for a skid loader, commonly known as a Bobcat, is probably over the top. But boys love their toys, so the Fecon Bull Hog mulcher and Gyro-Trac 400HL cutter head are awesome accessories. If you're *really* serious, go for something like the GT-140XL tractor (fecon.com and gyrotrac .net).

CARING FOR YOUR LAND

Forest stewardship is both a science and an art. Enhancing the resiliency of your trees against fire, beetles, and other disturbances while improving the aesthetics of your property is no simple matter. But with an understanding of the science of wildfire and the ecosystem in which you live, you can more effectively care for your land.

Depending on the size of your property, stewardship and fire mitigation can be a daunting task. As with climbing a high mountain, you need to break the ultimate goal into small steps.

I manage our 35 acres of ponderosa pine forest in the Colorado Front Range. We also have Douglas fir and aspen that I'm trying to encourage as well as über-flammable Rocky Mountain juniper that needs to be kept under control but not eradicated because it is good for local critters. As well, we have a seasonal creek that acts as a riparian zone with peachleaf willow, cottonwood, and a variety of shrubs. My goal has been to make our home safer and our ecosystem healthier. A professional forester looking to harvest timber certainly would do things differently. If we lived in a different region, I might do things differently, though many of these same concepts would still apply.

I also routinely break a primary safety rule of using a chain saw: never work alone. If I had to wait for someone to help, we'd be years behind on our stewardship efforts. This is the equivalent of free soloing in the climbing world: not entirely safe but not as dangerous as it sounds if you are acutely aware of the consequences. Do as I say, not as I do, and always have someone helping when cutting with a chain saw.

PHASE ONE

When you first start out, a huge task and possibly the wrong tools may doubly hamper you. Because you make the most gains closest to your home, cleaning up Zone 1 should represent about 70 percent of your effort, and the remaining 30 percent should constitute your first pass at Zone 2.

How long Phase One takes primarily depends on what, if anything, has already been done in the way of mitigation. Most people should be able to do the major projects with a couple weekends of effort.

But actually doing good fire mitigation in Zone 1 is easier said than done. This is where you may have to make some of your toughest decisions. That 20-foot juniper tree may look great, but it's a fireball waiting to torch your house. You love the blue spruce that your grandfather planted, but it has grown so big that it hangs over your roof. Those flashy ornamental plants under the front window are pleasant to look at . . . until they catch fire and superheat the glass above them.

If you plan to mitigate Zone 2 and keep your precious trees and shrubs next to the house, then *don't bother doing anything except creating an inventory.* You can clean out Zones 2 and 3 all you want—even put a fire break all the way around—and the fire department will still write off your house as a loss and won't defend it during a major fire event. Zone 1 is what will make or break the rest of your defenses.

This pine tree needs to lose at least the bottom five limbs, and the gutters will need regular cleaning.

Remember: It's the firebrands traveling a mile or more through the air that are probably going to burn your home to the ground.

So, yes, the juniper has to go; the spruce needs a good pruning; and the fountain and pampas grasses never should have been there in the first place. This reality doesn't mean that you must live amid a barren, stark landscape, though. You can have a great-looking, fire-resistant 30-foot perimeter around your house if you do some research.

There is no such thing as fireproof vegetation. The first 5 feet from your home (Zone 1A) should be kept low to the ground. A string trimmer is ideal for regular maintenance of this area because you can get into tight spaces. It's OK to have small clusters of flowers and other ornamental plants, but you don't want a large mass of plants or big shrubs even if they are fire-resistant. Trees should be pruned so they don't hang over the house or near a chimney.

Frequently water any plants in this inner zone. The best way to do this is to install drip irrigation with a timer. Using half-inch tubing, this is a fairly simple weekend project and will cost only $100 to $200, depending on how much area you are covering. Use a backflow preventer, a filter, a pressure regulator, and pressure-compensating emitters. A battery-operated timer is also highly recommended. However, homeowners on a well must remember to turn off the automated sprinkler if the power goes out to prevent draining the limited water supply (I learned this the hard way).

In this area, you can use mulch to conserve moisture and reduce weeds, but it can pose a risk. Gravel and stone, of course, are good if you like the look and don't mind picking out debris by hand. Large wood chips are relatively fire-resistant if you keep the area irrigated with sprinklers, but dried mulch allows fire to creep in almost undetected. Absolutely do *not* use pine needles or small wood chips for mulch, because they will bring the fire right to your home.

Some people irrigate all of Zone 1B (between 5 and 30 feet from the house) with sprinklers. If you live on the urban edge and have municipal water, your HOA bylaws may even require a green lawn. However, keeping an area this large watered—particularly during a drought—can prove expensive. Most people in intermix and rural areas tend to go with a more natural landscape and selectively water with drip irrigation. It's important to get out with the string trimmer once the grasses start to dry in the late spring. You may need to cut the grasses again after the summer monsoon because another long, dry spell often follows before winter.

Pathways and crushed stone can keep fire away.

In Zone 2 and beyond (from 30 feet out), there should be no watering other than very selective drip irrigation. This will reduce plant growth to minimize the amount of burnable vegetation. Make sure that excess water from Zone 1 doesn't flow into Zone 2.

Ideally, you want all of Zone 1 to be nearly horizontal, less than 1 foot of drop every 4 feet. If you have steeper terrain leading to your house, consider terracing by building short stone walls and backfilling. Even if you just level the downslope side of the house for Zone 1A, those 5 feet can keep a fire from rushing straight to your outer walls.

Pathways in Zone 1 and 2 will slow the spread of a fire. Plus, they're nice to walk on. It's easy to build paths using stepping stones; the tighter you place the stones, the less weed growth you'll have. We used flagstone and set it out along the path. After a few weeks of walking and adjusting position, I dug out underneath the stones to get them close to flush; slightly raised is better to help keep pebbles off the walkway.

In addition to trimming grasses in Zone 1, you need to remove dead branches from shrubs regularly and rake up needles and leaves. This fuel reduction can greatly slow the spread of surface fire. Several years of buildup from a single medium-size ponderosa pine can generate eight or more wheelbarrow loads of needles and pinecones.

You also need to inspect your home for unusual ember traps and fire hazards. For example: A doormat made of plant fiber can ignite right next to your door and siding. Also give proper consideration to wooden planters and lawn furniture on a deck or a pergola with a lattice. Bird nests are nice, but they can also act as mini fire pits, so clean them out after the chicks leave. Live trap any pack rats and drive them to a new home a few miles away, then clean out their nests.

Flickers rank among the most evil creatures on the planet. This giant woodpecker likes to wake homeowners in the predawn hours with drumming on the side of the house. Worse yet, flickers often make large holes in siding for their nests, which become entry points for embers. It can be difficult to scare flickers away, but building a nesting box nearby can help because they're territorial. Patching the holes in your siding won't be easy, as they're often high off the ground, but you have to do it to prevent water and possibly fire damage.

Fire-Resistant Plants

When selecting near-the-home plants, your best choices are short species with high moisture content such as wildflowers, ground covers, and succulents. Vegetable gardens are a great choice if you can figure out how to keep critters away. For shrubs, look for open branches with relatively few leaves instead of tight balls that you can't see through.

Any nearby trees should lose their leaves in the winter (deciduous species like aspen and oak). In terms of fire, these have several advantages over conifers, including leaves with higher water content and less-volatile sap. In the summer, deciduous species provide nice shade, and in the winter, they allow more solar gain to reduce your heating bill.

Most states in fire-prone regions have lists of recommended plants; do an Internet search for "Firewise plants Arizona" or wherever you live. Your local garden center should know which plants are best suited to your particular location—but don't count on it. In my experience, garden centers mostly focus on city dwellers, and their suggestions included highly flammable ornamentals and shrubs. Double-check with the Firewise lists before planting.

It may surprise you how large a selection of fire-resistant plants you have to choose from. In Colorado, for example, recommended plants include 89 species of flowers and ground covers, 33 species of small shrubs, and 24 species of large shrubs and trees. The list for Arizona includes 16 types of grasses, 31 different shrubs, and 25 species of trees. Florida's lists 11 trees, 15 shrubs, and 18 types of bedding plants, ground covers, and vines.

Propane Tank

The best solution for propane storage in high fire risk areas is an underground tank. This can be an expensive proposition, though, because you generally have to buy the tank instead of leasing one. The cost of bringing in a backhoe and digging the hole can also be significant.

If you already have an aboveground propane tank, make sure that the area around it is weeded and no trees hang over the tank. When exposed to high heat, the pressure-release valve should open, causing a jet of flame instead of a big explosion. If the heat is so intense that the liquid propane begins to boil, however, the valve won't be able to bleed the rising pressure fast enough—and *boom!*

Some people spread gravel or crushed rock under and around the tank, but this can trap a lot of pine needles and cones that are difficult to clean out. Bare ground is better as long as you keep it weed-free with a stirrup hoe or weed killer.

A propane tank enclosed by wood and surrounded by tall grass is an explosion waiting to happen.

Homeowners' associations sometimes require screens around "unsightly" propane tanks. Surrounding your tank with a stone or cinderblock wall gives it extra protection from radiant heat, and this is the second-best option to burying the tank. If there's already a wood fence around it, treat the wood with fire retardant and create a firebreak with gravel.

PHASE TWO

In the second level of your priorities, continue working on Zone 2 and get serious about the inner portion of Zone 3. You may also need to do some follow-up work in Zone 1, too, but you'll spend most of your time in the area from 30 to 200 feet from your house.

This is likely when you'll do your initial round of thinning the forest and clearing deadfall. Rather than wandering around with a chain saw cutting things down willy-nilly, walk your property a couple of times as you ponder the problem spots. Carry a roll of florescent flagging or a can of spray paint to mark trees destined for culling. As you walk around, think in terms of both fire mitigation and forest health. Keep the recommendations for tree spacing in Zones 2 and 3 in mind (see Chapter 2), and look out for ladder fuel that will carry a fire into the canopy. Also think about how you can make the remaining trees stronger, enhance the land for wildlife, and increase the natural beauty.

Scrawny, light-starved trees are unlikely to become vigorous just by removing a few trees around them, so they will always be more susceptible to disease and beetles. Dense stands of trees will already be competing for water, so a drought will hit them particularly hard. Snow-bent trees over 3 inches in diameter won't straighten themselves out again and will become permanent ladder fuel with their limbs touching the ground. Though mistletoe kills slowly, trees weakened by it may attract beetles that will eventually dine on healthy trees nearby.

On the other hand, it's nice to keep some "character" trees, too. These have lived an extraordinary life, and a logger would hate them. They may be crooked, split, growing sideways out of a rock, or have two trunks. Often all they need is a nice pruning to show off their charm and become more fire resistant.

Particularly in Zone 3, it's good to leave, or even create, about three snags per acre. These standing dead trees are valuable for woodpeckers and cavity-dwelling animals. After they fall, the logs provide homes for

Trees with character add interest to your property.

other creatures and insects as they decompose. Instead of cutting a tree out, you may want to "girdle" it by removing a section of bark all the way around the trunk.

Ideally, you want a mix of tree ages and species after you finish, though some forests, such as lodgepole pine, may be even-aged and single species. In Zone 2 you want to thin and prune considerably because this is your first line of defense against fire.

When selecting trees to remove, always look up. Instead of taking out this tree, removing that one next to it might open the canopy to give better separation. Proper spacing lets more light reach the ground and also reduces the likelihood of a crown fire spreading.

If your forest consists primarily of shallow-rooted trees, such as lodgepole pine and Engelmann spruce, think strategically about thinning. These trees are more susceptible to windthrow, so you want to reduce them in stages. By thinning a few, then waiting three to five years before thinning more, you allow the root system to expand so they can better withstand high winds. Another alternative is to leave somewhat dense clumps as windbreaks and cut out small meadows on the lee side.

Once you've marked trees for removal, it's time to get to work. The best time of year for tree cutting is the middle of September to early May so the odor of fresh-cut trees doesn't attract beetles. Exact details will depend on your situation, but you likely want to do most of the cutting in one fell swoop. That way you can process the downed trees and deal with disposal of the slash efficiently. Because you're working primarily within 200 feet of your home, this operation actually goes pretty quickly, perhaps taking a weekend or two.

After the trees are downed and cleared, go in with your pruning and pole saws to do some serious limbing on the trees still standing. Trees such as Douglas fir and Rocky Mountain juniper have thin branches that hang to the ground, making them ideal ladder fuels. Pruning these lower branches is very important for effective fire

A deer guard around a Douglas fir

mitigation. The pole saw can help you reach in and cut them off near the trunk without getting poked, but the pruning saw is helpful for touch-ups once you get in there.

Note that young thin-barked trees like Douglas fir are easily damaged and even killed by deer rubbing their antlers to remove velvet and mark territory. To prevent this, install a wire cage about twice the diameter of the trunk around the lower portion of the tree. In a decade or so, you'll need to remove it so the tree won't grow into the cage. Alternatively, you can cut lower branches so 2-inch stubs remain that will discourage bucks. Trees with thick bark, like ponderosa pine, don't need protection from deer.

In general, large-diameter trees (over 8 inches) in Zone 2 should be limbed to about 10 feet above the ground, while small-diameter trees should be limbed to about 6 feet. In Zone 3 limb big trees to about 6 feet and smaller trees to about 3 feet. This will give them resistance to crown fires while protecting your privacy.

You'll also notice a lot of dead branches high up in the canopy that can come out to let more light in and reduce the fuel load. Use your pole saw to remove as much of this as you can. For trees and large bushes near your home, consider using a pruning pole to snip the ends of a few branches for a nicer appearance.

Despite the thinning and limbing, your trees still remain susceptible to death from ground fire. Many older conifers have a deep accumulation of duff; those piles of dead needles and cones can accumulate from a few inches to several feet thick. This material allows fire to creep up to the tree's trunk, smoldering at high temperatures, where it damages the cambium. Although the tree may appear to have survived the fire, it will die in a few months.

Clearing the duff from the base of trees can help them survive a surface fire.

To prevent this kind of tree fatality, clear the duff from the base of trees to create a ring of bare ground about 12 inches wide. A Pulaski tool is ideal for this, because the hoe end is good for grubbing and the ax is useful for chopping off limbs that you uncover beneath the duff; a McLeod tool also works well.

You may need to evaluate a lot of native shrubs on your property because they not only make ideal ladder fuels and sources of firebrands, but also provide food and shelter for wildlife. In Zone 2 you probably want to remove about half of the shrubs, while in Zone 3 just those likely to cause problems with fire reaching into the canopy.

Raking and removing dead leaves, needles, and pinecones is essential in Zone 1, but it's also a good idea in Zone 2 to reduce the spread of ground fire. In high winds, this material serves as a source of firebrands that will bombard your house.

This is also a good time to inspect the power lines both on your property and in your neighborhood. Countless fires have started from power lines sparking in high winds. Look for any tree branches that appear close to the wires and any dead or dying trees that might fall and hit the wires or a pole. If you notice any hazards, call the power authority and get on their case until they send a crew.

The last step of this phase comes in late spring to early summer when you trim the tall grass in Zones 1 and 2. If you have a long driveway, be sure to trim the grass on either side because that's your escape route. You may need to trim this area again later in the summer if you get a lot of rain.

Once you've finished Phase Two, your home will have a much greater chance of surviving a fire. Over the next couple of years, you'll likely notice more wildlife visiting because you've improved their food supply and made it easier to spot predators.

Help Firefighters

It's a good idea to make your property more accessible for firefighters. During a large fire, it's likely not going to be the local volunteers defending your home; it will probably be a crew unfamiliar with the area because they came from the next county or even the next state over.

Make sure that street and home address signs are easy to read at night and in dense smoke. Forgo cutesy carved wooden signs for your home address, and install large reflective numbers that don't require electricity to read.

If you can, add turnouts to a long driveway, and enlarge the turnaround to make it easier for large fire trucks to get in and out. If there are bridges, culverts, or cattle guards on your property, make sure they can hold a 28-ton fire truck and clearly post weight limit signs. You also may want to mark your septic tank and leach fields to prevent a vehicle from driving over them.

Locked gates can delay emergency responders when time is critical, and they have contributed to fatalities. Train your local fire department on how to open the gate and keep it open for the duration of the emergency. Ideally, electronic gates should have a battery backup, but it's good to know how to open them manually as well.

PHASE THREE

When you reach this stage of stewardship, you're doing maintenance to everything done in Phases One and Two, and you're extending your efforts in caring for Zone 3. If you have a lot of land, this is when Zone 4 needs your attention.

During the few years after your initial efforts in Zones 2 and 3, walk the areas again and you'll surely notice a few more trees that should come out and limbs on other trees that should be pruned. There may be some trees that you left to see how they would fare with more light and water that never attained a healthy vigor. If you had snags, they may have fallen but not necessarily in the best location for preventing erosion. Some seedlings may have grown into ladder fuels.

After a heavy snowstorm, get out as soon as possible to check for damage to trees. In the winter you're more likely to find broken limbs and split or even snapped trunks that should be pruned. If you leave these unattended, the gaping wounds can invite bugs and infections when the weather warms.

When big snows hit in early spring, the trees are starting to run with sap, so they are more likely to bend over. For trees under 3 inches in diameter, knock off the snow with a broom, and they should recover. A larger tree can't straighten itself and will take a permanent set after a couple weeks without help. You may need a come-along winch to get it upright and some rope tied off to another tree to hold it up for about two months.

In Phase Three you'll also tackle some of the bigger projects in Zones 1 and 2 that give you more protection. This might include adding stone walkways, replacing wooden decks with more fire-resistant materials, or adding a pond that also serves as a water source for firefighters.

In our case, we revisited Zone 1A, that 5-foot perimeter next to the house. For years I had been using the string trimmer to keep grasses low to the ground, but our house was built long before wildfire posed a major threat in Colorado, so we have wood siding. We wanted greater protection from surface fire, so the most affordable solution was $1\frac{1}{2}$-inch decorative rock.

We used 3 tons of butter rock to encircle the house with a 3-foot perimeter and cover the entire area under the decks. (Helpful tip: Have the truck deliver *above* your house, not below.) For areas that receive little foot traffic, you only need to go 1 to 2 inches deep—far less than the purveyors' standard calculations—so 1 ton covers about 50 linear feet.

First, I laid down heavy-duty weed-barrier fabric, which normally comes in 36-inch widths. Look for commercial grade; most of the stuff sold at big-box stores is flimsy and easily punctured. Then I used landscape edging to keep the rocks from migrating. (A 2.5-pound sledgehammer is helpful for pounding stakes.)

After that, it was just a matter of hauling about eighty wheelbarrow loads of rock from the pile to the final location; a square-point transfer shovel is essential for this. Aside from the considerable sweat equity, the total cost ran about $1,200. While great for our home, it may be inadvisable if you have pine trees nearby. You'll have to pick the needles out by hand; neither a rake nor a blower will remove them without disturbing the rocks.

A bigger project was replacing the redwood decks with Class B capped composite decking (see Chapter 5). With over 700 square feet, this was a $25,000 investment that improved the appearance, value, and safety of our home. Unfortunately, it did not earn a discount from the insurance company (grrrr).

Another Phase Three project is planting shrubs and deciduous trees. We've added caragana, cotoneaster, lilac, and sumac shrubs— all of which have good wildlife value—as well as aspen and Siberian elm trees. All of these young plants require wire cages to keep the deer away and drip irrigation until they are well established.

Mistletoe

Keep a watchful eye out for dwarf mistletoe infestations. If you catch it early enough, you can save a tree by cutting off the infected branches. Heavily infested trees will die as the parasitic plant steals food and water. In the meantime, at the end of each summer, the nasty things shoot seeds as much as 60 feet out to infest other trees. Birds can also carry the sticky seeds on their feet.

To decide whether a mistletoe-infested tree should be removed, mentally divide it into thirds. For each section, rate it a 0 for no infestation, 1 if less than half the branches are affected, and 2 if more than half are infested. If the combined score is 3 or more, cut the tree down. Once a tree or branch is cut, the mistletoe dies, so no special disposal is required. Treat it just like normal slash.

Bark Beetles

While mistletoe is a slow-moving tree killer, Ips and mountain pine beetles can kill in under a year. Worse, each infested tree can spawn enough beetles to kill at least two nearby trees the next year—hence the exponential spread and the need for action if a tree is attacked. During droughts, trees produce less pitch, a primary defense against beetle attack.

If the tree's needles are red, it's already too late. The attack occurred about eight to ten months earlier. Most likely the beetles have already hatched and are attacking nearby trees. Walk around the trunk of the tree and look for masses of resin that resemble popcorn, generally from ground level to about 10 feet up. (Ips beetles tend to attack the top of the tree.) If you see this popcorn, cut away some bark and look for the telltale blue stain fungus.

If you have beetle-infested trees that are still green, you can't do anything to save them; the fungus is already inside. However, you can save the rest of your trees by removing the doomed trees before the beetle larvae hatch. There's no need to remove dead trees if you want to keep some snags, because the beetles have already gone.

One trick for drawing beetles away from prized trees is called "green chaining." This entails creating a pile of slash a good distance from other trees and adding fresh, green branches to the pile every couple of weeks during the flight season, typically spring and early summer. However, if you break the chain and don't keep feeding the pile, the beetles will move to trees within a quarter mile.

Once infested trees are cut, treat the slash normally. If you chip it, the material dries out so quickly that the beetle larvae will die, but the wood odor may attract more beetles. Covering the slash with clear plastic, called solarization, can heat up the pile enough (above 115°F) to kill most of the beetles; this requires a location with a lot of sunlight.

The tree trunks, however, still host the little buggers, so they require special treatment. If you have access to an industrial chipper, it can chip logs up to 10-inches in diameter and save you a lot of hassle. A more labor-intensive option is to strip the bark with a specialized tool called a bark spud ($60), though a flat nail bar will work, too. A 10-inch drawknife ($50) offers a slower alternative. Stripping the bark exposes the larvae, which soon die. Stripping bark is most easily done in the spring.

Another method of treating beetle trees is to lay an infested trunk out where it will get lots of sunlight during the summer so that the bark dries out. You have to rotate the logs 120° after a month and then again a month later to dry the wood fully and kill the bugs. A solar treatment using thick clear plastic can work, too, but is more problematic when working with heavy logs.

For a few important trees near your house, it may be worth the money to hire a contractor to spray them with permethrin. Other chemicals (carbaryl and bifenthrin) are approved for pine beetle, but they're much more toxic and probably best avoided. It costs around $10 to $25 per tree for a contractor to do the work, depending on how many trees and other factors. Involving your neighbors may lower the relative cost.

You can spray trees yourself, but it's hazardous work and requires getting all sides of a tree trunk for 30 feet. You don't want to breathe this stuff, and you'll likely be working on uneven terrain. I'm willing to do a lot myself, but I'd hire the guys with proper gear for this chore.

The spray must be applied in June before the beetles fly and is reapplied every year for about a decade. Some reports indicate that with the warming climate, the beetles are starting to breed twice a year, which means that it may be better to spray in May and possibly again in August.

Another option is to hang pheromone pouches on important trees to fool the bugs into dining elsewhere. Verbenone costs roughly $7 per pouch but reportedly works if the forest isn't already heavily infested with pine beetles.

We invite woodpeckers and nuthatches onto our property by offering them birdseed all year (black oil sunflower seeds are a favorite) and providing birdhouses and snags for nesting. Hopefully they will keep the beetles under control, and it's nice to have them around. If you live in bear country, put only enough feed out in the morning so that it's picked clean in a few hours.

Invasive Plants

Whether you live in the urban interface, the intermix, a rural area, or wildland, learn to spot and eradicate invasive species. These plants tend to spread rapidly and soon outpace indigenous flora. Among the worst offenders is tamarisk, which has strangled the banks of countless rivers and streams while sucking up enormous quantities of water. In the Southeast, everyone knows about kudzu, the fast-growing vine that has choked out millions of acres of forest.

Keeping your land native is no easy task, but it's worth the effort because you foster a healthier ecosystem more resistant to fire and pests and more attractive to fauna. Some invaders, like myrtle spurge and Scotch thistle, are easy to identify because they're so alien. But when it comes to grasses and weeds, you need a keen eye and a fair amount of knowledge to spot interlopers.

Every region has lists of invaders. These usually are broken down into categories that translate to Class A: seek and destroy; Class B: kill whenever you can; and Class C: don't let them spread.

PRUNING

With the right tools, pruning trees isn't difficult, but if you aren't careful, you can do more harm than good. Excess pruning, careless cutting, or pruning at the wrong time of year can weaken a tree.

Use a very sharp saw or pruner so that the cut is smooth, not ragged, for faster healing. Professional arborists sterilize their tools with alcohol or diluted bleach when working on diseased trees to prevent illness from spreading to other trees. This isn't necessary if your trees

Remove lower branches to keep fire out of the canopy.

are healthy. Don't waste your money on pruning sealer, because the tree will heal just as fast on its own.

The main criterion for effective pruning is to get close—but not too close. If you can hang a coat off the remaining stub, you didn't get close enough and the remaining wood will decay, making it easier for fungi and insects to attack. If you cut the branch off flush to the trunk, you've probably caused unnecessary damage that will take longer to heal.

Start your cut just outside the bark ridge, where the top of the branch meets the tree. The ideal angle is slightly less than parallel so that the branch collar (the bulge around the base of the branch) remains intact. If you need to rest, do so before the limb starts to droop, then finish the cut quickly to minimize damage.

For very thick branches or trees with bark that tears easily, cut them off in sections. By removing weight from the end, you reduce the chance of the limb cracking and damaging the trunk. For extra protection against tearing bark, first cut partway up from the bottom of the branch (an undercut) at least a foot away from the tree, then cut the branch off past this first cut, and finally prune near the trunk as normal.

If you notice branches growing toward the sky instead of straight out from the trunk, remove or cut them back. These have a weak V-shaped crotch that eventually will break from high winds or heavy snow, often leaving a nasty scar that heals poorly.

For branches dangling to the ground, you may not need to remove the entire branch. Instead, just cut the dangler back to an outward-growing section of the branch. A scrawny branch directly under a big healthy branch is never going to do well because it won't get much light; consider removing it.

If you intend to harvest your trees for lumber, prune them when young (about 3 to 4 inches in diameter) so the branches and resulting knots are small. As they mature, prune the trees to at least 17 feet up, but never remove more than a third of the canopy; this will yield a 16-foot log with a 1-foot stump.

No matter the species, you can prune dead branches at any time of the year because they won't ooze sap or attract beetles. Conifers also may be pruned all year long because their energy is stored in the needles. However, late fall and winter are best to keep the insects away.

Prune deciduous trees and shrubs in the winter if you want to encourage vigorous growth. They store their energy in their roots, so there are fewer buds to share the supply. Pruning these trees in the summer reduces the leaves that produce the food, so the next year's growth will be reduced.

Avoid pruning American elms, birches, fruit trees, and oaks after the beginning of April, when their sap is starting to run and the weather is warming. The sap can attract insects that carry fungi that will kill the trees.

BASICS OF TREE FELLING

In general, cutting trees down is a simple process. As long as you take the time to learn about the dangers, you can safely do it yourself—with a few notable exceptions. When you have a large tree near a structure or if there's any chance of hitting a power line, it's time to call a professional; the risk of a mishap is just too great. Also, don't mess with trees with extensive trunk rot because they're very unpredictable when they fall.

When standing next to a tree, somehow it doesn't look all that heavy. But a ponderosa pine 6 inches in diameter and 20 feet high weighs about 200 pounds. A tree 8 inches across and 30 feet tall weighs about 400 pounds, and a tree 12 inches wide and 40 feet high weighs well over 1,000 pounds. Combined with the force of gravity, almost any tree can cause grievous harm.

Complacency kills. Whether you're swinging an ax or running a chain saw, whether the tree is 4 or 24 inches in diameter, a casual attitude can result in serious injury or death. Even when you know all the risks, a false sense of confidence can get you into trouble. Wear protective gear—chaps, steel-toed boots, gloves, helmet—but don't let them substitute for proper caution. When something goes wrong, it happens in the blink of an eye, and the results are seldom pretty. That's why you should have a first-aid kit on your tool belt.

If you're new to felling trees, resist the temptation to fire up your new chain saw and start cutting. The Internet is full of videos of bozos doing dumb things while cutting trees. Don't be one of them. If you can, take a class in chain saw safety from a forest service or have an experienced friend show you proper technique. (Remember, though, that some old-timers have bad habits or use outdated techniques.)

Among the most important concepts to learn is kickback, a lightning-fast motion of the chain saw bar aimed right at your head. This usually happens when the upper tip of a running chain saw hits another log or branch, sending the bar up and back with tremendous velocity. Kickback can also happen when you're cutting from below with the top of the bar and the log pinches the chain, sending the saw straight back.

A thrown or broken chain could hit your face or right hand. Working with a chain saw above shoulder height is extremely dangerous because it's difficult to control if something goes wrong. Safety features like chain brakes and low-kickback chains also don't replace precaution. Always know where the tip of your bar is, and make sure it never encounters another log or branch.

When felling tall trees, the wind isn't your friend. Ideally, you want to do it on a calm day or in a steady, gentle breeze so the trees will fall when and where you want. Gusty days are particularly bad because the wind can suddenly push the tree in the wrong direction; this can lead to a pinched chain saw blade or worse. If you're out working and the wind picks up, call it a day or confine yourself to working on small stuff near the ground.

Preparing to Cut

Even if you're just going out to cut one small tree or buck some logs, put on your chaps, gloves, and helmet. Only fools run a chain saw without protective equipment. Fill your oil and gas tanks and give your chain saw an inspection to make sure it's ready to go (chain sharp and snug, chain brake works, etc.).

Firing up your gas-powered chain saw when it's cold can be problematic. See the section on fuel in Chapter 3 if you're really having a tough time. After bad gas, the top culprit of a balking chain saw is too much gas. Over-priming or cranking too much with the choke open can flood the cylinder with liquid fuel that won't ignite.

When starting cold, set the choke to open (press the decompression button if you have one) and crank no more than four times. You should hear and feel a pop as it tries to fire. If it doesn't, close the choke and crank again; it should start after a few pulls, but you can try eight times before trying with the choke open again.

If you kept pulling the cord with the choke open, you may have to wait ten to twenty minutes before trying again. You can also attempt to clear the flood by turning everything off (possibly even removing the sparkplug) and pulling the cord eight times.

Once it's running, let the saw warm up before going full throttle. Test the brake to make sure the chain comes to a full, rapid stop when activated. You can also check that the oiling system is working properly by pointing the bar tip at the ground and going full throttle for a few seconds; a slight spray of oil should be visible.

After the saw has been running a while, it should restart with a single pull. Particularly if you are using a brand-new chain, you may need to re-tension the chain once it has warmed and stretched a bit.

When handling your chain saw, your left hand goes on the handle, with your right on the trigger. Always wrap the thumb of your left hand around the handle so you have maximum control if something goes wrong. Leaving your thumb on top of the handle is less secure when a problem suddenly arises. If you are cutting horizontally, you can use the thumb of your right hand on the throttle instead of your trigger finger.

Don't rev the saw until you're at the wood and ready to cut. This should be obvious, but: Whenever you're walking around, carrying a running chain saw, the chain should be at full stop.

Though it may go against your initial instincts when holding a roaring beast, keep the chain saw close to your body when cutting. You have much more control when your upper arms are near your torso and your elbows are bent. As you extend your arms farther out and straighten your elbows, the chain saw becomes more dangerous. Cutting above shoulder height is likely to send you to the emergency room.

Whenever possible, cut with the section of the chain bar—either top or bottom—closest to the machine head. This greatly reduces the rotational force compared to cutting out near the tip. You may only cut with the bottom of the bar at first, but eventually you'll use the top of the bar nearly as often. If your saw has them, use the bumper spikes as a pivot for better control and cutting efficiency.

The chain doesn't stop the moment you release the trigger. Unless you hit the brake, it takes a few seconds for those rotating knives to halt. I once made that mistake, and it nearly cost me. Wearing chaps saved me a trip to the hospital.

After you've cut a tree down, inspect the sawdust. If the chain is sharp and filed properly, you should have a pile of longish chips. When the chain is dull, you'll have a pile of dust. A sharp chain pulls the chain saw through the wood, and a dull chain will make you want to push downward. It's worth taking the time either to swap out the chain or do a fast touch-up with a file so you save wear on the motor and yourself.

While cutting, be alert for soft spots that cut faster than normal and changes in the color of the sawdust. These can indicate a rotten trunk that may fall unpredictably. If you notice either, stop cutting and reevaluate the situation.

As the sawyer, you are responsible for the safety of others. Make sure that bystanders are well clear of the drop zone, which may not be where you planned. When limbing and bucking, make sure that nobody is standing behind you where they could get hurt if the saw kicks back.

Tree Felling Primer

1. Evaluate the tree and surroundings. Examine the tree from different angles to determine its natural lean; this isn't just the angle of the trunk but also includes all the branches that are sometimes heavier on one side. Often a tree has both a forward lean and a side lean. Also figure out where you want the tree to fall so that it won't hang on other trees or land in an inconvenient location for processing. If you're on a steep slope, avoid cutting the tree so that it falls uphill because it can bounce and slide. Check for dead limbs that might fall on you while cutting, affectionately known as "widow makers"—for a reason.

2. Clear the area around the tree so you have room to work safely. This may require removing small trees or brush that might hit your bar tip, cutting branches that want to stab you, or moving a loose rock for better footing.

3. Plan your escape route. Before you begin cutting, know exactly where you're going to run when the tree starts to fall. Normally this should be at a 45° angle from the direction of fall; visualize a Y with the stem pointed where the tree is aimed and the branches where you will escape. Obviously you don't want to be anywhere near the direction of fall because sometimes trees don't drop as desired. You also don't want to be behind the direction of fall because sometimes the butt of the tree will slip back violently—particularly if it hits other trees on the way down. You need to get at least 10 feet away as quickly as possible, which requires planning.

4. Plan your cut. Use the sighting line on your chain saw to aim your falling tree carefully. It's generally best to cut at about knee level so you have good control of the chain saw without straining your back. This will leave a stump about 2 feet tall that you can cut off near the ground later.

Aim with the black sighting line (above and below the logo).

5. Cut the notch (aka scarf). Sawyers frequently argue about different notching techniques, such as traditional and Humbolt, but for maximum safety you want a wide "mouth" that won't close up before the tree hits the ground. Make the first cut from the top at a fairly steep angle (over 60°), cutting downward into the first quarter of the

Working at knee to mid-thigh height gives you more control and safety. Make the initial cut at a steep angle and go a quarter of the way into the trunk. The bottom cut comes next and the back cut from the opposite side of the tree. The better your notch, the better your fell. Aim for a precision drop on the easy trees so you are prepared for the problem trees.

tree (roughly 60 percent of the diameter). Then make the bottom cut either horizontal or at an upward angle. While a wide "open-face" notch is desirable, the most important concern is making the two cuts meet precisely so the tree falls predictably. If you accidentally cut too deep, clean up the notch by taking out a thin slice as necessary.

6. Make the back cut. This is a horizontal cut either at the apex of the notch or just slightly (around 1 inch) higher. The cut should run parallel to the face of the notch and should stop 1 to $1^1/_2$ inches from the notch. It is vital that you leave this "hinge" material that will control the direction of the fall. Cutting too deep can result in the hinge giving way prematurely, and the tree can fall in any direction, possibly on you. It's better to leave a thicker hinge and give the tree a nudge by using wedges or a felling lever.

Due to the upper branches, this tree would have fallen to the left without the use of wedges. This notch was cut so the hinge would snap just before the trunk hit the ground.

7. Retreat! The moment the tree starts to tilt, stop cutting and get out of the way. Turn around and walk briskly in a straight line along your escape route; you're more likely to trip if you run or try to watch the tree fall. Often, the tree will start falling in slow motion before rapidly accelerating to the ground, but sometimes—particularly if you've cut too far into the hinge—it happens faster than a rattlesnake bite. It's best to hit the brake on your running chain saw and take it with you, but don't risk injury for something that can be repaired or replaced.

8. Inspect the scene. Look up to make sure branches aren't hanging in surrounding trees that might come down and whack you. Then inspect the stump to evaluate your performance; if the tree did something you didn't expect, the stump can give you clues from the cuts and hinge.

9. Clean up problems. If your tree is hung up in standing trees, plan your next course of action. If the hinge didn't break, you may need to finish the cut carefully.

The importance of a good notch and hinge cannot be overstated. The cuts that make these directly affect your accuracy and safety. The traditional notch that you may have learned takes a fairly narrow wedge from the tree (typically a 45° top cut and a horizontal bottom cut) with a back cut raised above the notch apex to create a step that can keep the butt of the tree from sliding backward. While effective, this notch creates a hinge that tends to snap when the tree has fallen halfway, thus losing directional control in the final moment.

Ideally, you want the notch face to be slightly less than the angle of the tree and ground. With a vertical trunk on horizontal ground, an 80° notch controls the tree almost all the way down and snaps the hinge as it lands. On a slope, you want to adjust the notch angle wider or narrower depending on whether the tree will fall downhill or uphill.

Beware the dutchman that is formed when one of the cuts in the notch is too deep, bypassing the apex. If you make a back cut into a dutchman, the hinge can break prematurely, and the tree can fall in the wrong spot or split vertically. Take the time to clean up your notch, and remember that the apex directs the fall. While a tree might have a natural lean, a good notch can change the direction it will fall by up to 45° without resorting to more complicated methods.

Making the back cut (also called a felling cut) at the apex has the advantage that it's easier to judge the width of the hinge. But if you're a bit higher, it shouldn't be a real problem. The main thing is that the back cut should run parallel to the notch apex so the hinge is even. Experienced sawyers can steer a tree by angling the hinge, but this can get you into trouble.

If the tree is 10 inches or larger in diameter, the bar will have space behind it as you're making the back cut. It's a good idea to insert a plastic felling wedge (tap it in with the palm of your hand) or felling lever to prevent the tree from settling back and pinching the bar. You're doing it right if this wedge keeps loosening or the lever handle lowers. But watch out if the wedge gets tighter or the lever handle rises because the tree is moving in the wrong direction. You may have to pound the wedge with a hammer or use the felling lever to give the tree a prod.

For trees under 5 inches, you can get away without making the bottom cut on the face. Simply make the top cut at about 45°, followed by the horizontal back cut, and the tree will gently bend over. This method saves time while still giving you good control of the fall.

Sometimes you need to make sure there's enough space on the ground for the tree to fall without hitting anything. There are all sorts of complicated methods for measuring a tree, but you don't need any of them as long as you have room to back up. Point your arm level at the tree and give it a thumbs-up. Align the base of your hand with the base of the tree, and then move forward or backward until the tip of your thumb aligns with the top of the tree. Now rotate your hand in the direction you plan on felling the tree (right or left), keeping the base of your hand aligned with the bottom of the tree. Where your thumb tip hits the ground is where the top of the tree will land.

Whether you leave a stump is a matter of preference. I like to cut them off as close to the ground as possible without risking damage to my chain. These stubs eventually decompose, but you can speed the process by drilling holes and filling with stump remover (potassium nitrate). If you intend to pull the stump with a winch, leave it fairly tall for better leverage. Burning a stump is a very bad idea.

If you're cutting trees on a steep slope and intend to leave them in place to decompose, they should end up parallel to the fall line. When a log lies perpendicular to the slope of a hill, it can roll if walked on or after it ignites, making it a hazard for firefighters.

Felling Problem Trees

Sometimes you run into a "problematic" tree. The tree might lean in the wrong direction from where you need it to fall. Perhaps the forward lean is OK, but it has a heavy top, giving it a side lean. Instead of rising vertically, it might be bent over at an angle. Or it could be partially or fully dead. All of these present unique issues that need to be factored into your decision-making process.

The three rules of cutting problem trees are: Assess, assess again, then reassess. If the tree is big enough to be a problem, it's probably been there for a long time. A few more days or weeks won't make the problem any worse as you evaluate your options. Charging in bull-headed can turn a problem into a crisis.

As mentioned earlier, with careful execution of your notch and hinge, you can often steer a tree up to 45° off its natural lean. But if you need a tree to drop opposite its lean or sideways, you'll need to employ more persuasion, and you might want to call a professional tree service.

For a small tree with a back lean, make the back cut first and then lightly set a wedge in the kerf. Then make a slight upward cut on the face side while still leaving a hinge. Finish it off by giving a push or driving the wedge further; a felling lever works well in this scenario.

With a tall, spindly pine tree easily blown by the wind, a come-along winch can effectively pull it into a more favorable position. Attach one end of the cable—preferably using a tow sling—as high as possible on the victim tree and then anchor the other to the base of a nearby tree for the best pulling power.

Wedges strategically pounded into the back cut can more effectively alter the trajectory of larger-diameter trees. It's possible to reverse a lean completely if it isn't too great. Of course, the odds of catastrophic failure are as high as the tree, so do your research before making a big mistake.

When a tree has a side lean, you can often correct it by driving wedges at an angle to the hinge instead of perpendicularly. Here again, it involves a bit of guesswork, experience, and luck. If it's a situation in which the tree absolutely has to fall in a precise spot, it's probably worth calling in the pros. If you go ahead yourself, consider using a pole saw to lighten the load on the heavy side of the tree.

It's easy to underestimate the dangers of cutting a tree with significant lean, say more than 30° off vertical. At first glance, it looks like an easy task because there's only one option as to where it will fall. But this seemingly benign situation can turn ugly when you start cutting, suddenly turning it into a dangerous "barber chair." The problem is that the trunk is under significant compression on the bottom and under an equal amount of tension on the top. When you start cutting the back cut, the tree can suddenly give way, breaking in two vertically and kicking the butt right up at you. A barber chair tree can cause serious injury or flat out kill you. Some species are more prone to barber-chairing, and other factors, such as snow loading, can also come into play.

How you handle a leaning tree depends on its size. Smaller-diameter trees are best handled with a wide notch, a quick back cut—good saw, sharp chain, fully revved—and a good escape plan. You want to get through most of the fibers before they have a chance to split so the hinge can do its job.

Large-diameter trees at risk of barber-chairing also start with an open-face notch. But instead of a back cut, you perform a bore cut (aka plunge) that creates the hinge but also leaves a back strap that holds the tree together. A bore cut is performed by starting with the bottom tip of the chain saw bar at an angle to the tree, then quickly rotating it perpendicularly so it cuts its way right through. Practice on a tall stump first. After you make the borehole, pull the saw out and cut the remainder from the outside (or a back cut below the bore, depending on the tree's angle), and get the hell out of the way.

Trees with a rotten core can be dangerous because all the forces are difficult to predict. Some wood is good, some isn't, and you won't know until it's on the ground. Again, this may be a job for a pro, so tread carefully. One option might be to use a come-along to apply tension in the general direction in which it should drop.

It's a good idea to leave some snags up for wildlife, but a dead tree can pose hazards if near a road or trail. The problem with felling a dead tree is that the dried wood doesn't hinge well and the core may have rotted, so the trunk may snap and fall unpredictably. The best solution is to apply some tension with a rope or come-along, but not too much because the root system may have rotted as well. Also beware that the vibration of cutting may cause a limb or even the upper trunk to fall.

Releasing Hung Trees

Sooner or later, if you cut many trees, you're going to hang one up in nearby standing trees. This can be a dangerous scenario because a tree can fall at any time. There are a few big don'ts to obey when dealing with a hung tree: Don't walk behind or underneath it—for obvious reasons. Don't try dropping another tree on the stuck tree because you'll likely just make the situation worse. Don't walk away and leave a tree hung up because, sooner or later, it will fall.

My first choice for releasing the offending tree is to use a cant hook (part of my felling lever) to rotate and cajole the trunk until something gives. This gives you fairly good control and opportunity to escape.

The second line of attack is to use a come-along and pull the butt out until the tree falls. As long as the butt isn't buried deep in the ground or lodged in rocks, this can be very effective, albeit a bit slow. If you can get a truck or ATV into the vicinity, you can try pulling the butt of the tree with a long tow strap.

Another solution is to start bucking the tree from the bottom, cutting off 16-inch sections starting at the butt. Because the hung tree is typically leaning at an angle, make an open-face notch on the top side and then make a back cut from the bottom. When the trunk gives way, the tree will swing in closer to the hang point, so be ready to run!

Girdling Trees

Rather than cutting down a tree, you may want to leave it standing so that it returns to the land naturally. When you girdle a tree, you interrupt the tissue (phloem) that carries nutrients, which essentially starves the plant. A deciduous tree will lose all of its leaves fairly quickly. Conifers will go through a red stage, in which all the needles dry up, that can last about two years before they eventually fall off.

The traditional method of girdling is to chop the bark away with a hatchet, using strokes from above and below, leaving a gap about 2 to 6 inches wide. This is effective but time-consuming and somewhat unsightly. A faster alternative is to use a chain saw and cut two rings around the entire tree several inches apart; make sure to saw all the way through the bark and into the tree a bit.

Processing Trees

Limbing and bucking trees is nearly as dangerous as dropping them. Don't underestimate this phase of the operation—just because a tree is lying on the ground doesn't mean it is safe.

When cutting the limbs off trees, you will sometimes find yourself in an awkward position with bad footing, making a slip with a running chain saw a real possibility. There's also a fairly high chance of kickback if you aren't vigilant about the location of the tip of the chain bar. Branches underneath the tree hold a great amount of tension, and when they give way, a lot of force releases and the tree may roll.

After all the limbs are off, you may want to buck the trunk into 16-inch sections for use as firewood. This is another great opportunity for chain saw kickback if you aren't paying attention. When working on a slope, you also run the risk of a log or tree rolling onto you or someone else below.

The limbs holding the tree off the ground are under tremendous pressure. This tree had been pruned but we decided to remove it to open the canopy.

Whether you process the tree where it fell or move it to a more convenient location will depend on terrain and accessibility. Because we're talking fire mitigation, the odds are we're also talking about rugged terrain. Sometimes it's easiest to cut it all up and haul out the slash and logs as best you can. Given the choice, I prefer to move the entire tree, or at least big sections of a tree, to a more favorable spot for the final dissection. Ideally, this will be where the slash piles will be created and the logs are accessible for hauling away.

With the right tools, like a pickeroon for manual labor and a choker chain or skidding tongs for using a winch, this is more efficient than hauling lots of parts. If I'm heading downhill and using a pickeroon, it's reasonable to drag a 25-foot, 10-inch diameter tree. On flat ground, you may need to cut those numbers in half. Going uphill requires some serious horsepower.

You can save yourself a ton of work by processing your trees in the late fall (after the fire season is over) and leaving them in place until the early spring. This gives the limbs several months to dry out, which can reduce weight by over half. The trunks won't lose as much water in that time but it can still be significant.

Limbing
Limbing trees can be backbreaking work. The ideal chain saw for limbing is lightweight because you're often using it at a full-arm extension and at odd angles. It also has a long bar so you aren't bending over as much.

When limbing, don't just squeeze the chain saw trigger and keep cutting, nor should you try to cut a second limb before you've finished with the first. These bad habits will bite you hard someday. Cut a limb, release the trigger, cut another limb, release the trigger, and so on. Keep a sharp eye on the bar tip at all times.

A spring pole is a small tree caught underneath a larger fallen tree. Because its roots anchor it, the spring pole can store a tremendous amount of force that, if cut improperly, can send you flying or the chain saw flying right at you. Similarly, limbs supporting a tree off the ground must be treated with caution because they're under high tension and the tree may roll when they're cut.

With spring poles and limbs under tension, it may require two or three cuts on larger branches to sever them safely. Try to figure out the stresses and make the first cut on the side experiencing compression. Make the second cut from the side under tension, but offset it by perhaps an inch and extend it past the first cut. Then you can make a finishing cut without the limb kicking back at you. It may sound complicated, but all of that can be done faster than the time it took you to read this paragraph.

For greatest safety, it's sometimes recommended that you cut the branches on the opposite side of the trunk. In reality, you'll probably start at one end of the tree and work your way to the other. Pay special attention when cutting on the side nearest you because saw kickback will send the chain right at your head.

One efficient technique is to start at the butt of the log and cut all the branches on the side nearest you as far as you can comfortably reach forward. Then rotate your chain saw horizontally and cut all the top branches, moving back toward the butt. Then rotate it vertically again and cut the branches on the opposite side, moving forward. Now you can take a step or two forward and cut some of the bottom limbs before working on the next top and side limbs.

Try to cut limbs off flush to the log so you don't leave stubs. Don't leave pointed stems on a trunk that could impale someone.

If small branches stand in your way, instead of stopping to grab them with your hand, you can often lift them with the tip of the bar when the chain isn't running, then send them flying with a quick rev of the throttle. Bigger limbs may need to be sectioned so you can move forward.

It's great if you have an assistant to pull limbs away as you cut them off. However, both of you must maintain situational awareness at all times—don't get tunnel vision.

Bucking

Once you remove the limbs, it's time to cut the log into firewood. This too can be a pain in the back, because you often have to bend over to work close to the ground. When possible, get the log up off the ground, which will also save your chain. The no-cost but harder way is to lift the log by hand and toss a small log underneath it a few feet from the end. Consider using a timberjack for easily lifting a log about 10 inches off the ground. An even better alternative is a free-standing or bumper-mounted log holder, like the Woodchuck, that grabs the butt and holds the log at about waist level.

A timberjack can lift a heavy log off the ground to protect your chain.

Buck the tree into 16-inch logs for firewood. The timberjack makes this chore easier by holding the log in the air.

When bucking a big log lying flat on the ground, it's often easiest to make a series of cuts 16 inches apart that go three-quarters of the way through. Then roll the log and make the finishing cuts from the top.

Matters get more complicated when the trunk is under tension on one side and compression on the other. A top bind occurs when two ends of the log are supported while the center is in the air. A bottom bind happens when one end of the log is raised up off the ground. There can also be side bind or end bind. Learn to identify situations in which directional pressures are stretching one side and compressing the other. Also be on the lookout for a log that might pivot and swing sideways when a portion is removed—you don't want to be the base-ball that gets hit by a giant bat!

Depending on the situation, you might use a small notch on the compression side followed by a back cut from the tension side; you might use bypass cuts; or you could cut partway through and insert a wedge so you can finish up without the kerf pinching closed. As you are cutting, keep an eye on the kerf to see whether it's opening (bottom bind) or closing (top bind). If you detect either, cut from a different side or use a wedge.

When working on a slope, you may need to chock the log so that it doesn't roll. For greatest safety, some recommend that you always buck from the uphill side to prevent a log from rolling onto you. I often prefer to work on smaller trees from the downhill side, because doing so requires less bending over and I'm in position to stop or direct a log before it can take off down the hill. It's usually best to start at the top of the tree and buck toward the butt end. This gradually reduces stress on the end with the most capacity to hurt you.

Cleaning Up

When it makes sense to process a tree where it lies, you have several options for removing the debris. If you have a truck and can get it there, that's a no-brainer—but be prepared for a stuck vehicle if you go four-wheeling. If the terrain isn't too bad and you've cut just one or two moderate-size trees, a good wheelbarrow works well for transport.

Cutting down half a dozen trees or more will generate giant heaps of slash that may need to be hauled away. In this case, try using one or two of the largest limbs as a sled and heap a lot of other limbs on top before dragging them away. Either a pickeroon or timber tongs (sometimes both) makes this vastly easier because you'll have a better grip and control of the pile.

Another method is to lay a slash sling or tow strap out and make your pile on top of it, then flip the rope over and connect one hook to the strap so it tightens down as you drag the other end of the strap.

This works well for moving heaps of smaller branches that otherwise tend to fall apart and leave behind a trail of debris.

When you have to move slash and firewood up a hill, two people can work as a team using a rope, pulley, and wheelbarrow. Attach a ratcheting pulley like the Petzl Mini Traxion ($85) to a tree or truck at the top of the slope. The person with the wheelbarrow at the bottom loads it up and attaches one end of the rope; he or she will guide and steady it on the way up. The other, preferably heavier, person then anchors the rope to his or her waist and counterhauls the wheelbarrow by walking down the slope. With the ratchet on the pulley, the team can take a rest without the wheelbarrow slipping.

Of course, if you have a power capstan or a winch on a truck, then dragging full-size logs and giant heaps of slash up a slope poses no problem. Especially when using a truck-mounted winch, a pulley is often required for a redirect.

SLASH DISPOSAL

A reality of effective fire mitigation is that it creates a lot of slash. All of the branches and logs need to be dealt with, or you've merely substituted one fire hazard for another. One study showed that thinning a forest without removing or burning the slash triples the amount of 1-hour fuels, quintuples the amount of 10-hour fuels, and nearly doubles the amount of 100-hour fuels.

Fire mitigation generates big piles of slash.

Though you'll have greatly reduced the chances of a devastating crown fire, the slash, if left untouched, increases the amount of fuel available for ground and surface fires. These fires will likely burn hotter and spread faster than a "normal" surface fire and lead to greater tree mortality.

Most homeowners have three realistic options for disposing of slash: hauling, chipping, and scattering. The fourth option, burning, is unrealistic for reasons we'll discuss. A fifth option, an air curtain burner, is an expensive specialty tool used by fire departments.

Hauling

If you have a relatively small and accessible lot, hauling the slash away may be your best option. While this eliminates fuel, it also deprives the soil of potential nutrients, which may or may not be a concern.

Many counties offer free collection sites for slash, assuming you have access to a truck or trailer. Unfortunately, these sites often are open only a few weekends per year, so they may be impractical. If you have beetle-kill wood, they likely won't accept it during the summer.

Another option is going to a commercial landfill, because they're open year-round during regular business hours. Around here, the fee runs about $5.50 per cubic yard. A small pickup truck filled to bed level holds about 2 cubic yards, and a large pickup holds about 3 cubic yards.

Straight tree trunks over $2^1/_2$ inches in diameter can be used for fence poles and posts as well as saw logs for lumber. To be acceptable, both ends must be cut straight at a 90° angle, with all limbs cut flush to the bark. The logs should be cut to standard lengths (8-foot, 10-foot, 12-foot, and 16-foot), plus 3 inches to allow trimming the rough ends. Trees that don't meet these requirements should be cut up into 16-inch logs for firewood.

Chipping

If you generate a lot of slash in areas not too far from a road, chipping may work best. This involves processing the branches with a portable home chipping machine or an incredibly powerful commercial grinder usually staffed by a two-person crew.

By running the tree branches through a chipper, you reduce the volume by a factor of around 4, so 40 cubic yards will reduce roughly to 10 cubic yards. In addition, the resulting smaller material decomposes faster because it has a much greater surface area and stays in closer contact with the soil.

On the other hand, when you chip logs suitable for firewood or lumber, the volume expands by a factor of approximately 3. That is, 10 cubic yards become 30. This means you're generating a much wider and deeper pile of more easily combustible material. Yes, it will decompose faster than if the logs were left intact, but the mulch will remain for a couple decades. If possible, it's better to haul off the logs or give the firewood away.

The chips from logs are rather large, roughly $1/2$ inch in diameter and 2 to 4 inches long. Normally, mulch like this is good at retaining moisture, which is one of the reasons gardeners like it. But when this material dries out in a drought, it burns like a giant bed of charcoal—fire can creep downhill easily through chipped wood, and the heat can scorch trees. Dried mulch also burns hot enough to sterilize the soil and kill roots that might otherwise resprout.

When you have big piles of slash, it's worth scheduling a visit with the big machine. To say commercial grinders are dangerous is an understatement—these things are so powerful that they can digest a 10-inch-diameter, 10-foot-long log in a few seconds. When an odd-shaped branch goes though, it whacks back and forth ferociously, so stay well out of the way.

Many fire departments in wildland areas have industrial chippers and offer the service at a reasonable rate. Our fire protection district charges $115 per hour, which includes a two-person crew. Over the past few years, our annual chipping bill has averaged around $400, which sounds expensive, but we have 35 acres that I've been working in stages, so that generates a lot of slash. Most homeowners with smaller lots would likely see a bill of perhaps $200 the first year of thinning and maybe $100 every other year for maintenance.

This is win-win for everyone: You financially support your local firefighters in the off-season, and they see that you're proactive about fire mitigation while becoming familiar with your property. You can rent smaller chippers from places like Sun Rental, but it's better to support your local fire department.

Because chipping is charged by the hour, it's in your best interest to help the crew by preparing the piles for efficiency. Make your slash piles close to the road, preferably on the uphill side, and stack them neatly with the ends facing the road. Make the piles longer rather than higher, no more than 5 feet tall. Piles should contain only woody limbs and branches; no grass clippings, leaves, weeds, or lumber.

After chipping big piles of slash, your best option is to haul it away to a landfill or compost facility. That way you're removing fuel from the area. Needless to say, you don't want to use this mulch anywhere near your house.

If hauling isn't an option, spread the piles of mulch out so they're only a couple inches thick and well away from the base of trees. Sprinkle the wood chips with a fertilizer high in nitrogen, such as 5-2-0 (avoid any with the second two numbers equal to or higher than the first) mixed with an equal amount of sugar. This will jump-start the microorganisms that break down the wood.

Wood chips are also a good adjunct to compost piles because they contain little nitrogen (a 225:1 carbon/nitrogen ratio). Normal food waste and lawn clippings are high in nitrogen (around 15:1) and tend to compact, so there's little airflow. Adding chips to the compost achieves a healthier 30:1 carbon/nitrogen ratio, and more oxygen reaches the microorganisms for fastest decomposition. For example, mixing three parts food and grass clippings with two parts wood chips will compost significantly faster than separate piles of each.

Lopping and Scattering

When hauling or chipping isn't an option, you may need to resort to lopping the branches and scattering them. If you're mitigating far from a road, particularly at the bottom of a steep slope where hauling uphill isn't practical, this may be your only practical option.

The key to effective lopping and scattering is dragging the branches out into open areas, away from other trees, then cutting them into small pieces. The goal is for all the slash to be spread out and stay close to the ground, where the higher moisture levels will speed decay. When you're done, nothing should rise up higher than 12 inches.

Lopping and scattering is problematic in dense forest because you can't get the fuel away from living trees. A surface fire here will burn so hot that most of the remaining trees will die even though it wasn't a crown fire. In this case, it's probably better to create slash piles, knowing that they may become bonfires. Locate piles as far from trees as possible. Though a hazard, they will decompose in a few decades and make great homes for critters in the meantime.

Open Burning

Forget it. The odds of getting both the right conditions and a burn permit are between slim and none. In theory, burning slash is a great alternative because it's inexpensive and returns nutrients, such as calcium carbonate (lime) and potassium, to the soil. But the reality is that you must navigate a slew of regulations before the weather gods deign to open even a narrow window of opportunity. Here in Colorado, that means at least 6 inches of snow on the ground, a favorable weather forecast, and good air quality.

What actually happens is that you'll create numerous heaps of slash, called jack piles, around your property that will sit there for years, drying out in the sun. You'll never actually get a permit to burn them because the rare days that that fire danger rating swings low also coincide with days during which the air quality index prevents burning.

Jack piles ready for burning, someday, in a county park. Pack the fuel tightly for a cleaner burn.

Those slash piles turn from fire mitigation to fire hazard. Just this scenario happened during the Fourmile Canyon Fire, west of Boulder, Colorado, where hundreds of jack piles ignited and became major sources of firebrands thrown by powerful winds.

Ideally, your local fire department will handle the permits and burn your jack piles but they likely have a long list of projects ahead of yours. If you're willing to navigate the labyrinth of regulations to get a burn permit, then make your slash piles no larger than 4 feet high and 6 feet in diameter. Pack them tightly—not just loose heaps—so they'll burn cleaner. A propane torch can help get the pile burning.

Carefully monitor the fire until the heat is gone. You must be 101 percent

Fire rings left from burning slash

sure it's all the way out! Use an infrared thermometer or your hand to make sure no hidden embers are burning. Numerous major fires have started days or even weeks after a fire was supposedly extinguished. Because the burned-out slash pile will likely leave a fire ring, periodically check the area for invasive weeds.

Using an Air Curtain Burner

The newest and arguably best method for slash disposal is the air curtain burner, which is essentially a portable firebox with a powerful fan to stoke the flames. The air jets are arranged so that smoke and particulates are held captive long enough to combust thoroughly.

The BurnBoss air curtain (airburners.com) is pulled on a trailer and lowered onto the ground. Because it has no bottom, the ash remains to fertilize soil after the burner is removed. These cost about $50,000 and require a fire crew on hand because they produce some sparks, but they can be a great community investment.

The advantages of an air curtain burner are many. The slash can be burned even when green, so any beetle larvae die before they emerge. The system is so efficient that huge piles can be consumed in a few hours. The high temperatures ensure very few emissions, though a burn permit is still required. Should it be necessary, turning off the fan and closing the lid can extinguish the fire quickly.

A chipper can reduce the volume of slash, but it doesn't reduce the mass. One ton is still one ton. The resulting mulch is bad for the soil because the low nitrogen content of the chips prompts microorganisms to take nitrogen from the ground (the reason why mulch is used to prevent weed growth). The wood chips also remain as a fuel source for ground fire and a source of firebrands. An air curtain burner reduces a ton of wood to mere pounds of ash that return nutrients to the soil and can do no harm in the future.

PREPARE YOUR HOME

Ultimately Zone 0 counts the most—your home. Prepping Zones 1, 2, and 3 is vitally important, but your home itself is the last defense. Preparing your home for wildfire encompasses a few simple tasks that increase fire resistance, such as blocking vents against firebrands and removing wood that touches the house. It may also include adding fire-suppression technologies or large projects like replacing wooden decks.

PASSIVE RESISTANCE

If you live in the Wildland Urban Interface, there's no such thing as a fireproof house that you wouldn't describe as a bunker. But you can do a lot to increase passive resistance to fire. Combined with creating a survivable space, these projects will help keep your home from igniting without any active participation. That means you can go away on vacation during fire season and not remain in constant fear that you might not have a home when you return.

Building Materials

If you're building a new home in a Red Zone, you'll quickly learn all the regulations imposed by local authorities and possibly your insurance company. Most areas now have a long list of requirements for fire-resistant building materials and practices. For starters: Single-pane windows are out; untreated wood decks and siding are out; untreated cedar shake roofing is absolutely out.

Existing homeowners, however, generally aren't required to upgrade to the latest standards unless they undertake a major renovation. When our home was built in 1992, it met or exceeded all of the regulations in place at the time. Since then, the average size of wildfires nationwide has doubled, and the average number of houses lost has tripled. It can prove ridiculously expensive to bring an existing house up to the latest codes. My wife and I would love to replace our cedar siding with the latest and greatest fire-resistant siding, but it isn't an affordable option in the near future. Many other homeowners are in the same boat.

If you have to prioritize, the building materials used for big horizontal surfaces—roof and decks—are the most important for maximum fire resistance. Vertical parts of the structure seldom catch fire merely from radiant heat; it's the little fire at the bottom of a wall that causes problems.

Class and Ratings

Fire ratings can be confusing. Dozens of resistance tests and standards apply around the world. California became the main driver for fire-resistant construction with the adoption of the Chapter 7A building codes in 2008. But, adding to the confusion, there are different classifications for flame spread for combustible materials and ratings for walls and roof systems.

The ASTM E-84 tunnel test compares different building materials for flame spread. Combustible products are labeled Class C or Class III if they have no additional treatments to slow flames. These have a flame spread rating of 76 to 200, with most construction wood ranging between 90 and 160.

The next step up in performance is a Class B or Class II rating, often achieved with a surface coating. These products have a flame spread rating between 26 and 75, which gives you a rough indication of how easily the product will burn.

The highest rating is Class A or Class I, and those products are often saturated or pressure treated with flame-retardant chemicals. Class A products have a maximum flame spread rating of 25, which makes them difficult to get started.

All Class A and B products are tested for ten minutes to achieve their rating. In California, for a product to be labeled "ignition resistant," it must maintain a flame spread rating of less than 26 for a full thirty minutes. This isn't a national standard, though, so buyers in other states need to know how a manufacturer defines ignition resistant.

Don't get too bogged down in the minutiae of flame spread, heat release rates, or penetration for various products; there's a lot of marketing hype included. Given variances between labs and testing methodology, even when using a test standard, it's difficult to make real comparisons.

Materials like cement, metal, and glass are considered noncombustible. While they won't burn, they may have other limitations depending on design and construction. For example, cement and glass can crack under high heat, and aluminum can melt.

While using Class A or ignition-resistant building materials is important, that's just the starting point. Overall construction matters too. Putting Class A shingles on top of Class C roofing paper and particle board can give you a Class C roof. Burning embers won't ignite the shingles, but the heat can transfer to layers underneath and cause them to combust.

Fire ratings for construction are based on ASTM E-119, which compares complete assemblies of materials for walls, roofs, and more. This testing gives the time it takes for the structural integrity to fail. A two-hour exterior wall lasts longer than a one-hour wall, which is better than a non-rated wall. A four-hour wall has the highest rating and comes with a corresponding price. For a typical house built without consideration of wildfire, the walls will provide about forty-five minutes of protection.

To achieve a Class A rating, a roof must have a maximum flame spread of 6 feet during the test. In addition, if it's made with combustible materials, the roof must not burn through when a large wooden lattice that weighs 4.4 pounds is ignited on the surface. It must also resist fifteen cycles of an intermittent flame.

Decks

Decks made from redwood or cedar look great at first. But the attraction wears off along with the finish, and you'll discover how much maintenance they require. Pressure-treated pine is less expensive and a bit more durable, but it's not as nice visually, and it comes with concerns about chemical toxicity.

The bigger issue is that wood decks and framing are flammable unless treated with a fire retardant. In some areas, particularly in California, you can purchase wood impregnated at the sawmill to give it a Class A or ignition-resistant rating. This is commonly called FRTW, for fire-resistant treated wood, or FRX, and costs about 25 percent more than untreated wood. An environmentally friendlier option is wood soaked in liquid glass and then baked for a Class A fire rating without chemicals (timbersilwood.com).

If pretreated wood isn't available, you can treat the wood with a product like Fire Kote 100 (firechemicals.com) or Flame Stop II (flamestop.com), applied like stain with a brush or sprayer. This costs about $35 per 100 square feet and is supposed to last about five years. It goes on clear and penetrates into the wood to give it Class A resistance. After the wood has dried for forty-eight hours, it can be stained or painted with water-based products.

A deck with fire-resistant materials, including furniture when the cushions are removed. Trex Transcend decking has a Class B fire rating and requires minimal maintenance.

If you're applying it to an existing deck, you must remove the old stain first with a power washer and wood stain stripper. This is a two-step process, starting with the stripper (about $20 per 100 square feet) and the pressure washer set to about 1,000 psi. You must then neutralize the wood with an acidic wood brightener, which also costs about $20 per 100 square feet. Altogether, it's about $1 per square foot, plus a lot of labor, to make an old deck fire resistant . . . and you have to repeat the procedure every few years.

Another way to increase the fire resistance of an older deck is to replace the support posts with heaver timbers. By going from 4-by-4-inch posts to 6-by-6-inch posts, you decrease the surface-to-volume ratio, so they'll take longer to ignite and burn. In many wildfire hazard sites, new timber construction for deck framing also requires 3-by-8-inch joists and 6-by-12-inch beams. Add a fire-retardant treatment for even more insurance.

If building from scratch or completely replacing all your decks, the material of choice is a fire-rated capped composite made of recycled materials (finely ground wood, melted grocery bags, etc.) with a protective plastic cap: Fiberon Horizon, TimberTech Evolutions, or Trex Transcend. Early generations of composite decking had numerous

Composite decking with heavy timbers greatly increases fire resistance.

problems that have largely been solved by the external caps. The new materials resist scratching and staining and have a more natural look.

Ranging in price from around $6 to $10 per square foot, capped composited decks cost two to three times more than decks made from commonly used wood. But synthetic decks more than make up for it with increased longevity with a little maintenance. (There's no such thing as a maintenance-free deck.) Plus, the 95 percent recycled content means you're saving trees and aren't applying chemicals every few years.

Not all composites, even from the same manufacturer, have a fire rating. In California, the state fire marshal requires every deck in the Wildland Urban Interface to have a Class B rating, so a good selection of materials meets this criteria. If you want Class A–rated decks, you'll find very few options.

Although cellular PVC decks can be made resistant to flame spread, they also melt under relatively low heat (220°F) and can lose structural integrity. This is a case in which a Class A rating doesn't mean a product is ideal for wildfire zones.

Assuming that you've performed all the other fire-mitigation tasks around your house, it can be better to leave the space underneath a deck open. An enclosed deck sealed enough to keep firebrands out may also have problems with rot from moisture. With an open deck, you must have a noncombustible base (concrete, crushed rock, or bare ground) and resist the temptation to store flammable materials under it.

Framing

With fire-resistant treatments, the wood in traditional "stick frame" construction has a Class A rating. Depending on the materials selected, the walls and roof can be brought up to as much protection as desired using layers of gypsum board or other underlay materials.

In addition, the structure of a wood-frame house can be made more fire resistant with insulation. Once the standard, fiberglass batting has largely been replaced by blown-in and spray-on insulations that do a more effective job of filling voids. They're also easier to install. Cotton batting is a more expensive alternative for do-it-yourselfers, but it's also a lot less irritating to skin and lungs.

Loose fiberglass, rock wool, and cellulose (treated with boric acid or borax) are nontoxic and resistant to fire. Any of these can be a good choice as long as it's blown in at high density (more than 2.6 pounds per cubic foot). Because cellulose is made from about 75 percent recycled newspaper and is less air-permeable than fiberglass, it's now considered a superior "green" insulation.

Foam insulation boards (polystyrene, polyisocyanurate, and polyurethane) can be made fire resistant, but the halogenated organic chemicals used in them (HBCD, TCPP, and blowing agents) may be unhealthy when trapped indoors. These are generally a better choice for outside the home. Similarly, there are concerns about the off-gassing of spray polyurethane foam (SPF), though new versions made without isocyanates may be safer.

While wood-frame construction is still the most prevalent, there are new alternatives that deserve consideration as well. When deciding on which method to choose, consider all factors such as transportation, labor, and longevity. You may discover that traditional isn't necessarily best.

Instead of stud and plywood or oriented strand board (OSB) construction, homes built with structural insulated panels (SIPs) are faster to assemble, stronger, and more durable; Greenix (sipsupply .com), ThermaSAVE (thermasave.us), and Thermocore (thermocore .com) are among available brands. Made by sandwiching polystyrene or urethane foam between outer layers of plywood or OSB, SIPs have good insulation and flame-resistance properties.

Another alternative is using autoclaved aerated concrete (AAC), blocks that contain a mixture of concrete, aluminum powder, and air (aerconaac.com). These are much lighter than standard concrete and have great insulating power. Because AAC is molded under pressure, it can be made in many shapes and sizes that allow for fast construction.

Instead of layering foam between wood, it can also be used for the outer layers of insulated concrete forms (ICF). With this method, the foam is stacked like Legos to become the mold for a 4- to 6-inch layer of concrete (along with rebar). After the concrete has cured, the foam remains in place for backing stucco on the exterior and gypsum board inside. The foam is fire retardant and the concrete can't burn, so houses with this construction have a good chance in a wildfire.

Exterior Siding

While the exterior walls of your home certainly affect the fire resistance of the structure, for most homes in the Wildland Urban Interface, the material is less important than other factors such as windows and roofing. As long as you've done your mitigating around the house, there won't be enough radiant heat from vegetation to ignite wood siding.

Exterior siding does make a real difference if a house or shed 20 feet away catches fire. Unlike a crown fire that passes through quickly, a building fire can continue long enough for radiant heat to ignite your home. Therefore, it's more important for homes on the urban edge to have ignition-resistant siding than homes that are sur-rounded by forest.

Arguably the worst choice for any building in a Red Zone is vinyl siding because it will melt and fall away from the wall at relatively low temperatures. After only a minute of high heat, the vinyl is basi-cally gone, and the backing material must provide all the protection.

Wood siding can still be a reasonable choice as long as proper construction techniques and mitigation are performed. Plain bevel clapboard siding should be avoided because fire can easily penetrate the joints. Siding with shiplap or tongue-and-groove joints provides greater protection from flame ingress.

The wood for new construction should be treated at least to a Class B fire-resistance level so flames are less likely to spread upward. The treatments will leach out over time, so you should reapply fire retardant on wood not protected by stain or paint.

Unfortunately, there are no good options for improving the fire resistance of an existing wood exterior already stained or painted. It isn't practical to strip the siding down to bare wood that will accept a fire-resistant coating. There's also no such thing as fireproof exterior paint. Hardscaping next to the house and reducing hazards in Zone 1 are your best bets.

Beware of scams espousing ceramic coatings that are much thicker than regular latex paint. These companies have a reputation for employing hard-sell tactics, bogus claims, pseudoscience, and unfulfilled warranties. Among the lies are phrases like "Never paint your home again,""Class A fire rating," and "25-year guarantee." What they don't tell you: The warranty comes from the contractor instead of the parent company, and it is usually nontransferable if you sell the house; they will point fingers and claim improper preparation when the paint starts peeling; and they don't have a track record of more than a decade.

Corners have a high surface-to-volume ratio, so these are more likely to catch fire than the walls. Inside corners compound this problem, because that's also where leaves and firebrands tend to accumulate. Pay attention to making the corners of your house flame resistant.

A noncombustible exterior will provide slightly greater protection for your home than wood siding. But the extra cost may not provide as much insurance as many people think. Choose brick, stone, or stucco for aesthetic reasons but not for keeping wildfire at bay.

The traditional method of applying stucco—a mix of Portland cement, sand, lime, and water—requires two base coats and a finish coat for a combined thickness of at least $3/4$ inch. This is both labor intensive and, if applied incorrectly, can lead to cracking that can be expensive to repair. Traditional stucco isn't waterproof so it requires a waterproof paint or sealant but new stucco can be mixed with a polymer to give more protection. Eventually, all stucco buildings will experience cracking; regions with large temperature swings experience this sooner. A few hairline cracks aren't a problem, but you'll need to fix cracks wider than a nickel to prevent damage to the structure.

The newer alternative to three-coat stucco goes by the misnomer "one-coat stucco," which is actually applied as two coats. It's basically the same concept, except that acrylic and glass fibers are added to the cement mix for greater strength and flexibility. This system reduces labor costs and is typically only $1/2$ inch thick, yet it can be as durable as traditional stucco.

Adding to the confusion is an alternative often called synthetic stucco, which contains no cement. Dryvit is one popular brand. This method consists of covering the building with a layer of expanded polystyrene foam board, then coating that with about $1/8$ inch of polymer material held in place by fiberglass mesh, over which goes a finish coat. Properly known as an exterior insulation finish system (EIFS), it looks like traditional stucco, has a higher R-value, and is noncombustible. From a distance, it can be difficult to tell them apart. But if you knock on EIFS, it will sound hollow, while both three-coat and one-coat stucco sound solid.

For builders, EIFS is relatively fast and cheap. From a homeowner's perspective, both hail and woodpeckers easily damage it because the coating is thin and soft, and this damage can be very expensive to repair. Because EIFS is totally waterproof and cannot breathe like traditional stucco, it can also lead to major issues with mold and rot of the wood frame unless the builder installed proper drainage and added a $1/4$-inch ventilation gap between the stucco and the sheathing.

Alternatives include fiber cement siding that looks like wood shingles (certainteed.com and jameshardie.com). Other companies offer concrete log siding that looks like wood and requires no maintenance (everlog.com and knotalog.com). You can choose a veneer of artificial stone made from cast cement (daltile.com), natural sliced stone (nsvi.com), or thin brick siding half an inch thick (brickit.com). Some artificial stone is made from polyurethane, which will burn, so double-check.

With many construction techniques, the bottom edge of the siding material is often left exposed with large gaps that can act as entry points for embers or flames. This is an insidious danger because embers often accumulate at the base of walls. A fire inside a wall can go undetected for a long time before smoke or flames become visible—at which point it's probably too late.

These base gaps should be sealed with wire mesh, fire-resistant foam, or metal flashing. Drains may be needed for moisture control, however, so make sure they're not sealed accidentally.

Roofing
When designing a new home, keep in mind that the more complex the roof, the greater the chance for fire. Every inside corner offers a place for leaves, needles, and embers to accumulate. Few people are diligent about clearing roof debris.

A roof can achieve a Class A fire rating either by using naturally fire-resistant exterior materials (stand-alone roof) or by using a combination of materials in the construction (assembly-rated roof). Even when stand-alone materials are used, it's wise to build with additional fire-resistant materials for greater protection.

One way to achieve an assembly-rated Class A roof is to use a fire-resistant underlayer made from fiber-impregnated gypsum—such as DensDeck (gp.com) or Securock (usg.com)—atop plywood. Another option is using fire-rated cementious-coated (FRCC) oriented strand board, such as FlameBlock (lpcorp.com), instead of the plywood/gypsum combo. This coating of magnesium oxide releases water under extreme heat, which greatly extends the burn-through time.

By far, asphalt shingles reinforced with fiberglass are the most common roofing material in the United States. If you want a different

This roof is a fire magnet. The old wooden shake has many large gaps ideally suited for catching firebrands. That skylight probably has a pile of pine needles at the top and likely isn't fire-rated.

look than the standard three-tab shingles, some laminated shingles resemble stone or wood (certainteed.com and tamko.com).

A relatively new alternative is molded tiles made of recycled rubber and plastic that look like slate or shake (ecostarllc.com). With the proper underlayments, a roof with these tiles has a Class A rating. The roof can also be exceptionally long-lasting and maintenance-free compared to those utilizing natural materials.

Though it seems counterintuitive, a wood shake roof can achieve a Class A rating if the wood is treated with fire retardant and the appropriate underlayments are used. If you have an older shake roof, products like Shingle Kote (firechemicals.com) can bring the wood up to a Class A rating. With any wood roof, you have to reapply the treatment every few years to maintain fire resistance.

Roofs made of copper or steel have a stand-alone Class A rating. However, because aluminum has a much lower melting point, it requires proper underlayment to achieve the Class A rating by assembly. When properly designed, an aluminum roof can be very durable, and it can give you the satisfaction of knowing it came from recycled beer cans. Metal roofs are often smooth and slick, so it's easy to slip and fall when walking on them; they also avalanche snowfall easily.

Clay-barrel and cement roof tiles are popular in Southern California and Arizona, among other areas that don't get much snow. They're great in terms of fire resistance as long as all the holes and gaps are plugged to keep firebrands out. Walking on a tile roof can crack the tiles if you step in the wrong spot, which can be a costly mistake. Depending on the style, you'll need to step either in the valley or on a seam. Ask an expert before inspecting your roof.

If your home or business has a flat roof, you can apply an acrylic coating called PermaKote Plus (hytechsales.com) to give it a Class A rating. This is a thick, rubbery coating applied as two coats over a primer coating. The system works on just about any material for protection from fire.

If your home lies in "Hail Alley" along the Colorado Front Range, you should also consider the hail rating of a roof. The strongest roofing material has a Class 4 rating, though Class 3 may suffice in areas with less-intense storms. A metal roof can have a high rating so water won't leak in, but some can easily dent in a major hail storm.

Windows

Scientists studying wildfires discovered that windows can break due to the temperature differential between the edge of the glass covered by the frame and the unprotected glass, which causes different rates of expansion—the bigger the window, the bigger the problem. Once a crack develops, sections of glass can burst, and suddenly you have a huge entrance into your house for firebrands.

The solution is what you most likely have in a modern home to keep your heating and cooling bills down: thermal windows. Thermo-pane windows provide an additional layer of protection because an extra layer of glass has to break before flames and embers can enter.

Standard insulated glass units (IGUs) consist of two layers of plain annealed glass separated by a space of dry air. These will last for decades, but eventually the seal will fail and moisture will get inside, causing fogging and a reduction in insulation. Windows on the sunny side of the house will fail first.

An owner of an existing home, due to the extremely high cost, probably won't replace double-glazed windows unless the glass has cracked or fogged heavily. Even in a cold climate, it can take decades to recoup the expense of higher-efficiency windows with lower heating bills.

When it does come time to replace windows—which often requires a building permit—or build a home, be forewarned that new building codes can limit your options. Giant bay windows are discouraged because smaller windows (2 by 2 feet) have less temperature differential between the center and the edges, which makes them more resistant to cracking. In addition, small windows hold broken pieces of glass in place better, so they give more protection even when broken.

If it's in the budget, go with double-glazed windows with tempered glass on the outer layer for the best protection. Tempered glass has much higher strength and resistance to heat exposure than annealed glass, so it's less likely to break. Low-emissive (low-E) coatings on windows can make them so reflective that it's possible to set dry grass or wood on fire.

Recently a number of manufacturers have begun to offer clear ceramic or glass with special coatings that make them more fire resistant; brands include Superlite (safti.com), Firelite (fireglass.com), Keralite (vetrotech.com), Pyrosafe (firesafe-glass.com), and Pyrostop (pilkington.com). These will be expensive but look better than standard fire glass with wire mesh inside.

The frame around the glass also makes a difference in the fire resistance of your home. Steel frames give the most protection because they can't burn or melt, but they cost more and less of a selection is available. Both wood and aluminum perform reasonably well in fire tests; the worst choice is vinyl frames.

While you may not be in a hurry to replace your windows, skylights from the 1970s and '80s often consist of cheap Plexiglas domes, making them top candidates for upgrades. These can easily melt and often have an accumulation of detritus. It's wise to replace them with flat tempered glass over a layer of fire-resistant polished wire glass in a low-profile frame that won't trap a lot of leaves and needles.

Of course, all of this discussion assumes that your windows are closed. Many mountain homes, don't have air-conditioning, and often owners leave the windows open during fire season to keep the house cool. One solution to this problem is to install windows that have a heat-activated fusible link (fyre-tec.com and nissenco.com). When the window frame reaches a specified temperature, the link breaks, and the window closes by itself. Steel rolling doors and shutters are also available, though they are expensive and decidedly industrial-looking.

Even if you have double-glazed windows or better, it's wise to use fire-retardant drapes and shades. If you have time before evacuation, closing the window coverings can give your home more protection from heat building up inside.

Some experts advocate installing shutters for all the windows and making plywood covers for vents into your house. The theory goes that you can quickly run around closing shutters and hanging covers. The reality is you may not be home or have have time before evacuation. Your home needs to survive all by itself. If you have an old vacation cabin with single-pane windows, consider making plywood storm shutters to hang whenever you're gone for an extended period. The wood can burn, but it's still better protection from radiant heat and flying embers than nothing.

For open windows and doors, install vinyl-coated fiberglass insect screening. Many people mistakenly call this plastic screen, but the fiberglass is necessary for durability. Compared to metal screen, it absorbs radiant heat better, so glass has a better chance of withstanding a fire.

Doors
The exterior doors of your home, another entry for approaching wildfire, need to have good weather seals and withstand twenty minutes

of intense heat and direct flame. Many composite entry doors are made with a fiberglass skin and a fire-resistant foam core, but they tend to be ugly. Even greater protection can be achieved with steel doors that offer up to ninety minutes of fire resistance, albeit at the sacrifice of attractiveness.

If you like the look and feel of wooden doors, they should be solid with a minimum of $1^1/_4$-inch thickness in the panels and $1^3/_8$-inch thickness in the stiles and rails. Doors with windows, including French and sliding patio doors, should have at least one layer of tempered glass.

The garage doors also must be fire resistant. By their very nature, these doors are harder to seal against wind, so there's a chance of firebrands blowing into the garage. For this reason, the door into the house should be fire rated, self-closing, and have good seals. Be sure that the garage door has an easy-to-operate disconnect from the electric opener in case you need to open or close it with the power out. An exterior handle on the garage door is also a good idea so that firefighters can open it from the outside if necessary.

Vents

When you walk around your house, you'll notice a number of vents up high and below the roof. Those near the peak of the roof exhaust air to prevent moisture buildup in the winter and overheating in the summer. These can be an entry point for embers in high winds. The vents under the eaves pull air in. Those intake vents have been responsible for many destroyed homes during wildfires because firebrands can also be pulled inside. Even the best nonflammable roof will be defeated if the fire starts on the inside.

The $1/_4$-inch mesh that was likely used on the attic and under-eave vents when the house was built doesn't do enough to stop embers. It's important to cover these vents with $1/_8$-inch galvanized or stainless steel mesh screen. This is a fairly simple do-it-yourself job if you have a good ladder. If you're building or doing a major remodel to the exterior, consider installing Brandguard vents (brandguardvents .com). These have overlapping baffles specifically designed to keep firebrands out.

Chimneys

If your house has a chimney or stovepipe, install a spark arrestor with a rain cap. This will prevent setting your own house on fire by accident, and it keeps firebrands from entering. Equally important, a chimney cap keeps water out, thus preventing an expensive repair. It also blocks critters from entering; raccoons are notorious, but squirrels and birds also like to nest in chimneys.

Chimney caps are made from galvanized steel (cheap, unattractive, and quickly rusts away), aluminum (cheap with low durability), stainless steel (durable and looks nice), or copper (durable and shows the neighbors you have money to burn). For most homeowners, stainless steel caps are the best combination of performance, price, and aesthetics.

All chimney caps should have ⅝-inch mesh for the spark arrestor to keep firebrands from entering; these are sometimes called California-style chimney caps. Although ¾-inch mesh was once the standard for spark arrestors, it has no performance advantage over the smaller mesh, and the price difference is negligible.

If you regularly burn wood in your fireplace, inspect the flue at least once a year for creosote buildup. This requires shining a powerful flashlight up the chimney and scratching the wall above the damper. If you have an ⅛ inch of creosote buildup or more, schedule a professional cleaning by a chimney sweep. If there is ¼ inch or more, don't use the fireplace at all. You run the very serious risk of burning your house down.

There are no hard rules as to how often you need to hire a chimney sweep, because it depends on the frequency of your fires, the type of wood you burn (softwood like pine requires more frequent cleaning than hardwood), and the efficiency of your fireplace (the better the combustion, the less buildup). If you burn a lot of fake logs (Duraflame, etc.), you'll need to clean more often, because these are inefficient and put a lot of ash up the chimney.

Don't be fooled by so-called creosote-removal treatments (logs for fireplaces and granules for airtight stoves) that supposedly clean your chimney just by burning them. At best, these can delay a proper cleaning with brushes, though reports from users are mixed—some say they work, others say they do nothing—and they're rather expensive, for what they are, at about $20 each. There's no substitute for a thorough annual chimney inspection and perhaps cleaning if you burn a lot of wood.

Gutters

Gutters are usually made of galvanized steel, aluminum, or vinyl. If you're building a new home or replacing gutters, heavy-gauge (.032-inch) aluminum is arguably the best value in the long run. If you already have gutters that are working properly, it isn't worth replacing them for the sake of fire protection. Although vinyl gutters can burn, they will likely melt and fall away from the house. Whatever the gutter material, the leading edge of the roof should have a metal drip edge so no wood is exposed.

The real concern is keeping debris out of the gutters, no matter the material, because tree litter is what sets houses on fire. The unfortunate reality is that rain gutters are great accumulators of highly combustible materials.

Rain gutters are ideal collectors of fire starters—this house is toast.

Even if you have a nonflammable metal roof, you can lose your house if the gutters aren't clean because the burning litter will ignite the understructure. As an extra incentive, clogged gutters can also lead to major structural damage from water seeping into walls.

You have two choices to combat this problem: manual cleaning or clog prevention. Manual cleaning involves getting up on a ladder possibly two or three times a year, which can be dangerous and quickly becomes tiresome. You can prevent clogged rain gutters by removing nearby tree branches and installing gutter guards. Even with this protection, you should still get up on a ladder occasionally to inspect your gutters.

If cleaning your gutters is unappealing, gutter guards prevent leaves and needles from piling up. Increasingly, this is becoming a requirement for new homes and major remodels. Dozens of companies sell gutter guards, and all claim their product is the best. But the reality is that many are a poor choice for homes in the Red Zone.

Rule out any gutter guards made of foam or plastic because firebrands can set them on fire. If trees surround your house, then dismiss metal screen guards with large holes because they easily clog with needles, oak catkins, and maple whirlybirds. Also avoid any system that screws into the roof because that invites water damage and may void your home warranty.

This leaves you with either metal surface-tension gutter guards or micromesh guards. The former are better than nothing but are still prone to clogging. While the company may offer a free cleaning service, you have to schedule an inspection and then a later visit from a crew, so they're not exactly hassle-free.

Currently, the best systems appear to be stainless steel micromesh guards from GutterDome, GutterGlove Pro, GutterRX, and Leaf Solution. These generally aren't do-it-yourself projects, and you can expect to pay around $25 per foot for installation. A typical home has about 160 feet of gutters, so that's about $4,000 total. Of the do-it-yourself guards, your best option is the Amerimax Gutter Shingle (amerimax.com), which costs about $4 per foot; anything cheaper is a waste of time and money.

For those in snow country, be advised that gutter guards don't cause ice dams, but they can exacerbate them. The root cause of ice dams is inadequate insulation and/or ventilation in the roof, or air leakage into the attic. However, gutter guards that are horizontal instead of sloped will hold snow instead of allowing it to slide off.

Enclosed Spaces

A savable home can turn into a total loss if you allow flammable stuff to accumulate in those out-of-sight storage spaces around the house. Diligently keep burnable clutter out from under your decks, and you don't need to screen this space off. This includes resisting the urge to become a pack rat and raking out piles of leaves.

If the storage space under a deck, patio, or porch is absolutely needed, make it resistant to firebrands while providing ventilation to prevent rot. You have lots of options for enclosing these spaces but make sure to use $1/8$ inch stainless steel mesh for the screen.

Fences

A common element in many post-fire analysis reports is that wooden fences carried flames directly to houses that were consumed. The debris that often collects at the bottom of a fence gives an extra boost to the already flammable wood.

Whether you have a classic 6-foot privacy fence or an open split-rail property fence, you need to separate it from your house with a firebreak of some sort. A popular option is to attach a metal gate between the fence and the house. But you could also build a stone column or go all out and get a wrought-iron fence.

Assuming you're keeping a cedar fence, you would do well to apply fire retardant and give it a gravel safety perimeter to keep grass fire away. This should be at least 1 foot wide on each side, with a weed barrier underneath for minimal maintenance. Remember, even if it isn't attached to your house, that fence can become a source of firebrands once it gets burning.

Internal Sprinkler System

Most moderate-size houses in unincorporated areas don't have internal sprinkler systems like those you see in businesses and hotels. That will change over the next decade as more counties mandate their installation on new construction and major remodels. For example, in Boulder County they're mandated on all large homes (above 4,500 square feet) since 1995, but it applies to homes of any size beginning in 2013.

The reasoning is that many nonurban fire departments depend on volunteers. When a fire is called in, the firefighters must leave home or work and go to the fire station for their gear before heading to a blaze. Therefore, response time can be considerably longer than in a city. With sprinklers installed, they may not be able to save your house, but they have a much greater chance of saving the entire neighborhood.

An internal sprinkler system puts at least one head in each room. When something like a kitchen flare-up or a couch fire raises temperatures at the ceiling to 155°F, the sprinkler sprays 260 gallons of water in ten minutes to extinguish the flames.

When installed in new construction, a sprinkler system costs about $1.50 per square foot, so an extra $4,500 for a 3,000-square-foot house. But if you're remodeling and are required to install sprinklers throughout the entire structure, the cost can run as much as $5 per square foot. On the other hand, you may get a 5 to 15 percent reduction on your insurance premiums, so it's worth checking beforehand.

Computer Backups

In this day and age, backing up your computer files on disks or a portable hard drive makes little sense unless you have over a terabyte of data. Even if you are diligent about keeping the backups current (liar), you still face the hassle of off-site storage. As long as you have a high-speed Internet connection, an automated backup system is the way to go.

At present, the two leading contenders for online backups are BackBlaze and CrashPlan+, both of which cost $50 per year. Depending on the size of your hard drive, the initial backup can take days, weeks, or even months. But this all happens in the background and doesn't affect computer performance unless sending large files, in which case you can just pause the backup.

Because photographs are often the most precious items lost in a fire, back them up digitally, too. This means scanning the prints and slides so you can store them on a hard drive *and* cloud server. Even if you have the technology, you probably don't have the time to scan all of your images. Fortunately, there are services that do a great job for a reasonable price. Among the best known are ScanCafe (scancafe .com) and Larsen Digital (slidescanning.com).

Fire-Resistant Safe

At first glance, a fire-resistant safe to keep vital documents and possessions protected looks like a good idea. But in reality many just offer a false sense of security. A burglar safe is often a lousy fire safe because of minimal insulation, and they aren't waterproof.

The problem with most economy fire safes is that they're designed for urban settings where the fire department arrives on the scene within five minutes. More often than not, the fire is put out before the entire structure is consumed. These safes are at least waterproof, though, so efforts to put out the fire won't harm what's inside.

If you look at images of houses after a major wildfire, however, it's obvious that practically nothing remains. These fires burn hotter and much longer because the fire departments are simply overwhelmed. The contents of the average fire safe from a big-box store will turn to ashes in these conditions.

Cheap fire safes are designed to keep their contents below 350°F when exposed to 1,700°F for one hour. These may be called Class C, but some companies use their own testing and ratings instead of Underwriters' Laboratory (UL). While that might prevent paper from burning, objects like film and fabric have little chance.

The next step up is a Class B safe, though it gets a bit more complicated at this level because two standards apply: UL and the Korean Industrial Standards (KIS). Safes that meet either standard are pretty good because they keep the contents protected for two hours at 1,850°F. Without going into all the details, UL-certified safes are a bit better due to more demanding testing.

If you have truly valuable objects that must be protected, then you're looking at Class A safes. These offer four hours of protection from 2,000°F while keeping the contents to 350°F. There also 'tweeners, like a three-hour safe, all the way up to the highest-end "data safes" that keep contents below 125°F.

A proper fire safe makes for rather poor burglar protection because it should have thin sheet-metal walls to reduce heat buildup. These are adequate to prevent pilfering from the casual thief, but that's about it. If serious burglar protection is your major concern, avoid any safe with fireboard no matter how fancy the lock appears. Short of going exotic, the only real protection from fire *and* burglary is a safe-deposit box at your bank.

The size of the safe is another major factor in price. The smallest decent fireproof safe (0.7 cubic feet, KIS-certified) weighs around 90 pounds and costs $300. If you want more storage space and protection, a 1.3-cubic-foot safe starts at $1,500 and weighs 450 pounds at the low end and hits $3,700 and 1,100 pounds at the high end; see brownsafe.com for more details.

Should you decide to purchase a fire safe, the next question is where to put it. Two concerns: Heat rises, and these things are *way* heavy. Your best option is ground level next to concrete foundation walls if possible. Temperatures will be cooler, and off to the side is more protected from the impact of falling objects.

Another consideration is that most fire safes foster high-humidity environments; much of their thermal protection comes from a water-retaining mix of concrete and vermiculite that releases steam at high heat. Anything you put inside a fire safe that can rust or otherwise be damaged by moisture must be sealed in airtight bags; coating metal and wood with Renaissance Wax is a great extra protection.

Fire Bunker

On February 7, 2009, the Black Saturday Bushfires killed 164 people in Australia and injured another 414. This tragedy has led to a rethinking of the usual advice about evacuation—at least in some areas.

If your home is remote, and especially if you only have one exit route, you might consider building a fire bunker. Similar in concept to a bomb shelter, this is a fortified room intended as a place of last refuge. Most people can't evacuate whenever there is high fire danger, and if a fire is about to hit, it can be more dangerous to leave than to stay put, especially at night or when the smoke is so thick that you can't see the end of your car (see Chapter 8).

While good in theory, a fire bunker could also become your final resting place if inadequately designed and constructed. Currently, there are no standards in America for fire bunkers, so most of the research comes from Australia, and even that's minimal. This is an area ripe for fly-by-night companies that make all sorts of claims but won't be around to pay off your relatives after the fire.

If you decide you want a fire bunker, it can cost around $10,000 to $20,000, and you may have to call it a "wine cellar" for a building permit. Cheaper than that likely means you've skimped and created a false sense of security. Do it right, or don't bother.

For a fire bunker to be effective, it must keep the radiant heat out for at least one hour as the flame front passes by and residual fires die down. It needs to be solidly constructed so something heavy won't come crashing in, and it must be completely airtight or have an adequate auxiliary air supply because an intense fire will suck oxygen out.

The location of your fire bunker is also a critical decision. One option is to build a cellar, but that runs the risk of the entire house collapsing on it during the fire, so a bombproof ceiling is essential. This shelter should have an external exit, perhaps with a cement block wall a few feet in front of the door to block radiant heat. If you build outside, it needs to lie at least 30 feet from any structure—but it should be no more than 120 feet from the house so you can reach it quickly. Don't build downhill because that's where a flame front will likely approach. Don't build uphill if it will take too long to reach. Make sure the path is obvious even in the dark.

The construction can be fire-rated plasterboard, heavy timber, nonporous concrete, or a combination of these materials. Concrete exposed to intense heat can decompose explosively, called spalling, so it should be covered by dirt on the outside and not contain rebar, which heats and expands faster. Four layers of fire-rated plasterboard with an exterior of compressed-fiber cement board is one option for an aboveground shelter.

The fire door must be set in a steel frame built to the dimensions of your walls. Consider having the door open inward so falling debris can't block it. To prevent accidental entrapment, the door shouldn't have a lock—particularly if you have children. Depending on space, you might look into a tunnel entrance with an outer and inner door or a dogleg made of stone or concrete to block radiant heat.

There's an obvious temptation to add amenities like phone lines, electricity, and a window or periscope so you have an idea of what's going on outside. But these luxuries also create many potential points of failure in your air seal. All points of entry must be sealed with heat-proof caulk like Fire Stop (firechemicals.com). If you insist on a window, it should have a removable cover and an external thermometer so you know to open it only after things have cooled off outside.

An external vent is a good idea to bring in extra air after the fire has passed but it's still too hot to go outside. The vent can also prevent problems with mold during the 99.99 percent of the time the bunker isn't in use. Any vents require an airtight seal that you can close off right after entering.

With or without vents, you may want to consider an additional air supply. If you build a shelter to hold your family, an extra guest or two could become problematic. One option is to keep a scuba tank or three in the shelter; a used standard aluminum 80 can often be picked up on eBay for $50. These don't even need regulators or masks if you don't plan on leaving the bunker.

Resist the temptation to use the fire bunker as a storage space. The more junk you put inside, the less air you'll have when you need it most. Otherwise, plan on building it bigger so you can bring in extra food, water, and clothing to survive for the next few days, plus valuables like photo albums and such.

ACTIVE SUPPRESSION

Be ready to put a small fire out fast! Then do what you can for a major fire. Options run from simple sprinklers to full-blown suppression systems that would make a volunteer fire department jealous.

A significant percentage of wildfires start by mishaps near homes such as a power line hitting a tree limb and showering sparks on the ground or the muffler from an engine igniting a grass fire. If possible, call the fire department first. If it's safe to do so, try to put out the flames before they arrive.

Fire Extinguishers

A house fire doubles in size every thirty seconds, so every home should have multiple fire extinguishers readily available. You need one for the kitchen to handle flare-ups and accidents. Every car and truck should have an extinguisher, both for you and so you can help if you encounter a fire. It's also good to have an extinguisher near your workbench. Homeowners in the Red Zone should have several extinguishers for wood and grass fires, too.

In the kitchen, you need an extinguisher capable of putting out a grease fire without splashing: either the Kidde FX10K ($25) or the First Alert Kitchen ($20). Instead of a high-pressure stream, a kitchen fire extinguisher emits a heavy mist. Sodium bicarbonate (baking soda) fills these extinguishers, which won't harm appliances. However, they can't put out burning paper, wood, or fabric. Don't trust any aerosol can fire extinguisher; they're cheap but far less effective.

Other locations in the house, as well as cars, should have small, multipurpose fire extinguishers, such as the Kidde FA110 ($30). In the garage, you might want a larger one, like the Kidde Pro 10 ($60). In the United States, these are called ABC extinguishers because they handle solid materials that leave an ash (A) and flammable liquids that bubble (B), and won't zap you if there's an electrical current (C). Other countries use different rating systems, but the concepts are the same.

ABC extinguishers use dry chemicals—a mix of monoammonium phosphate and ammonium sulfate—to create a thin layer of dust that blocks oxygen from reaching the fire. Effective on any type of fire likely to be encountered outside an industrial setting, they do make a tremendous mess, but that's a small trade-off. Most inexpensive dry chemical extinguishers aren't refillable, though the pricier Pro models can be recharged for about $20.

Extinguishers are also rated by capacity, which is designated by the

Home fire extinguishers: Kidde Pro 10, Amerex 240, and Kidde FA110

number in front of the letter. A 1-A extinguisher has the equivalent of 1 gallon of water on a wood fire, and a 4-A has four times that. It's more complicated with Class B ratings, but all you need to know is that the lower number (usually 10) is more than adequate unless you work on a NASCAR team.

While you need a selection of ABC fire extinguishers, it's also a good idea to have several Class A extinguishers that spray water. These 2-foot-tall silver cylinders hold 2.5 gallons and are pumped up to 100 psi with an air compressor or bicycle pump. The Amerex 240 and Badger WP-61 are good, but avoid the Kidde Pro 2.5 because it lacks a Schrader valve, so you can't refill it yourself. These normally sell for around $120, but you can find good used air-pressurized water (APW) extinguishers on eBay for about $50.

Sometimes called water cans, these giant squirt guns have many advantages over dry chemical extinguishers on grass and wood fires. For starters, you can and should practice with them, because refills are free. You'll never know how it's going to squirt until you try it, and during an emergency is less than ideal. With any extinguisher, aim at the base of the fire, not the flames.

After the APW extinguisher is completely discharged, unscrew the top, remove the valve, and, leaving the plastic funnel in place, use a hose to fill the tank until water bubbles out. (The funnel keeps the proper air space.) Reassemble and pressurize till the needle is in the green on the gauge. To improve efficacy, add $\frac{1}{3}$ cup of dish soap to the water. This acts as a wetting agent (surfactant) so water doesn't bead up and roll off.

APW extinguishers shoot out a powerful water stream over 40 feet and last about 55 seconds. You can put your thumb over the nozzle to create a fan of water that soaks a larger area. This helps conserve water. Try both on a sidewalk to see how the fan covers the area more efficiently.

For even better performance, convert a water can into a compressed air foam (CAF) fire extinguisher. Foam is about five times more effective than water at knocking down a fire. Unfortunately, Class A foam is sold only in concentrates that come in expensive 5-gallon pails, and you need only a cup. You might be able to beg some from your local fire department, or you can make a reasonable substitute at home.

This conversion simply requires opening the water can and drilling with a $^3/_{32}$-inch bit all the way through the pickup tube (creating two holes) about a foot down from the top. Then cut the nozzle off from the rubber hose just above the metal ferrule so the extinguisher has a wider mouth.

Fill the tank with 1 gallon of water and, if you can't find Class A foam, add $1^1/_2$ cups of dish soap and 1 cup of glycerin, which you can get from a good drugstore. The holes in the pickup tube pull air in to mix with the soapy water, and the glycerin makes the soap bubbles more durable. This produces about 6 gallons of foam that blocks oxygen and cools the flame.

Another option is to fill your extinguisher with 2.5 gallons of fire gel. FireIce (fireice.com) offers six premeasured cans of concentrate ($50) that creates a long-lasting gel. When sprayed on a wood fire, this cools and blocks oxygen much more effectively than plain water, plus it stays in place longer to prevent reignition.

Inspect all fire extinguishers at least once a year, and make sure they have adequate pressure. This just requires a glance at the gauge but also ensure that rapid access isn't blocked. Also look inside the nozzles for obstructions. I recently found that a wasp had made a nest inside one and completely blocked the opening so I added aluminum foil covers

Hoses

For putting out fires near your house, every outside spigot should have a 100-foot garden hose attached. While 50 feet is a more common length, it comes up awfully short for protection. Even if you have quick-connect attachments, in an emergency it's too time-consuming to haul a hose from the front of the house to the back. That said, quick-connects do give you the option of combining two hoses if you need a 200-foot run in a hurry.

The best option for a hose is $5/8$ inch in diameter with brass fittings such as the Apex NeverKink, Gilmor Flexogen, or Tuff-Guard. A $1/2$-inch hose is lighter but won't deliver as much water, while a $3/4$-inch hose is so heavy that coiling and dragging it are a chore.

Ideally, each hose should have a high-flow nozzle attached. Often called a fireman's nozzle, the good ones are mostly metal and cost $20 to $30 (Bon-Aire and Nelson). Standard garden nozzles don't deliver as much water, and most break too easily. If you use a brass quick-connect with shut-off, you can swap nozzles without shutting the hose off at the spigot.

A good-quality hose can cost $60 to $90, so take care of it. It's best to turn off the water at the spigot after use and drain the hose to remove the water pressure. If you leave the hose pressurized, the water can expand from heating in the sun and lead to premature failure.

Prevent UV degradation by keeping hoses in the shade or using a winding reel. A hose reel helps, but the cheap ones break easily. The best reels have a moving guide to coil the hose neatly and easily. A hose reel also makes it easier to bring a hose inside until after a fire has passed. (It won't do you any good after it's melted.)

For homeowners with a hot tub elevated on a deck or slope, put a quick-connect on the drain and keep a hose nearby. If your electricity goes out, this will give you enough water pressure to send out a good stream of water, particularly if you have a sweeper nozzle ($6). A standard water hose isn't designed for 106°F water, so it will collapse easily at a sharp corner. Hot water hoses tend to be stiff, heavy, and expensive. One solution is a piece of stiff tubing big enough to go over the hose and give a smooth radius over a deck edge.

Many homes have 50 to 80 gallons of water in a hot water tank. When there is no power, this can be tapped by using the spigot at the bottom, perhaps by running a hose outside.

Well Pressure Tanks

Houses that rely on wells instead of city water have a couple problems in an emergency. Running a well pump for too long can drain the well and burn out the motor, which can prove very costly. This is why you shouldn't run a sprinkler system nonstop. If the power goes out, the well pump stops working, and you run out of water when the pressure tank drains.

The bladder tanks on most houses typically have an actual capacity of around 15 gallons of water, which certainly doesn't go far. Upgrading your pressure tank to an 85-gallon model is easy and relatively inexpensive (spend more for a better warranty); it's taller rather than wider, so it takes up the same footprint as the smaller tank. An 85-gallon tank can't halt a full-blown fire, but it's helpful for putting out spot fires.

If you have the space and funds, go bigger or even add another pressure tank. There is no downside to upsizing your pressure tanks. In addition to more emergency capacity, it reduces wear and tear on the well pump because it doesn't have to cycle as often.

Fire Cistern

When you live beyond a municipal water system, fire defense becomes more problematic. Without a standby generator, well water is unavailable because electricity is routinely cut to threatened neighborhoods; fallen live power lines pose a serious threat to firefighters. Even if power remains on, a well can't deliver water fast enough for fire suppression.

One solution is to install a fire cistern that holds 1,800 to 2,400 gallons of water, enough to battle most house fires. Another option is to install a community cistern with at least 10,000 gallons of water where tankers can refill. Many counties in fire areas are now mandating cisterns as requirements for new building permits.

For a fire cistern to be effective, it must be located 50 to 75 feet from the house. Closer and the fire department can't use it if the house is burning. Fire hoses are normally 200 feet long (four precon-nected 50-foot lengths) and need to reach the backside of a house, so the cistern can't lie too far away either. The cistern needs to be located near the turnaround that the fire engines will use, and it can't be used for other purposes, such as a sprinkler system.

A standard concrete cistern that holds 1,800 gallons is about 10 feet long, 7 feet wide, and 8 feet tall. It will weigh about 8 tons before you fill it up, so you'll need heavy machinery to bury it. The total cost, including a dry hydrant, runs about $2,500, though it could rise much higher if blasting is required.

A community cistern can cost upwards of $45,000 to install, but the expense is spread throughout the fire district. Homeowners typi-cally contribute to a cistern fund. We have a community cistern on our property. Technically, we leased the land to the fire department, so, in addition to having 10,000 gallons of water nearby, we don't have to do any maintenance, and the fire department keeps it topped off.

Of course, a pond or swimming pool also makes for a great water supply. Even a hot tub can provide 200 to 500 gallons of water—better than nothing. Using foam or gel systems can turn that into the equivalent of between 800 and 2,000 gallons of water.

Water Pumping Systems

Without a pumping system, a fire cistern, swimming pool, or nearby river, still leaves you in a bad situation. The farther you are from a fire station, particularly one not staffed full-time, the more you may have to take matters into your own hands.

A pump for firefighting must deliver both high volume and high pressure. For home defense, you want a pump that can discharge 15 to 30 gallons per minute. More than that will waste water that's in short supply.

The pump also needs to be able to deliver that water at 100 psi at the nozzle. A 1-inch fire hose loses about 30 psi every 100 feet from friction, so the pump should be putting out at least 160 psi at the head. Without that level of pressure, you don't have enough height and distance, which puts you too close to the flames. Look at the pump performance curve, and you'll see that the greater the discharge, the lower the pressure.

For some homeowners, a great system is the Wildfire Hot Tub Package (primopumps.com). It's a complete outfit with a gas-powered engine and pump, plus all the accessories, that costs either $800 or $1,000 depending on the configuration you choose. Fairly small and portable (40 pounds), it delivers almost 100 psi at 30 gpm, which is far greater than a well offers. The next step is their Home Firefighting Cart System, which costs about $4,500. This weighs over 200 pounds, hence the need for the cart, and requires a large supply of water, such as a swimming pool or fire cistern. Delivering 160 psi at 30 gpm, this package would make firefighters happy.

If you're caring for a ranch, summer camp, or similar large property, a wide range of truck-mounted, trailer-pulled, and stationary firefighting systems are available. These start at $7,000 and can easily exceed $20,000 for full-blown systems.

Assuming the pump is powerful enough, you're well beyond using a garden hose for fighting fire. For distances up to 200 feet, a 1-inch-diameter single-jacket fire hose ($90 for 50 feet) offers a good combination of flow and maneuverability. If you need to go much farther, use a $1^1/_2$-inch hose for the initial lay to maintain pressure (less friction) and a 1-inch hose at the end for ease of handling.

Flame-Retardant Spray

If the grass around your house is crispy brown and the forecast shows no significant rain in the long range, consider spraying your yard with a treatment like Unishield TG-300 (firechemicals.com), a flame retardant for dry grass and brush. The company claims it's biodegradable, not harmful to animals, and will last all season. At a cost of around $600 to cover 1 acre, applying fire-retardant spray every year when the grasses dry up can be an expensive proposition. It's also no substitute for trimming everything in Zone 2. But if it's a bad fire year, this may be worth your money for the extra protection.

Fire Foam

Because water is often in short supply, you want to maximize what you have. Using Class A foam or gel can stretch your water supply by three to five times. The slower evaporation rate of these materials also can greatly extend the length of protection versus plain water.

There are many types of firefighting foams. Class A is great on wood-type fires, but it doesn't work for other fires. Nor should you use any other foam for protecting against wildfire. Some foams contain protein to increase longevity, but they can stain so badly that you may need to repaint the entire house afterward.

The air bubbles in foam help cool and smother fires, while the surfactant reduces water tension so it penetrates better. Class A foam is also ideal for establishing a long-lasting wet line in grass and vegetation to act as a fire break. All of this is enhanced further if the foam is injected with compressed air (CAFS) to create a light, thick blanket that quickly cools a fire.

The easiest and least expensive foaming system for home use is Foam-Fast ($150, foamfast.com), which attaches to a garden hose. It consists of a long canister with a nozzle on the end and comes with three solid cartridges that last up to one hour each.

More elaborate systems use compressed gas, such as nitrogen, to create foam; because this can be stored in tanks, the systems can still work when the power goes out. The Aegis 2000 is half the size of a refrigerator and holds enough foam to cover 5,000 square feet. The $12,000 system sits on a concrete pad next to your house, and when a fire threatens, you hose the house down. In cold climates, though, the 200-gallon water tank should be located indoors.

From the perspective of firefighters, foam is great. However, from the perspective of an evacuating homeowner, the big drawback is its relatively short life. The foam itself might last about two hours—wind and humidity playing big factors—and then the water soon evaporates.

Fire Gel

While foam essentially forms a blanket of water with air-filled bubbles, fire gel consists of a layer of slow-drying, water-filled bubbles. The advantage of gel is that the moisture content can last up to thirty-six hours. Realistically, on a hot, windy day, gel will dry out in about six to eight hours. But even after it's completely dried, misting it with water can regenerate the gel. If you've been evacuated, the fire department just has to set a nozzle to a 30 percent fog pattern, and your house gets another boost of protection.

Fire gel comes in a concentrate of superabsorbent polymers, a surfactant, and either a mineral oil or a vegetable oil. This concentrate is mixed with water using a mixing eductor attached to a hose. These systems work best with 100 psi but can get by with the lower pressure of a garden hose attached to the house (in which case the gel won't be as wet).

When you spray the gel, it creates a layer of water encapsulated in the polymers. The thicker you spray, the longer the gel will last before drying out. It's clingy stuff, so it will stay in place on vertical surfaces—even glass windows—better than foam.

Barricade (firegel.com) was the original fire-blocking gel, but a number of competitors are now available. A Barricade kit, consisting of an eductor that attaches to your garden hose and 4 gallons of gel concentrate, costs $375 and covers roughly 2,400

Barricade fire gel and eductor

square feet. FireIce (fireice.com) sells a pressure washer system for between $1,500 and $2,200. This extends the reach of spray, but the system may be impractical to move around rugged terrain.

When fire is approaching, spray the gel on flammable walls, windows, and decks as well as surrounding vegetation. Be careful when walking on sloping surfaces because it's very slick, like a thick layer of soap. Both companies claim that their products are nontoxic, environmentally safe, and won't harm paint. After you return, you'll need to use a pressure washer to remove the gel from your home.

Fire Wrap

The short duration of foam and gel creates a problem if you have to evacuate for many days or have a cabin in a remote area. For protection that lasts days or weeks, you can wrap entire structures with a radiant barrier of aluminized glass fabric. When fire approaches, the material shields from firebrands as well as 95 percent of the radiant heat.

Even without power or water, two or three people can cover a building in half a day. The rolls weigh up to 62 pounds, and you'll have to work on rooftops and ladders, so it's a dangerous task that you have to reverse when you return. It may take up to 15,000 staples and many rolls of high-temperature tape to seal a cabin from embers and hold up against strong winds.

Offered in rolls from 5 by 150 feet to 12 by 60 feet (around $750), the Firezat Fire Shield (firezat.com) is reusable and lasts for years. It may take three to six rolls to cover a building. If you live where fire is likely to come from one direction, such as atop a slope, you may only need to protect the roof and walls on that side.

External Sprinkler Systems

Rooftop sprinklers will wet your roof, gutters, decks, and surrounding vegetation as long they have water pressure. Ideally, you should run the sprinklers for several hours before a fire arrives to saturate the surroundings. But there are some significant drawbacks to sprinklers as well.

Roof Saver Sprinklers (roofsaversprinklers.com) are designed to sit on the peak of a roof and stay in place without screws or anchor weights. They come with a good-quality garden hose and a bracket to keep everything in place. These cost $180 each and cover about a 100-foot-diameter circle, so you may need several to provide full coverage.

The main drawbacks to rooftop sprinklers are dependence on a water supply and adequate pressure. If you're in the boonies, the well may run dry from continuous pumping and the motor could burn out. Also, without a standby generator, the power may go out and your pump won't work at all, in which case you'll have no water.

If you live on the urban edge and have municipal water, pressure likely will drop dramatically during a big fire as everyone tries to wet down his or her property. The fire department may request that people *not* use their hoses and sprinklers so that firefighters have enough water pressure to fight the fire properly.

For sprinklers to be effective, you need a significant water supply because you aren't getting the multiplying effects of foam or gel. A system that sprays 5 gallons of water per minute will use 7,200 gallons in twenty-four hours. You'll need a large lake or river to provide adequate water for days of threat. You also may need a large fuel supply for a standby generator. If your sprinkler system runs out of water or fuel on day four of an evac, you've lost that layer of protection. An empty fire cistern when things turn ugly on day six is problematic for firefighters.

At least one company (wildfiresprinkler.com) specializes in sprinkler systems for homes that have a good water supply available. Their system uses a propane-powered pump and can cover an acre with 60 gallons per minute for as long as the fuel lasts. Prices start at $7,500, but it's likely to run much higher for a complete installation.

Standby Generator

A portable generator is adequate for powering a few appliances for a short while, but, if you want to run your furnace, well, and other critical systems, your best option is a standby generator running on propane or natural gas. These have an automatic transfer switch that starts the engine and charges the electric panel within ten seconds of a power failure.

Sometimes bigger is better. While a smaller 14 kW generator appears less expensive, it may require much higher labor costs because the service panel must be rewired for specific circuits. A larger 20 kW generator can power the entire house with only a single breaker switch.

Depending on size, location, and other factors, a standby generator is likely to cost from $6,000 to $12,000 for most homeowners. Both Generac and Kohler are respected names. For colder regions, you also need some extra parts to keep the engine ready, and you may need a larger propane tank to last a long power outage.

Fire-Retardant Systems

Once the water has evaporated, neither foam nor gel offers substantial protection from fire. In the case of a truly massive fire, homeowners may be evacuated for a week or more. For maximum protection, you may want a fire-retardant system.

Similar to what the Forest Service drops from air tankers, fire retardants work by changing the chemical process of fire to produce carbon and steam instead of flames. Once laid down, a fire retardant continues to work for six months or until it is removed by several days of rain.

Fire retardants used for aerial attack contain an iron oxide coloring agent so pilots can tell what areas have been treated, as well as corrosion inhibitors and flow conditioners. Much of the environmental concern stems from these additives—in particular, sodium ferrocyanide (yellow prussiate of soda, or YPS). None of these chemicals are used in fire retardants designed for home defense.

A house protected by a fire-retardant system, such as Firebreak (firebreaksystems.com), requires a fire cistern full of water, a 120-gallon or larger tank of the retardant, and pressurized tanks of nitrogen to spray the mixture. Rather than putting out a fire, the water in this case distributes the retardant. Sprinklers are mounted on the roof and possibly in the defensible space area for maximum distribution. It's best if the system is built into a new house, but retrofitting is possible.

You can activate the system manually by opening a valve, by phone with a code, and even automatically via a fire sensor. The cost of a Firebreak system starts at $14,000, but realistically you're looking at $20,000 to $50,000. Unfortunately, your insurance premiums won't go down, but you may be required to install one of these systems if building in a very high-risk location.

Fire Sensors

A number of companies have developed special cameras or sensors designed to detect wildfires. These can be tied into fire-retardant or sprinkler systems to protect property while you're away.

The Fire Scout (fire-scout.com) detects the ultraviolet signature given off by flames and can spot a fire a quarter mile away. It can also detect the arcing of power lines—an all-too-frequent occurrence in windstorms—up to 1 mile away. The device then notifies the fire department. The sensors used by FlameSniffer (flamesniffer.com) have a radius of 1,000 feet. A network of posts is placed around a home or neighborhood that detects both flames and firebrands and then activates a sprinkler system that comes with the package. The price of these systems is site dependent; suffice it to say, they aren't cheap.

A more sophisticated system called FireAlert (ambientalert.com) uses a dual-band infrared sensor to detect fires up to 6 miles away in any direction. It can also monitor the progress of a fire and trigger an alarm or set of sprinklers when flames get too close. At present, FireWatch (firewatchamerica.com) represents the state of the art in remote detection. Rather than looking for flames, the sensor examines changes in water vapor molecules and can detect a smoke plume over 10 miles away. At a cost of around $1.5 million, it's technology well suited to counties where nipping a fire in the bud can save many times that.

Wildfire Protection Service

Wealthy homeowners have one more option for protecting their property: contract firefighters. In most western states, Chubb Insurance includes this service with the mansion owner's policy. When a fire breaks out in the area, fully equipped teams of certified wildland firefighters go to insured houses and take preventive action, such as spraying gel. These private firefighters work in coordination with the Incident Management Team. Their job is to protect structures in advance of a fire, get out of the way, and then do what they can afterward. Their presence essentially frees other firefighters to work elsewhere.

COMMUNITY PROJECTS

On a larger scale, it's wise to engage your neighbors to join discussions of wildfire. Firewise (firewise.org) is a national program administered by the National Fire Protection Association that encourages homeowners to work together to address their shared wildfire risk.

To become part of the recognized Firewise Communities/USA program, a community is required to follow a five-step process. This includes performing a community assessment, holding an annual Firewise activity day, and submitting documentation. Nearly 1,000 localities across the nation are recognized as Firewise Communities.

Another avenue for communities to follow is the development of a Community Wildfire Protection Plan. At a minimum, a CWPP requires collaboration with local and state governments to draft a fuel reduction plan and make recommendations on how to decrease the ignitability of area structures. It also requires a lot of time spent in meetings and on paperwork. The payoff comes when your area is more likely to qualify for state and federal grants that help pay for large-scale projects such as major firebreaks.

Truly local events can be a lot more fun with less hassle. An example of this is the Saws and Slaws Day held in Nederland, Colorado (sawsand slaws.com). This grassroots event consists of neighbors and volunteers performing fire mitigation on several properties in the morning and then having a potluck in the afternoon. The "forestry and food" theme nicely helps build community as well as reduce fire danger.

Fund-raisers for firefighters, such as the Fight Fire with Beer Festival in Boulder (firefighterappreciationweek.org), are also popular events that can serve as good educational tools if planned effectively. Often organized around a local band of musicians, with food and beer provided by restaurants and breweries, these tend to be large parties. With a little forethought, they can also be a great opportunity to teach the public about what firefighters actually do, the gear they use, and the dangers they face. This knowledge in turn leads to greater support of fire departments and mitigation efforts.

FIREARM SAFETY

If you have guns in the house, the ammunition poses minimal danger to anyone during a fire—with one major exception. Unloaded cartridges will auto-ignite when heated to around 320°F, but the bullets will have no velocity. Gunpowder cooks off before the primer detonates, and the lighter shell casing actually becomes a weak projectile.

However, if you have a gun with a round in the chamber, it can discharge potentially lethal bullets when heated. A revolver will fire one rifled bullet and send high-velocity shrapnel from the other chambers. A semiautomatic pistol, rifle, or shotgun that is Condition 1 (magazine loaded, with a round in the chamber) will discharge a round, and it can possibly even continue to fire until the magazine is empty.

Ideally, loaded guns for home defense should be kept in a Class B fire-resistant safe whenever you leave the house. Unfortunately, most gun safes aren't fire-rated to that level, but at least the steel will slow the bullets. The worst gun safes come from mass-discounters; these typically have fairly thin 12-gauge steel on the door and even thinner steel on the other sides.

If you keep a gun loaded in the nightstand or closet when not at home—not smart if you have children—leave it in Condition 3 (no round in the chamber). Any gun not needed for protection should be completely unloaded.

In only three years, sixty-three fires were apparently started by gunfire—just in Utah. When a forest is tinder dry, a steel-jacketed or steel-core bullet glancing off a rock can create sparks that start a fire. Solid copper bullets easily ignite fires because they get so hot. Even worse are tracer and incendiary rounds, which are designed to light things up. It's even possible for lead bullets to start a fire if they hit a flat, immovable target; they may not spark, but they become hot enough to ignite dried grass. This is one reason why steel targets are designed to rotate or flop down when hit.

There has also been an alarming increase in the popularity of binary explosive targets, despite bans in many areas. In 2012 idiots shooting at exploding targets caused at least twenty-two wildfires, including the 7,600-acre Goat Fire near Pateros, Washington. If you must get your yee-haws out, shoot at milk jugs or soda cans filled with water, watermelons, potatoes, or squash. Watch Hickock45 on YouTube for examples of fun and safe shooting, and pick up your trash afterward!

PREPARE YOUR FINANCES

If you do nothing else suggested in this book, you *must* prepare an inventory and talk to your insurance agent. After every major wildland fire in which houses burn, local media always run follow-up pieces a few months and even years later on how some victims are still suffering. Sadly, most of that pain is self-inflicted because they didn't prepare.

INVENTORY

The best mitigation in the world offers no fail-safe guarantee against total loss in the case of a major firestorm. Many victims agonize over the heartbreaking process of trying to remember every last thing that they owned. After a fire, it can take hundreds of hours to reconstruct an inventory that will list thousands of items—and you'll never remember everything.

Preparing a proper inventory *before* you need it will save time, prevent tremendous anguish, and ensure a faster claims process with the highest payback. It isn't exactly fun, but it is a huge investment in your mental and financial well-being.

Once you start adding it all up, it may shock you what it costs to replace your stuff. All the yard tools for fire mitigation can easily add up to $3,500. Houseplants and pots can quickly surpass $5,000 if you have to go to a nursery and start over from scratch. If you are into cooking, the knife block in the kitchen could hold $1,500 worth of Japanese knives, and small appliances and cookware may exceed $5,000.

Even though your homeowner's policy probably has a provision for contents that gives you perhaps 70 percent of the insured value of the house, insurance companies resist paying out that much. Without good documentation, an adjustor will lowball you on value.

There are many paper-based inventory lists available for free, but don't waste your time with them. The pencil method is arduous to start, difficult to update, and requires off-site storage. Thankfully, the daunting task of creating a thorough inventory has become much easier thanks to modern technology. Mac users with an iPhone or iPad can download a program called Home Inventory ($20, binary formations.com), a well-designed database that allows you to go by room, category, or collection to catalog everything you own.

On its own, Home Inventory resembles a lot of other software designed for this purpose. Where it really shines, though, is the free integration with your device's camera, which allows you to add photos of your belongings quickly. For example, I can go into the family room and take a bunch of photos of the stereo and furniture. The photos automatically load into my database and attach to the descriptions already entered for each item. If I left something off the list, I can add it from the device and take a picture.

With Home Inventory, you can also shoot video of a collection and save it into the database. Manuals in PDF form are easily attached as well, and you can either photograph or scan receipts from within the program. It's also easy to add notes that help determine value, such as upgrades to a computer or the provenance of an antique. The program tracks warranty information and gives a wide range of reports, too.

To get started, first make a list of every room in the house, making sure to include places like the attic, garage, shed, and decks. You may want to treat collections—stamps, baseball cards, guns, jewelry, rare books—as separate "locations" because they often require their own insurance rider.

Go through each room, and enter the contents into the program. I prefer to enter as many items as I can see while using my laptop, then go back later to fill in details and add photos. As a rough guideline, I separately document only objects valued over $50. When taking photographs, be sure to get a macro shot of the serial number or any other vital information, such as a signature on an autographed book, identifying marks on valuable pottery, and so forth.

To estimate value for items that you've had a while and no longer have a receipt, use Amazon.com, eBay.com, Etsy.com, or the like. It may take a bit of guesstimation, but it at least gives a reasonable idea of replacement prices. Antiques and handcrafts may take more research to determine current value, so record as much information as possible to help with the appraisal.

When you reach closets and dressers, in many cases you can simply approximate the contents. For example: a closet might hold 10 dresses, 12 pairs of blue jeans, and 15 pairs of cowboy boots; a dresser contains 6 pairs of pants, 8 pairs of shorts, and 20 T-shirts. With those estimates, the adjustor will give you an approximate value. As always, document especially valuable items—a wedding dress or a bespoke Italian suit—separately.

Take a similar approach in the kitchen. The pantry may contain 50 jars and cans of food and condiments probably worth $500 altogether. The freezer likely holds a few hundred dollars worth of food. The spice rack has 30 bottles at an average cost of $5 each. A wine cellar might contain 25 bottles of red and 10 bottles of white "drinking wines." Also document and photograph each bottle of special wine valued over $50. Oenophiles often have bottles worth hundreds of dollars apiece.

Your collection of music can also add up fast. The average price for a CD is $15, and you may have several hundred. If any are collector's editions, they can be worth considerably more. These days, vinyl records are making a comeback, so if you have boxes of them sitting in the basement, document them, too.

Your photos are, of course, invaluable to you, but the insurance company doesn't reimburse for memories. However, you are covered for the cost of the film and processing as well as storage systems. I have about 10,000 slides in hanging files, so that's roughly 285 rolls of film at about $25 each, which tots up to around $8,000 just in raw costs. Photo albums full of prints also add up quickly. If you have prints hanging on walls, include the cost of printing, matting, and framing.

Some valuable items may not seem like they'd cost much to people unfamiliar with a particular sport or hobby. For example, high performance outdoor equipment costs a lot, and one of each piece often isn't enough. Few adjustors would easily accept that a pack can be worth $400, a sleeping bag $600, or a bicycle $4,000—let alone that there were many packs, bags, and bikes.

Once the inventory is complete, it's a simple matter of adding new items as you acquire them and deleting items that you divested. It's also easy to generate reports and even print packing lists for trips or if you move.

If all of that still sounds like too much for you, at the very least you should record a photo and video inventory of your household contents. Many smartphones, tablets, and laptop computers have the capability. Go room by room and open all the drawers and closets as you proceed. When making a video, describe the contents aloud so you have a visual and audio record.

If you can't do that, there are companies that provide an inventory service. For around $500, they'll send a trained team to go through your entire house and create an inventory. When hiring a home inventory service, make sure that they are licensed, bonded, and insured; also request a signed confidentiality agreement.

Securing the Inventory

A detailed inventory does you no good if it burns up with everything else, so you need to have off-site storage for what is one of your most valuable possessions: a document worth tens of thousands of dollars to your final payout, not to mention untold stress.

The great thing about creating a digital inventory is that every-thing can be stored automatically on a cloud server, such as Dropbox or iCloud, with password protection. (Use software like 1Password so you have greater security with strong passwords.) This makes updat-ing the files effortless and gives you access to them from anywhere.

Otherwise, you need to keep a physical copy of your inventory in a secure off-site location (bank, office, relative, etc.). As mentioned in the previous chapter, a fire safe is inadequate protection for such a vital record. Even a USB thumb drive is a hassle—whenever you make changes, such as a major purchase, you have to update the inventory manually.

INSURANCE

Your home is probably your single biggest asset. If you have a mort-gage, you have to have at least minimal coverage. In the event of total loss from wildfire, that level of insurance will make your lender happy yet possibly leave you homeless *and* penniless.

When it comes to insurance, the biggest mistake you can make is to assume that you're covered. Very few people truly understand the fine print of their homeowner's insurance policy—not even agents. It's written in obtuse legal jargon that is designed to obfuscate and requires specially trained lawyers to decipher. Starting in 2015, Colorado will require all policies be written at the tenth grade reading level. Just because it "makes sense" that something should be covered doesn't make that coverage a fact. While it might be the right thing to do, getting a speedy reimbursement probably isn't in the contract.

Renters may assume that the landowner's policy covers their per-sonal belongings and will reimburse them for living expenses. In fact, they have zero coverage unless they purchase a renter's policy, which is usually fairly inexpensive.

Another common mistake is believing that you can get by with less coverage for a lower premium. This is wishful thinking at its best, and people who have gone through it are seldom happy with the harsh reality of the aftermath. A few unfortunate truths remain when it comes to homeowner's insurance: Loyalty doesn't matter, rebuilding costs more than planned, rebuilding takes longer than expected, depreciation hurts, and your most valuable possessions may not be covered.

Your twenty years of loyalty to the insurance company, faithfully making payments on time, doesn't mean diddly-squat to them when it comes time to make a major claim. Your original agent probably retired, and the claims adjustor is a shark brought in from out of state to handle a huge disaster. He or she will go by the book and try to avoid paying every last penny.

If you live in the Red Zone, there's a good chance that you don't have enough coverage. A survey of 160 residents who lost homes in the 2010 Fourmile Canyon Fire west of Boulder revealed that nearly two-thirds were underinsured. One reason for this conundrum is that insurance companies use software, such as Xactimate, to estimate the construction cost of a house. This is designed for crappy tract houses in massive developments where builders get volume pricing. Homes in locations where wildfires occur tend to be one-offs and hopefully have a bit of character. Another possible reason for underinsurance is basing the policy on the market value of your home, which may have decreased in an economic downturn. Meanwhile, building costs keep climbing and can even spike during local shortages after a large disaster.

If you have an older home, complying with new housing codes (Law and Ordinance, or LAO, in insurance-speak) can also be a lot more expensive since you built your castle. Many policies don't cover the cost of code changes or building permits, so be sure you have LAO coverage, often an extra 10 percent or a $25,000 flat rate. These required upgrades can easily add 20 percent to construction costs, so even this coverage can leave you short. Starting in 2014, all homes in Colorado must have 25 percent LAO coverage.

Home improvements—remodeling bathrooms and the kitchen, adding decks and patios—can greatly enhance the value of your home.

Many insurance companies require notification of any upgrades that increase a home's value more than $5,000.

The standard term limit on living costs is one year, because insurance companies want people to rebuild quickly. However, in mountain areas, everything takes longer, and one year frequently isn't enough. Some policies allow for two years, but you have to make sure it's in the contract.

The cheapest policies will replace property at its depreciated value. That $1,000 television you bought five years ago may be worth only $250, even if you have to spend $750 to replace it. Depreciation is where insurance adjustors can work you over on every last item that you once owned.

Insurance Pitfalls

You can avoid unpleasant surprises from your insurance company, but it isn't easy. Herein lies the rub. You can't count on your insurance agent to offer you a sound policy that covers all of your needs. The agent will sound sincere and profess to know what you need, but he or she can't do full diligence . . . which is your job. To get a good policy that truly covers what you expect requires research and getting answers to the right questions.

Start with the actual square footage of your house. This number can be significantly larger than the square footage of living space, often used for estimates or taxation. It includes the garage, attic, and basement if you have them, as well as attached decks and outbuildings. Then get an unbiased estimate on the cost to rebuild your house from at least one local contractor or assessor; this may cost $250 or more, but it's the most accurate value. It's important that the contractor or assessor be familiar with the latest building codes as well as pending changes.

Alternatively, you can use a website like AccuCoverage.com and HMFacts.com to get a replacement estimate for around $10. These provide detailed questionnaires that get you in the ballpark for home value. However, they likely won't account for unique features that require additional cost and labor.

The replacement cost of a house differs substantially from a real estate appraisal, which fluctuates with the market. Rebuilding can also cost more than new home construction because of factors like demolition and debris removal, loss of economies of scale, pesky building codes, additional fees for site accessibility, and higher labor costs.

When you talk to insurance agents, get quotes only for full replacement coverage. If you have a mortgage, you'll be required to have "All Risks" coverage because it offers protection against anything not specifically excluded. Once you own the home, you have the option of reducing premiums but switching to "Named Perils" coverage. This costs less because it only covers what's explicitly spelled out, such as fire and wind damage.

Don't be tempted by cheaper options, such as actual cash or fair market value, which is the depreciated value. This will leave you underinsured when it really matters. Be certain the policy spells out replacement cost, which covers the actual price to purchase an equivalent item, regardless of the age or condition of the original.

The standard policy is divided into sections. Coverage A is what covers your house and everything attached to it. If you have a shed, barn, or detached garage, those fall under Coverage B, which is often 10 percent of the house.

Most of your personal property falls into Coverage C, typically 70 percent of the dwelling value. If your house is valued at $300,000, you probably have at least $200,000 of property insurance as part of the policy. It sounds like a lot, but the devil is in the details. Combined with depreciation, lack of an inventory, and all the exclusions of things people "thought" were insured, an actual payout on that property might be only $100,000, which doesn't go far these days.

Most of the good stuff—art, antiques, cash, firearms, home office equipment, jewelry—probably isn't covered beyond a shockingly low, fixed amount unless you pay more for endorsements. When you purchase a rider or floater policy for these "scheduled" items, it goes on top of your "unscheduled" property in Coverage C.

Even if you have LAO coverage for building code changes, it's wise to request an Extended Replacement Cost (ERC) endorsement that's at least 20 percent coverage above the limit. (Colorado recently mandated a minimum of 10 percent ERC for all homeowners, but more is better.) This gives your $300,000 home $360,000 of protection, which may allow you to purchase a new home or rebuild how you'd like. This extra coverage usually applies only to your house, however, and not its contents. Be sure to clarify whether this ERC will be paid out if you relocate instead of rebuild.

This additional replacement coverage is important because most policies don't include infrastructure such as driveways, power and phone lines, or detached solar arrays. Your well and septic system may be damaged and will need to be brought up to code—a very expensive prospect—before you receive a certificate of occupancy.

Be certain that you have Coverage D for Loss of Use and that the Additional Living Expense (ALE) limit is for a minimum of two years. This covers your rent and other expenses during the rebuilding process. Many policies set this coverage for one year, which isn't nearly enough. After a major fire, it can take six months even to get a building permit, and weather and other delays can add significant time as well. If possible, the ALE should cover you for three years.

Removal of debris from a house that has burned to the ground can be painfully expensive, often costing around $20,000. If hazardous waste is suspected, the disposal price can skyrocket to $50,000 or more. Houses built before around 1985 often contain asbestos and other nastiness, and your house remains may be declared hazardous automatically unless you can prove otherwise. Not all policies include debris removal, so be sure it is in the contract.

Also check that your insurance policy covers re-landscaping costs; many don't. Removing dead trees and bushes and replacing them with new landscaping can be an expensive proposition. If it's available, insurance for landscaping is also a percentage of your dwelling coverage, with a cap value on trees.

Even with a policy for full replacement cost, you probably won't get a check for the total amount. Most policies pay out only for actual cash value (the depreciated price) up front, and you don't get final payment until the house or possessions have been replaced. This means you must purchase equivalent items even if you don't want them and send in copies of the receipts. It's a backward system because it actually penalizes you for thrifty shopping.

If you can document losses that are about 30 percent greater than your coverage, you may be able to bypass this tedious shopping and documenting exercise. At that point, the insurance company may agree to pay the full amount of coverage. This lets you purchase what you want, when you want, for the price you want.

There are nineteen states with a Valued Policy Law that ensures you're paid in full after total loss due to fire. Check if your state has this law, and find out the details. While nice if you need it, the Valued Policy Law applies only to your house and not its contents, and it doesn't kick in unless the dwelling is declared a total loss. If anything reusable remains, such as the foundation, you're out of luck—again.

You don't necessarily have to rebuild in the same location to receive a full payout from the insurance company. The value of your land isn't included in the policy, however. If you build or buy a home elsewhere, you still own the land from your original home (and have to pay taxes on it).

You can lower your insurance premium by 25 percent or more if you opt for a higher deductible. This might be a good idea, because some companies drop clients who dare to make even a small claim; two or three within a few years is begging for trouble. The agent likely won't volunteer that the company has a "use it and lose it" philosophy until it's time to renew your insurance. Ask what will happen to your rates if you make a claim, and find a different agent if you don't get a straight answer.

Another way to save money is by bundling home insurance with car and life insurance policies. This can save from 5 to 15 percent annually. But you need to make sure the auto coverage also meets your requirements.

Shopping for home insurance isn't easy, because it is difficult to compare policies. Currently, no online resources offer a comparison of coverage, and companies are loath to show you the complete policy until it has been purchased. This is where the fine print bites you in the ass unless you thoroughly understand what's in it.

Remember, just because an insurance agent told you something would be covered doesn't make it so. Unless you actually see it in writing, the coverage does not exist. And check your policy every year because deductibles can go up dramatically without warning.

Flood Insurance

While homeowner's insurance covers most types of loss, the notable exception is flooding. This may not seem like much of an issue if you live so far from a creek that you can't see or hear it. But flash floods and mudflows are common after major forest fires. Terrain that appears benign may suddenly turn into a torrent of water and mud. The average flood insurance claim is around $28,000, and roughly 20 percent of those claims come from medium- to low-risk areas.

Your only protection is to purchase flood insurance from the National Flood Insurance Program, administered by the Federal Emergency Management Agency (FEMA). This costs around $600 for a standard home, though the actual figure depends on several factors. The kicker here is that flood insurance doesn't take effect until thirty days after the documents are signed. Learn more by visiting floodsmart.gov and filling out the flood risk profile. You'll work with a local agent to get the right policy.

If your home survived a wildfire, look into flood insurance right away. You may need this coverage for a decade until the plant life in the area has recovered sufficiently to hold everything in place.

EVACUATION PLANNING

The emotional stress created by an approaching fire is immense. No matter how tough you think you are, you *will* feel overwhelmed and frightened. Information on what's happening will be scarce and often conflicting. Do your family and yourself a huge favor by planning for evacuation ahead of time. Failure to do so will intensify the crisis and can prove fatal. Remember the five Ps: Proper Planning Prevents Poor Performance!

COMMUNICATION PLANNING

When fire happens, finding out what's going on becomes a top priority for anyone in the Red Zone. Reports have attributed numerous deaths in recent years to a failure of the Reverse 911 system to notify the victims of impending disaster. The bottom line: Have multiple methods of receiving emergency notifications.

Part of the problem is a failure on the part of residents to check their listing at their county emergency management office. If you don't register, you won't receive notification via cell phone, e-mail, or text. In addition, many people log in and discover incorrect information for their landlines. Make sure that *all* of your phone numbers and e-mail addresses are registered.

In Colorado, the success rate for Reverse 911 (also called Enhanced 911 or E911) is only about 50 percent. In large events, such as an oncoming wildfire or earthquake, about 20 percent of calls fail to connect because the circuits overload with everyone calling family members to check on their safety. Because cellular service is easily overwhelmed in disasters, it's wise to keep a landline to your house. At least one phone must be hardwired because cordless phones don't work when the power goes out. Don't count on using Skype or other Internet phone services because bandwidth can be in short supply even if you have power.

Handheld transceiver radios can also be useful for staying in touch with one another during an evacuation. If you have a portable 2 meter/440 MHz ham radio, you can modify it to transmit on police and fire bands (called a MARS/CAP mod) so you can speak directly to emergency personnel. This is legal during an emergency but can send you to jail and garner hefty fines at any other time.

It is also wise to create a community phone tree. (See "Neighborhood Watch" later in this chapter.) This way, if one person spots smoke nearby, word can get out quickly to all the neighbors instead of waiting for a Reverse 911 call that may never come.

The final method of notification is a sheriff deputy or firefighter coming to your house to check on occupants—if they can. In 2012 lack of access may have contributed to two fatalities in Colorado. At the Lower North Fork Fire, a chain blocking a driveway kept a firefighter away from a home where a victim died, and at the High Park Fire, a locked gate prevented a deputy from warning another victim. Both of these deaths might have been prevented if emergency services had been notified in advance how to access the property, perhaps with the code to a keypad or lockbox.

In addition to ensuring that you receive official warnings, you also need a communication plan for contacting one another during an emergency. Phone lines can clog quickly, so text messaging is often a better way to handle network disruptions.

In a large-scale event, it can be easier to call long distance than across town. Therefore, everyone in your home should know to contact a designated family member or friend who lives in a different region of the country to notify one another of their whereabouts.

Every member of the household should carry contact information for the entire family stored in his or her cell phone. Designate key contacts as ICE1 (In Case of Emergency), ICE2, ICE3, and so on. This allows paramedics or police to call the proper person quickly if an accident happens. Under your own information, note any allergies to medications (penicillin, sulfa drugs, etc.). Also include family doctors and veterinarians among your contacts. It's a good idea to have the local phone number for reservation desks of nearby hotels so you can get a head start on finding a place to stay. (In a large emergency, they're going to book up fast.)

Print this contact information on a card for your wallet, purse, or book bag. The card acts as an important backup in case you lose your phone or the battery dies. Make sure that your children's day care or school also has multiple contacts in case of emergency.

The last part of your communication plan is to designate a meeting place away from your home. This could be a grocery store parking lot, a church, a hotel, or any other good location beyond the danger zone.

EVACUATION VEHICLES

During fire season, keep the gas tanks in your evacuation cars and trucks at least half full. Also keep the windshield wiper fluid container completely full, because ash may rain down hard. If you have a truck that sits unused much of the time, make sure it has a good battery so it will start when needed.

Each vehicle should have basic supplies, including snacks and water bottle, flashlight, first-aid kit and medications, fire extinguisher, basic tool kit, road flares, jumper cables, extra keys, cash, warm clothes, and special items for infant, elderly, or disabled family members.

Store an unopened package of Wet Wipes in each vehicle so you can clean the smoke from the inside of the windshield. They also come as a welcome relief when you want to wipe down after all that sweat and fear.

Keep cell phone car chargers in all vehicles so you can stay juiced up. If you have multiple vehicles and will be forming a convoy, it can be helpful to have two-way radios to communicate. Your cell phones may not work due to terrain and overloaded circuits.

In colder climates, heavy wool blankets are a better emergency choice than sleeping bags because they are fire-resistant and block radiant heat; they are also useful for first aid. These should be made of at least 80 percent wool—100 percent if you can find them—and weigh roughly 5 pounds for a standard 62-by-80-inch size. Among the best are Swedish officer's, Italian officer's, and German military blankets. They cost in the $50 to $100 range, and you want at least two blankets per vehicle.

In warmer climates, a lighter-weight wool blanket (about 3 pounds) will suffice. You can find 80 percent wool US Army blankets at surplus stores for about $30, but there are many fakes with much lower wool content. Harbor Freight sells an 80 percent wool blanket for $10 that's adequate for emergency use.

Depending on your situation, you may want a set of bolt cutters to open a locked gate. A chain saw may be necessary to cut fallen trees. A folding shovel and come-along winch could be invaluable for freeing a stuck vehicle.

EVACUATION KIT

A popular discussion among survivalists is what they pack in their "bug-out bag," essentially a portable pack preloaded with all the essentials to survive for at least three days. These "preppers" are anticipating apocalyptic disaster scenarios in which power and water grids go down and society ceases to function under rule of law. While perhaps a bit extreme, they do offer some good advice for the less paranoid.

Every household in the Red Zone should prepare an evacuation kit with supplies for each resident and store it in an accessible location, such as the garage or your evacuation vehicle. Pack a duffel or suitcase with the goal of surviving for seventy-two hours at a friend's house, hotel, or evacuation center.

A good bug-out bag must literally be grab-and-go. That means all of the supplies are true spares so you don't waste even ten seconds looking for something not already in it. While soft by survivalist standards, this kit can reduce stress during the first frantic hours of evacuation.

Evacuation Kit	
Long pants	Shorts
Long-sleeved shirt	2 T-shirts
Underwear	Socks
Contact lenses	Medications
Headache pills	Deodorant
Toothbrush	Book or card game
$50 cash	Energy bar and water

Note: The evacuation kit is *not* the same as a disaster kit. If you live in an area at serious risk of earthquakes, hurricanes, or massive snow/ice storms, you also need a "hunker-down" cache. This includes three days of food per person (plus a can opener), 3 gallons of water per person, a battery-powered AM/FM radio with spare batteries, flashlight with spare batteries, first-aid kit, whistle, personal sanitation supplies (moist towelettes, garbage bags and plastic ties, toilet paper, feminine napkins), and a wrench to turn off utilities. Also consider a shotgun and pistol with ammunition if you're willing to train with them.

It's also wise to keep a hunker-down kit with at least one day of supplies at work. This includes food and water, first-aid kit, flashlight, required medicines, and shoes suitable for walking a long distance.

EVACUATION LIST

When the reality of evacuation hits you, you'll feel a huge rush. The sudden prospect of losing everything kicks mental clarity out the door. Countless fire victims have expressed deep regrets about the photo album or the family heirloom that they failed to grab in the moments of panic as they were rushing away.

Prevent a huge amount of mental agony by preparing a detailed evacuation list ahead of time. This not only includes what to take with you, but also what tasks need to be done before you hotfoot it out of there. Where possible, pre-pack tote boxes with evacuation items like documents and pet supplies.

A good evacuation list is broken down by time frames: five minutes, one hour, and six-plus hours, each of which is divided into a packing list and a to-do list. Because you hopefully already have an evacuation kit prepared, the thirty-seconds-to-get-out scenario is already covered.

These lists are very detailed about the locations of items, because you may be out of town and a friend or house sitter will need the information. Print the lists and put them in an envelope taped to the refrigerator or in some other prominent location.

Five-Minute Lists

Your evac list starts with what honestly can be done in five actual minutes. This has to be realistic based on the layout of your house and your degree of fitness. Overburdening the list defeats the purpose. This is your opportunity to think about what is truly important in your life as well as what's vital to protecting your property.

The five-minute list takes true introspection: These are the objects that can't be replaced. Your pets are obvious, but do you know exactly where their carriers are? Photo albums and family videos may be scattered all over the house. Heirloom jewelry might be in a safe, but can you remember the combination under stress?

Everyone in the family who is old enough should participate in creating this grab list. Your kids might surprise you with what they consider most important, and your spouse might be more sentimental than you realized.

Start by pre-packing a document box with vital papers and labeling it prominently. Also keep a backup address book with info on friends, insurance agencies, doctors, and so on. Toss in a local map so you can find alternative escape routes if necessary.

Document Box	
Birth certificates	Passports
House deed	Mortgage documents
Property records	Insurance papers
School paperwork	Medical files
Marriage license	Legal documents
Tax files	Military service and discharge papers
House plans	Banking information
Local road map	Investment files
Recent utility bills	Pet vaccination records
Copies of driver's license and credit cards	List of service providers with account info

Consider, too, that an evacuation can last for many days, and you may still have to work even though it feels like the world should stop. If you have papers and books important to your job or schoolwork, keep them ready during high fire danger so they can be grabbed easily along with your computer.

A few items you might not think about may make your evacuation less stressful. For example, it sounds odd to grab dirty laundry, but that's what you wore in the past few days, so it's probably clothes you like, and you can wash them at a Laundromat. During evacuation, you're going to be living on your cell phone, and finding a charge isn't always easy, so bring the appropriate cables. If you own good binoculars or a spotting scope, they might help you check on your home during the evacuation.

Five-Minute Evacuation List	
Take	**Location**
Pets	Carriers in garage, pet food in closet
Document box	Upstairs office closet, labeled EVAC
Laptop computer	Office
Hard drive	Attached to computer in office
Photo albums	Living room coffee table, bedroom on left
Top filing cabinet drawer	Office cabinet on left
Jewelry	Wall safe (combination: 1234)
Camera bag	Office closet
Dirty laundry	Hamper in basement
Cell phone chargers	Kitchen counter
Binoculars	Gear closet
Prescription medicine	Bathroom counter
Extra contact lenses and glasses	Bathroom drawer, left column, top
Wedding album	Living room table

As with the packing list, you also need to prepare a list of the most critical tasks that can help protect your home from fire. You can also help make the firefighters' job easier.

Closing the windows and fireplace flue will keep firebrands out and reduce airflow and smoke damage. Similarly, turn off attic fans, whole house fans, air conditioners, swamp coolers, and interior fans, which will pull smoke and ash inside otherwise.

Lowering metal shades or closing storm shutters can greatly reduce radiant heat that might set combustibles on fire. Fabric drapes or paper shades potentially can ignite, however, so they should be opened all the way or removed. Also move overstuffed furniture away from windows and sliding glass doors.

Cutting off propane or natural gas coming into the house can keep a bad situation from getting worse. Do this at the valve where the gas enters your house; if you have time, shut it off at the tank also.

Turning on inside and porch lights helps firefighters find your home at night or in heavy smoke. The lights also tell them at a glance whether electric lines are working. (If you have a generator running, they likely will hear it unless the wind is howling.)

Unless you believe that looting poses a greater risk to your home than it burning to the ground, leave the doors unlocked so firefighters

Five-Minute To-Do List	
Task	**Details**
Close all windows	
Close fireplace flue	Rotate lever to left
Turn off fans and air-conditioning	Switch on hallway wall
Close metal window shades and storm shutters	
Remove or fully open drapes and paper shades	
Unlock all doors	
Move furniture away from windows	Living room
Bring in seat cushions	Patio furniture on deck
Turn on exterior lights	
Turn off propane to house	Outside back door, turn lever down
Close garage door	Unlock by pulling release pin
Remove ice holder from freezer	Set in sink

can check inside for possible fire from embers blown in through vents. Keep the garage door closed to prevent firebrands from entering, but leave it unlocked. Garage door openers don't work without power, so pull the release pin on the chain (add internal and external handles if the door lacks them).

The last item on the list—removing the ice holder from freezer—may seem absurd, but it's based on personal experience. Our kitchen has a hardwood floor, and the refrigerator has an icemaker in the door. During our long evacuation while the power was out, all the ice melted, and the water drained onto the floor. By the time we returned, the floor had warped, and a large section required replacement. Because the flooring covers the entire main floor, repairmen had to sand and varnish everything, which meant moving all the furniture. That one little ice holder made for another two weeks of mayhem, including three more days of evacuation while the varnish dried.

One-Hour Lists

If lucky, you'll get the automated warning, "Be prepared to evacuate." Though you aren't required to leave at that moment, take it seriously and start packing. Emergency services will not initiate Reverse 911 with this message unless there's a distinct possibility of the situation deteriorating rapidly.

This advance warning might happen if the fire is miles away but the conditions are ripe for rapid advancement. Emergency officials will also factor in the size of the population at risk, the number of emergency vehicles that may need to get into the area, and the nature of the roads (wide and straight versus narrow and twisty, number of exit points, etc.).

The one-hour lists begin with everything on the five-minute lists, then you start working down in priority. Anything you don't pack, you may never see again. Any task you don't complete might increase the odds of losing it all.

This list includes family heirlooms and sentimental items that can't be replaced. It also includes items that can help you stay sane during a long evacuation, such as a supply of clean clothes. My list includes mountain bikes so we can both get a workout to relieve stress and have alternative transportation.

When the follow-up "leave now" call comes, put on protective clothing in case the evacuation doesn't go well—a blocked road, for example. Even if it's 100°F outside, wear long pants and a long-sleeved shirt made of fire-resistant fabric (wool or cotton, not synthetic). Put on good hiking boots or running shoes, not flip-flops. Take some leather work gloves in case you have to grab something hot, like a door handle, and a bandana to protect your face.

The one-hour to-do list takes care of the last details that can help save your home. Hopefully, you've already done everything to create a survivable space. If you procrastinated, then at least pull combustibles like firewood and scrap lumber away from the house.

One-Hour Evacuation List	
Take	**Location**
Pet food and bowls	Basement closet
Photo albums	Guest bedroom
Desktop computer and monitor	Office
Family photos	Hallway
Antique vase	Living room, upper shelf
Small painting	Bedroom, above dresser
Big print	Living room
Clean clothes and shoes	Bedroom closet
Pet toys	TV room
Mountain bikes	Garage
Hiking packs	Storeroom, middle cabinet
Case of 1982 Petrus	Wine cellar, left side

Sometimes it's the little details—a broom on the porch or a door-mat that you bring inside—that can prevent the big burn. Simple tasks like closing all inside doors to reduce air circulation don't take long.

Your pets will certainly be stressed from picking up on your stress and perhaps the smell of smoke. Herding all your critters into one room can save you the frustration of finding their hiding places when you get the call to leave. (See the "Pet Evacuation" section for more details.)

Bring water hoses inside until the fire front passes to protect them from melting. Turn off sprinklers before you leave to protect the water supply. Again, do what you can to help firefighters protect your

One-Hour To-Do List	
Task	Details
Move pets to guest room	
Make sure all hoses are attached	Leave spigots closed
Remove propane tank from grill	Place in garage
Change into long pants and long-sleeved shirt	
Point vehicles outwards	Leave keys in ignition
Move sofa away from window	Living room
Bring deck chair pillows inside	
Move wooden furniture off deck	Place downwind away from house
Close all interior doors	Turn on light in rooms with windows
Place fire extinguisher outside	Silver one in garage, red one in storeroom
Place chain saw and fire tools outside	Garage
Turn off propane at tank	Round knob under lid
Spray house with fire gel	Storeroom, attach to hose
Place extension ladder outside	Lay flat on ground
Make note for firefighters	Tape to garage door

home. If you have a portable pump for a pond, hot tub, or creek, get it ready for them to use.

Move your ladder to where it can be set up to reach your roof. If you have tools that might be useful—such as a McLeod, shovel, and chain saw—set them outside. Sure, they probably have all that stuff on the trucks, but it can save precious time if they can grab equipment right where they need it.

If you leave any vehicles behind, make sure they don't block the driveway or turnaround. If there's time, face each car outward, and leave the key in the ignition so it can be driven away with the greatest ease.

Write the firefighters a note with pertinent information—where flammable fuels are stored, location of power cutoffs, location of water supplies such as a hot tub or pond, contact information, confirm that everyone and pets have been evacuated, and so forth. Be sure to thank the firefighters for their efforts. Heck, even put out some snacks and fluids!

Six-Hour Lists

These lists differ a bit because you probably won't be given an actual time frame until evacuation. Typically you'll get an alert for a potential evacuation, in which case you get the five-minute and one-hour packing stuff ready, and you start with the to-do lists. You might also be watching a wildfire on the news that's 30 miles away and thinking to yourself, *There's a chance that sucker could head this way.*

Another possibility happened to us. On the fourth day of the Fourmile Canyon Fire, the winds died down entirely, but forecasters predicted a major windstorm that night. My wife and I were allowed back up to our house for a couple of hours to grab anything we could. This is when it really helped to have a game plan, because we had been out of town when the fire started.

Depending on the situation, you may need to check on neighbors and make sure they are prepared to leave. You might even want to pre-evacuate some of your more valuable possessions. For example, you might rent a storage locker where you can keep things like a book collection, power tools, and outdoor equipment. This is the sort of stuff you may not use all the time, but, when you look at your home inventory, they really add up. This also may an opportunity to knock off a few honey-do projects that you've been putting off.

PRACTICE RUNS

A couple years ago, our local volunteer fire department (Boulder Mountain Fire Protection District—beyond excellent) organized a practice evacuation of the entire district. This was a full-scale operation coordinated weeks in advance with all of the firefighters, auxiliary members, and much of the neighborhood involved.

On a designated Saturday, test evacuation calls went out to the entire fire district. Firefighters rushed to their stations, donned their gear, and went to the pretend fire line. The volunteers for the "Third Arm"—active non-firefighters who help out at many levels—donned their safety vests, put out signs, and managed intersections for traffic control. A large percentage of the neighbors jumped in their cars and evacuated to the designated location, where we were served coffee and donuts.

All together, over 500 people spent part of their Saturday giving a stress test to the emergency system. The information gained was invaluable: discovering issues with communication, problems with traffic flow, and logistics of handling infirm residents. A community-wide disaster drill is rarely practiced, yet it's the only way to discover weaknesses before the actual emergency arises.

Even if your local fire department isn't this sophisticated, you can learn a lot by performing small-scale drills with your family. This includes making sure all the kids know escape routes from their bedrooms in case of a house fire. Run through different scenarios and figure out how everyone should react. For example, what do you do when one of you is at work, one of you is at home, and the kids are at a friend's house? What will you do if someone is at the house who can't drive and the roads are closed?

Those who can drive should be intimately familiar with at least two different evacuation routes—at night—to a designated meeting place. Remember: If you're driving in a panic to escape, emergency vehicles will be driving toward the fire. An accident in heavy smoke can make a bad situation much worse. The more you practice, the less likely someone will panic in a real emergency. Calm thinking can prevent fatal errors.

NEIGHBORHOOD WATCH

You also need a backup plan for when you're away. The best solution may be to form a coalition with your immediate neighbors. Sometimes called a Neighborhood Pod, this group should consist of four to six adjacent households, depending on your locale.

While those in the Pod must look after their own household first, they also provide mutual aid to one another to the extent that they're able. The best way to get organized is with a potluck, barbecue, or brunch. Start with a meeting that lasts no longer than an hour, and socialize after.

During the Pod meeting, discuss each other's special needs: young children, elderly parents, disabilities, and pets. Understand that your neighbors may be too preoccupied with their own evacuation to assist, but empower them to help if they can.

Establish an emergency phone tree where one person calls three others to disseminate information quickly. For the phone tree to work, a designated person must activate the calling (plus a backup person). Each person then contacts the people on his or her list, leaving messages if necessary. The people at the bottom of the tree then contact the initiator to confirm that notifications are complete. Test the phone tree after it's set up, and update it once a year.

A Pod meeting is also a great time to bring up what mitigation work has and hasn't been done on each property. Before the meeting ends, schedule a follow-up meeting for six months later.

The main outcome of your Pod meeting should be a set of realistic goals shared among neighbors. Somebody can compile and distribute the contact information list. Somebody else can share the information with anyone who couldn't attend. Another person can take charge of the next party and sending out a reminder a week or two in advance.

If you have a whole neighborhood watching out, you'll be able to sleep a lot easier when you go away on vacation. You also become safer as a community if everyone starts working on fire mitigation projects together.

PET EVACUATION

When the Fourmile Canyon Fire struck, my wife and I were out of town. We had just sat down for the flight back to Denver when we heard about a fire west of our house. Immediately recognizing the danger, we got hold of a neighbor and asked her to get our cats just as they shut the doors of the plane.

We weren't allowed back to our house for four days. It's hard to imagine how we'd have felt if our pets were still up there. Whenever a major fire erupts, police officers blocking roads into the area come face to face with panicked homeowners desperate to get their pets. People often get into shouting matches and occasionally run blockades. Several victims of the 2003 Cedar Fire near San Diego were horse owners who reentered the fire area to rescue their animals.

These scenarios happen so often that pet evacuation is now considered standard procedure with many emergency services. Helping pet owners forms part of the mission of serving the community and enhancing public safety.

Some local fire departments have residents fill out a form for each pet with its name, breed, gender, dietary information, need-to-know personality traits, consent for medical treatment if required, owner contact information, veterinarian contact information, and alternate caretaker contact. All of this goes into their database, and an animal emergency response team can be sent in during a crisis.

If you're away, a neighbor or animal rescue person may need to evacuate your fur kids. You can make this task much easier and safer by providing them with a pet evacuation kit with helpful supplies and information. This includes a method for getting them safely into a vehicle, such as a crate for big animals and a blanket or pillowcase for small animals. If you have dogs, offer suggestions on how a stranger might approach them safely—and warn if biting is likely! If you have cats, tell the responders their favorite hiding places.

Unfortunately, evacuation centers sometimes don't allow pets, an absurd restriction that forces victims to make hard choices about where to stay when already stressed about losing their homes.

Pet Evacuation Kit	
Take	**Location**
Leash and/or harness	Closet next to door
Pet crate	Garage shelves
Muzzle	In pet crate
Heavy leather gloves	Garage shelves
Pillowcase, towel, or blanket	Bathroom pantry
Masking tape and pen	In pet crate
Pet food	Kitchen pantry
Food and water bowls	Basement
Pet medication	Kitchen pantry, next to food
Pet bed	Bedroom
Litter box	Basement

Fortunately, some hotels will waive their normal no-pet clause for evacuees. But you may want to create a list of kennels, veterinary hospitals, and animal shelters in your area just in case.

LIVESTOCK EVACUATION

During one of the fires in Colorado, a spokesperson stated that more trailers were needed to get livestock out of the area without realizing that trained animal evacuation volunteers were already on the way. When this went out over the TV news, ranchers from around the region rushed to the area with trailers. Unfortunately, when they arrived at roadblocks, the sheriff was allowing only official evacuators to enter the area. The ensuing traffic jam of trucks with big trailers made it difficult for rescue and fire personnel to get to the fire.

If you have horses or livestock, when the fire danger runs high, have a trailer ready to hit the road. Beyond that basic requirement, it's important both for you and the animals to practice loading in a hurry—not at a leisurely pace. When an actual fire is approaching, all animals will be extremely nervous, so any handling out of the ordinary will only compound the situation. You can guarantee that any loose board in a trailer, hole in a fence, or sharp edge on equipment will rear its head when the stress level maxes out.

Alpacas, llamas, and horses in particular will panic at an oncoming fire. Once their flight instinct kicks in, they will be almost unmanageable for days after the fire danger has passed. It will require as many experienced handlers as you can wrangle to get the animals loaded onto trailers. If you can't do this in a timely manner, you may have to make the hard decision about whether human lives are more important.

If the situation becomes particularly dire, your only recourse is to open gates or cut fences and set the animals free to fend for themselves. Ideally, you've microchipped them for later identification.

Other options include attaching a luggage tag to the tail with a zip-tie and even spray-painting your phone number on the animal's side.

Don't leave a halter or headstall on any animal set free or left in a holding pen; these can snag on a fence, tree, or other obstruction. Similarly, never tether animals together when a fire is approaching.

If animals must be left behind, post information about the type and number on your barn for emergency crews. Notify authorities ASAP if you release animals because they are at risk of injury from other causes and may pose a danger to firefighters.

WHEN THE FIRE ROARS

The fear and frustration that accompany a mandatory fire evacuation throw everything in turmoil. You have no idea if you'll have a home when it's over. Suddenly your life goes on hold—or at least you want it to because you may still have work or school obligations. You develop an insatiable thirst for knowledge, yet answers come slow.

FIRE WATCH

When the land is parched, lightning storms are cause for anxiety. After a storm rolls through, especially without significant rain, break out the binoculars to scan for smoke. Also turn on your smart phone or radio scanner to listen for sheriff and fire personnel as they respond to calls. This can give you a vital heads-up if problems are brewing.

Many emergency services now use lightning detectors that pinpoint both positive and negative strikes. When the fire hazard is high, they often send first responders to investigate even without a report.

If you spot something that might be smoke, keep a careful eye on it for at least a minute. Unfortunately, it can be difficult to tell the difference between smoke and rising water vapors, called "water dogs." These form quickly after a rainstorm due to the temperature difference between the warm ground and cool air. Water dogs sometimes form vertical columns that rise from the ground and then tend to flatten out. In general, water dogs are white and have very little apparent movement, while smoke is darker gray and tends to billow and swirl. The water dog column may slowly drift across the landscape, while smoke has a single point of origin from which it rises.

If in doubt, call 911 and report your suspicions. Even if you just smell smoke and don't know where it's coming from, err on the side of caution and call it in. Smoke from distant fires can sometimes move in and smell quite strong but there's usually a haze in the air, while a fresh fire gives off a strong smell without much haze.

When you call in a possible fire, unless you feel threatened, remain at your location so you can direct firefighters and possibly show them your vantage point. If your house is diffi-

This means it's time to be on full alert and have your evacuation kit ready.

cult to locate, give the 911 operator a description of your vehicle and drive to the end of your driveway to meet the fire department. If you can speed them to a fire by even a few minutes, it can make a huge difference in the outcome.

EVACUATE *NOW!*

It might be a Reverse 911 call. It might be a sheriff or firefighter banging on your door. It might just be the sight or even smell of smoke. Whatever it is, don't ignore the warning. Forest fires can travel at 14 miles per hour, grass fires double that, and firebrands can travel at 60 mph, so pay heed and get the hell out.

When conditions are right, wildfires can make huge, unpredictable runs in minutes. That fire three ridges and 5 miles away can be on your doorstep before you know it. The couple who died in the 2013 Black Forest Fire, which destroyed 511 homes in Colorado, was found in their garage with the car doors open. They were overcome while packing to leave and wasted precious time on things that didn't matter, like ammunition and propane tanks.

When entire subdivisions are threatened, such as in the Waldo Canyon Fire, from which 32,000 people evacuated, normally quiet roads will suddenly become clogged with traffic as thousands flee. Every single driver is stressed to the max, yet bumper-to-bumper traffic reduces travel to a crawl. What usually takes minutes can turn into an hours-long terrifying escape. Your best bet is to leave early and beat the rush.

Beware the trap of macho hubris thwarting female wisdom. Many stories tell of husbands who want to wait it out when wives are urging evacuation. Under the high stress of the situation, arguments often don't end well. It's far better to come to a clear understanding that everyone leaves when the evacuation order is issued or when smoke is thick from a certain direction.

Most states have two levels of evacuation: voluntary and mandatory. When authorities issue a voluntary evacuation order, it's particularly important for those with special needs who will require extra time. Many fire departments maintain a list of people who require assistance. Some states, such as Ohio and Texas, give law enforcement legal authority to remove people by force during a mandatory evacuation. Other states, like California and Maryland, make it a Class 2 misdemeanor for violating an emergency restriction. Several states also make you liable for any costs of a rescue after failure to comply with an evacuation order. In all jurisdictions, law officers have the authority to remove minor children if the parents refuse to leave.

More than likely, if you refuse to leave, the sheriff will simply ask for the contact information of your next of kin and warn you that a rescue operation will not come. They don't have time to waste arguing with fools bent on dying.

The longer you delay in making your decision to leave, the more you tie up resources. When a house has been cleared of occupants, it is marked with colored flagging, and incident command is notified. This information affects planning and strategy. If you try to evacuate long after a closure, you may find roads blocked by fire trucks.

EVACUATION PROCEDURE

Start by grabbing your evacuation kit and throwing it in the car. Then go through your five-minute lists and get ready to roll. Delegate jobs, and try to remain calm. Only after your first tasks are complete can you start thinking about your one-hour lists. Keep an eye on the clock, and make sure nobody is dallying. If you're hauling a stock trailer, hitch it up and have your truck ready so you don't have to back up. Load the animals quickly, but try not to stress them too much; they will already smell the smoke. Take a last-minute look around, and make sure you have all the vitals from your evacuation lists. Even though this may be the last time you see your home, you need to focus on getting everyone to safety.

Once you decide to evacuate, get all the way out. Don't drive around trying to see what's happening. Don't stop alongside the road to look at the oncoming fire, because you'll create more traffic congestion. Turning around because you forgot something is absolutely wrong and could cause an accident.

When driving out, turn on your headlights and emergency blinkers; the smoke can be so thick that other vehicles may have a hard time seeing you. Expect large oncoming vehicles around every corner and be ready to pull to the side. Pulse your horn if you're concerned that others can't see your vehicle.

If more than one vehicle is evacuating, stay close together and use radios if you have them. If you have a truck and a car, the bigger vehicle should go first because it can better handle unexpected obstacles like rockfall.

Avoid driving too fast because visibility can deteriorate suddenly; many cars have hit trees or plunged off the road during evacuations. Adding to the problem, panicked livestock and wildlife may be on the road, too, as well as downed trees or even power lines.

Roll the windows up to keep embers out, and run the air conditioner in recirculation mode to stay cool. If you have to stop for any reason, get to the side of the road so other vehicles can pass. Don't turn off the engine; it may be difficult to restart with all the smoke in the air.

If a power line falls on your car, stop and do not get out! As long as you stay inside, you will not get electrocuted. A downed power line can kill you two different ways. The most obvious is direct contact either with the line itself or any conducting object that it touches, such as your car. If you must leave the vehicle, you need to jump so that you never touch the metal.

The more insidious cause of fatality is called "step potential" and occurs when you walk on energized ground; the difference in voltage just 18 inches away can send an arc through your body. To prevent this, either hop away or shuffle your feet so they both remain in contact with the ground. Move at least 20 yards away on dry ground and 40 yards on wet ground.

EVACUATION LIVING

After you reach safety, stop at the evacuation center and let them know you're OK. Even if you aren't staying there, you can find useful information and help from aid organizations and insurance representatives. If animals had to be left behind, the staff may be able to have a trained team enter the evacuation zone to retrieve them.

All expenses incurred during a mandatory evacuation should be reimbursed by your homeowner's policy, and there is no deductible. An extended evacuation can easily cost a family $2,000 to $5,000 by the time it's over.

Contact your insurance agent as soon as possible—don't wait to learn the status of your house. Some companies will cut an advance payment for evacuation expenses. This is when you start taking notes about the person you spoke to, such as name, title, and contact information. Start a folder for receipts for lodging, meals, clothing, fuel, car rental, and incidental expenses like toiletries. Remember: No receipt, you treat.

Staying with family or friends is likely the best option during an evacuation, assuming you don't wear out your welcome. During our evacuation, my wife and I were fortunate that good friends put us and our cats up—an act of kindness for which we remain eternally grateful. If that isn't possible, you may want to stay at a hotel. However, local hotels fill up quickly, so try to get a reservation as soon as you reach safety. Mind the earlier tips about pet policies and storing the numbers for nearby hotels in your emergency contacts list.

As a last resort, particularly if you have no insurance, you may have to stay at an evacuation center, often a school gymnasium. The Red Cross will be there with cots and other assistance. It's a noisy place, so be sure to bring earplugs; a sleep mask may be helpful, too.

If you are unfortunate enough to be evacked for weeks, months, or even years, you'll need alternative housing. Insurance covers this, too, but you may need assistance finding a longer-term solution.

If you know the fire burned through your neighborhood, regardless of whether your home is still standing, you may want a tetanus booster. If it's been more than a decade or you just can't remember, getting the shot makes for a wise precaution because you will likely be clearing debris. (Tetanus is a puncture wound infection, which you can get from any object, rusty or otherwise.)

SMOKE PROTECTION

When a forest burns, the smoke contains fine particulate matter and hundreds of chemical compounds, including carbon monoxide, nitrogen oxides, hydrocarbons, acrolein, formaldehyde, and benzene. Sometimes the smoke burns so thick that streetlights will turn on in the middle of the day.

If visibility is only 1.5 to 3 miles, the air quality is considered unhealthy, and you should reduce heavy or prolonged exertion. When visibility falls to just 1 to 1.5 miles, the air quality is considered very unhealthy. When you can see less than a mile, the air is hazardous.

In 2011, over 200 million people in the United States, nearly two-thirds of the population, were affected for a week or more by smoke from wildfires. This haze covered an area fifty times larger than the area consumed by fire. Indeed, 6 of the 20 states with the worst air did not even have major fires within their borders.

Among the symptoms of exposure to heavy smoke are coughing, scratchy throat, irritated sinuses, shortness of breath, chest pain, headache, stinging eyes, and a runny nose. People with asthma, lung problems, or heart disease may feel their condition worsen. Even after you evacuate, you could be in for some misery caused by smoke; children and the elderly are particularly sensitive.

Though the cooling can be a relief, don't count on an air conditioner to clean the air. Most air-conditioning systems have no intake filtration to remove smoke particulates. If your house has central air, replace the furnace filter with the best available; this can remove at least some of what circulates inside.

If you are forced to remain in an area with heavy smoke, you can get some relief by wearing respiratory and eye protection. Unfortunately, neither of these is a good option if you're working hard. The mask makes breathing harder, and glasses tend to fog. Better than nothing, a standard dust mask or a bandana won't filter out fine particles of smoke. You need an N95 breathing mask with an exhalation valve; these don't fit children, and they don't work if you have a beard. The mask must fit snugly enough that it's difficult to remove when you inhale and hold your breath. If it fits loosely, it isn't working.

Many of the respiratory problems from smoke arise because of damaged or paralyzed cilia. These are the tiny hairs deep inside the nose, sinuses, and smaller airways of the lungs that act like tiny oars to sweep foreign particles eventually to the stomach. When the cilia stop beating, the body produces more mucous, which has no way of getting out. You can help your cilia by making sure you have an adequate intake of vitamin A from a good multivitamin. Also stay hydrated; tea is particularly effective at stimulating cilia.

If you're coughing up thick phlegm, consider taking proteolytic enzyme tablets that contain bromelain and papain. Also called pro-teases, these digest protein and can thin mucous, thus soothing your throat. (They also help with clearing your ears for flying or scuba div-ing.) Stomach acid destroys them, so choose tablets that either melt in your mouth or have an enteric coating so they pass into the gut. Most health food stores carry the tablets in the vitamin section.

If your nasal passages and sinuses are irritated, try the Grossan Breathe-ease Nasal Moisturizing Kit or NeilMed Sinus Rinse ($15). These don't burn or sting like nasal sprays with preservatives or plain saline solutions. Avoid taking antihistamines, which may cause exces-sive drying of mucous and make you drowsy.

For those with severe problems, the best option is pulsatile sinus irrigation. This is performed with an $80 machine (Grossan Hydro Pulse or SinuPulse Elite) that's more effective and less messy than neti pots, bulbs, or syringes.

For eye protection where a lot of ash is falling, you can wear clear goggles, but most of these don't keep out smoke. One solution, as long as you don't require prescription glasses, is to go to a kitchen store and buy a pair of RSVP Onion Goggles ($20). Because smoke also irritates your eyes, you may want to use artificial tears. Among the best prod-ucts for irritated eyes is Allergan Refresh Optive ($10). Avoid products like Visine, which constrict the blood vessels in your eyes, or gels that tend to blur vision and leave your eyelids crusty. You can also take omega-3 oil supplements (flaxseed or fish oil) to help with eye dryness.

STAY TUNED

Whether you are threatened by wildfire or under evacuation orders, you *will* be desperate for information. Two news briefings per day by the Incident Command Team won't come close to satisfying your thirst for knowledge. Finding out what's going on—and whether you still have a home—becomes a high priority.

Well-meaning officials, citing a right to privacy, sometimes embargo information about what structures have burned. But with fire evacuations frequently lasting a week, nobody wants to wait several days to discover whether they have a home to which they can return. Instead, homeowners have to sort through rumors and read a stream of nonsense on Twitter to learn anything. During the Fourmile Canyon Fire, we heard twice that our entire neighborhood had burned to the ground. If you're lucky, local television stations and newspapers will update websites throughout the day. But often it's a stream of recycled drivel based on press briefings hours earlier.

Some localities are getting better about using social media to deliver reliable information. In Australia, the Country Fire Authority has created free apps called FireReady for all the mobile platforms. Among the best in the United States is San Diego County, which offers a free phone app called SD Emergency that provides a wealth of information. Many other counties have Twitter feeds and websites devoted to emergency information, though updates are often sporadic.

My preferred source of information is to get it straight from the fire lines. I listen in on sheriff and fire department channels with a portable ham radio. You can purchase a RadioShack or Uniden handheld scanner for around $100. To find the proper frequencies, visit RadioReference.com and search the database. I also have an app on my iPhone called 5-0 Radio Pro, which is well worth the $3. It doesn't include all the channels a radio scanner can pick up, but it's very convenient. The main drawback is that you need a good cell connection so, unlike a scanner, it won't work with a weak signal.

In some areas, ham radio operators band together to create an emergency radio network independent from the standard infrastructure. In a major disaster, these people can communicate when power lines, landlines, cell phones, and Internet services are down. They assist emergency personnel, relay information, and increase resilience of communities.

You can also check the Incident Information System (inciweb.org) for updates on your fire. There's also an app called US Fires that mirrors this information on your iPhone. Unfortunately, InciWeb often has outdated information and can be slow to load, so it often isn't worth the bother.

People outside of mainstream media and emergency services increasingly are stepping in to fill the information void. One example is ColoradoFireMaps.com, which strives to release accurate and understandable maps as soon as possible.

Another excellent resource is the Wildfire Today blog by Bill Gabbert (wildfiretoday.com). A retired wildland firefighter, he has many connections and often has better insights than traditional journalists. Another interesting source of information is the Wildland Fire Hotlist forum (wlfhotlist.com), where many firefighters hang out on the Web. Just by lurking you can get a lot of details not available through mainstream media.

Another possible source of intel on your home is Weather Underground (wunderground.com), which has live reports from many backyard weather stations. By looking at the map, you can pick stations near your house (or your actual house if you have a station connected to the Internet) to get a better idea of local conditions. If a station isn't updating, it could mean the power is out . . . or the home is gone.

Though it's more about fire potential than active fires, the US Forest Service Wildland Fire Assessment System (wfas.net) has a lot of information that might affect your decision to leave on vacation or stay home.

WORST-CASE SCENARIO

You're trapped! The fire moved so fast that the roads are overrun, and the smoke is so thick you can barely see five feet. Or maybe you were out camping and didn't learn about a fire until it was too late. If you panic, you die. Some basic tactics can at least give you a fighting chance.

Most fire victims die by inhaling superheated air that damages the lungs so badly that suffocation results. To survive a wildfire, you must protect your airway and reduce radiant heat as much as possible.

Contrary to oft-given advice, do *not* cover your mouth or body with a wet cloth. The water will create steam that will burn you. Instead, you want a dry cloth to filter some of the smoke. For tangible proof, consider that a steam room is tolerable to 115°F, but you can handle a dry sauna up to 200°F.

Caught at Home

If you missed the window of opportunity to evacuate, sheltering at home is a much better option than getting caught in the open. Although it may get very hot inside, it will likely be four to five times hotter outside. Call 911 if possible to notify authorities of your situation.

Follow all steps in the five-minute to-do list: Close all exterior doors and windows to reduce smoke and heat. Close Venetian blinds and fire-resistant window coverings, but fully open or remove light-weight window shades that can easily ignite. Move overstuffed furniture away from windows and sliding glass doors. Shut all interior doors to reduce the spread of fire. Turn off the gas line leading to your house.

Because you will likely lose power, homes on wells will have a limited supply of water; don't count on your standby generator surviving. Assuming that you have time before the fire hits, fill sinks, bathtubs and buckets with cold water. This will give you a supply of water to douse spot fires and embers before help arrives. Soak towels, large rags, and burlap sacks in the water so they can easily be tossed on flames. Also get all of your fire extinguishers out and ready to use.

If you have fire foam or gel, coat as much of your house and immediate surroundings as possible, particularly on the side where the fire is most likely to approach. Watering the lawn helps raise the humidity for an extended period, but plain water on nonabsorbent surfaces like roofs and decks will evaporate too quickly to be effective.

As long as you have power, activate sprinklers or use your garden hose to saturate the lawn. Turn off the sprinklers as soon as the power goes out, though, so you have whatever water is in the pressure tank after the fire passes. As discussed in Chapter 5, running sprinklers too long runs the risk of draining the well and burning out the pump, leaving you without water even after the power comes back on.

Keep your family together and move to a protected area, preferably on the opposite side of the house from where the fire is approaching. Have everyone put on cotton long-sleeved shirts and pants, and shelter on the floor underneath heavy wool blankets.

Stay away from windows—they can shatter from the heat—and outside walls, but make sure you have two exit routes. If the room begins to fill with smoke, lie on the floor and cover your face with a dry towel. Always stay as low to the ground as possible; even a few inches higher can mean deadly temperatures and gases.

Don't leave the building unless it catches on fire! It takes about one hour for a typical house to burn down, so your best bet is to stay inside as long as possible. Hopefully by then, the fire will have passed and everything will have cooled to a tolerable level outside.

After the fire front has passed, you need to leap into damage-control mode. Countless homes have burned to the ground long after the initial fire passed due to firebrands. After the flames have passed, take turns maintaining a fire watch for at least twenty-four hours.

Before going outside, prepare for intense smoke and firebrands raining down. Don fire-resistant long clothing (cotton or wool) as well as a hat, leather gloves, clear goggles for eye protection, and a bandana covering your mouth and nose. A wool blanket can also give good protection from heat and embers. Venture out slowly, staying low to the ground where temperatures are cooler. Once it's safe to move around, bring the water hoses and fire extinguishers from inside and attach the hoses to the spigots. Concentrate on the base of any flames on the structure and get them out right away.

Check your decks and roof, particularly the gutters, for burning embers and extinguish them. Look up in your attic and down in the crawlspaces for hidden embers. Inspect nearby woodpiles, wooden fences, and trees to make sure they aren't burning.

If your water supply is running low, you can use a shovel to smother small flames and embers with dirt. You can even attach a hose to the outlet on your water heater or hot tub as an extra source of water.

Once the fire has burned through, it may be safer to stay at home than attempt to drive out. If possible, call 911 again and let them know your situation.

Caught in the Car

While the best option is to evacuate and the second best option is to shelter in a building, your chance of survival is better in a vehicle than out in the open. If the smoke becomes so thick that you can barely see the end of the hood, it's too dangerous to keep driving.

At some point you have to decide about survival inside the vehicle. Although it will get intensely hot, you still have more protection than if you were outside. Don't worry about the gas tank exploding; it's extremely rare and the least of your concerns.

If you're driving and it looks like you're about to be overrun, find a safe place to park that has little vegetation nearby. Try to point your car toward the direction of the fire so you have the most protection from heat. Keep the motor running. Avoid parking in a narrow canyon or atop a saddle where the fire will funnel. If possible, park next to a building, cliff, or steep road bank that will block radiant heat. You are better off in a parking lot or grass meadow than a narrow road with overhanging tree branches.

Call 911 if you have cell phone service to let them know your situation and location, and don't hang up. Curl into the floor well so you're as low as possible. Pull a wool blanket over top of you for insulation from the heat. Because flames can funnel underneath vehicles, you are better off inside it than hiding below.

No matter what happens, don't get out and run until the fire front has passed. It will get brutally hot, the winds will buffet your car, and smoke and sparks may enter. But you still have to stay inside. During the Painted Cave Fire near Santa Barbara, California, a Hotshot crew in their trucks and civilians in two passenger cars survived a direct hit from a wall of flames for over five minutes.

Once the fire has passed, get out and evaluate the situation. If the engine is still running or will restart, and the tires aren't on fire, drive to safety. Otherwise, you may have to evacuate on foot by staying in the black (burned-out areas). Leave a note on the car telling rescuers of your plan.

Caught in the Open

It's a true worst-case scenario when you're caught by wildfire without any form of shelter. Unless it's a low-burning grass fire, you have no chance at all of running through the flames to escape—one breath of superheated air and you're history.

If you're out on a hike or bike ride and spot smoke, note the location and call it into 911 as soon as possible. Then look for the best escape route based on terrain and wind conditions. This should always be away from the fire even if it means moving away from your car at the trailhead.

Your best hope is to seek refuge in an area that won't burn and is far from the flames. This could mean treading water in a river or pond, preferably with a flotation device of some sort and something to cover your head. You might find a wide, sandy beach or a giant scree field where you can cower. Or perhaps you can circle around to an area that has already burned—the "black" is a favorite safe zone of firefighters.

Avoid areas of heavy vegetation, especially if you have to cross a steep slope. Streambeds can be dangerous because the sidewalls tend to funnel wind and the extra water means a lot of plant growth that's often dry during fire season. Don't shelter at the top of a slope or in a saddle. Instead, look for the lee side of a large rock or ridge. No matter how many times you hear it, don't soak fabric in water and wrap it around you. Again, it will just turn to steam and cause serious burns.

If those options aren't available, find a depression such as a ditch or creek bottom. Clear away anything flammable like leaves and dry grass. Then lie down with your mouth close to the ground and your hands covering your face.

As bad as it gets, fight the urge to panic and run. The air temperature will be many times greater just a few inches above the ground and even worse at head height. Though it will seem like an eternity, the worst of the fire usually will pass in sixty seconds.

Fire Shelters

Wildland firefighters carry an emergency shelter derisively called a "shake and bake." This is a one-person, thermal-resistant tent that can greatly increase the odds of survival. These can be bought online and are available to anyone. If you live in a particularly remote area, it might be worth considering purchasing fire shelters for everyone in the house. But consider some caveats.

If you look on auction websites and surplus stores, you may find relatively inexpensive fire shelters that come in a yellow case (around $50). These are the old-generation A-frame-style shelters issued before 2002, and they offer little more than a false sense of security.

The only fire shelters worth having are the new-generation half-cylinder models that come in a blue case. The regular ($360) fits a person up to 6-foot, 1-inch, while the large ($410) fits to 6-foot, 6-inch and has more girth, so it might be better for an adult and child. These shelters weigh 4 to 5 pounds each and are about the size of a loaf of bread when packed.

The new-generation fire shelters have two layers of fabric with aluminum foil that both reflects and insulates. The rounded shape also reflects heat while providing maximum interior volume. Inside are grab loops that are pulled up to the elbows.

It requires practice to use a fire shelter, particularly because it will likely be deployed during violent winds. Once a shelter has been opened, it cannot be folded back into its carrying case. For that reason, they also sell practice shelters ($140) that come in a red case.

The general idea is first to clear the ground down to mineral soil. Then quickly shake open the shelter, step in it, sit down, and roll over. Point your feet toward the oncoming flames and lie flat on your stomach with your mouth next to the ground.

Firefighters have reported entrapment times of ten to ninety minutes, sometimes with multiple flame fronts. They are also wearing Nomex clothing, which gives them additional protection. However, all nineteen firefighters killed in the 2013 Yarnell Fire in Arizona had deployed their shelters to no avail.

FIRE FIGHT

The actual process of fighting wildfires remains a mystery to many people, starting with the mass media. All too often television and newspaper reporters disseminate nonsense and long-debunked myths.

This chapter will give you some insight into what is done to protect lives and property. Perhaps with a little understanding, you won't be one of the idiots who sues the local fire department because "not enough was being done" or "they weren't fast enough."

FIRE MANAGEMENT

For the past three decades, wildfires have been fought using the Incident Command System that ensures a chain of command and continuity of structure as the fire grows. Other countries use similar systems, though details vary.

When a wildland fire "incident" is detected, it is categorized by severity and a management team determines an initial attack. Factors that determine severity include terrain, wind speed, air temperature, humidity, dryness of fuels, and predicted weather.

A Type 5 incident is small enough that a rural fire department can handle the problem. The first officer on the scene is designated Incident Commander and is in charge for the first six to twelve hours unless the situation escalates. It usually takes two to six firefighters a few hours to put Type 5 incidents out and mop up.

A Type 4 fire may require all the resources in the county or fire district. However, it's still a fairly simple fire that may not require activating a management team.

When the fire is larger, more complex, or at risk of blowing up into something major, a Type 3 Incident Management Team (IMT) is activated for an extended attack. Because bigger fires often cross multiple jurisdictions, Type 3 teams consist of county and state personnel who have trained for defined roles. Most fires that will take longer than twenty-four hours to control are escalated to Type 3 status.

When it gets grim, a federal IMT is brought in. Until 2013, there were about thirty-eight Type 2 teams and sixteen Type 1 teams (the numbers

An Ironwood Hotshot from Tucson, Arizona, performs mop-up on the Fourmile Canyon Fire. Type 1 and 2 teams routinely travel long distances to the worst fires.

fluctuating somewhat over the years), the latter having the most training and experience. However, moving forward, these will be consolidated into forty "Complex IMTs" around the country.

In really bad years, many large fires rage at the same time. To control resources throughout a region, one of four Area Command Teams may be activated. While this team doesn't direct operations on individual fires, it does provide logistical and administrative support.

Most IMTs have a similar structure and are set up so each person reports to only one boss, thus preventing conflicting orders. At the top of the totem pole is an Incident Commander (normally one person but sometimes two or more in complicated situations that call for a Unified Command) in charge of everything. Reporting to him or her is a Command Staff and a General Staff.

The Command Staff consists first of a safety officer who monitors conditions and ensures all personnel are kept out of harm's way. The liaison officer interacts with all other agencies (sheriff, ambulance, etc.) involved with the fire. The public information officer communicates with homeowners and media.

The General Staff includes an operations chief who actively directs all personnel in the field. A planning chief collects information about the fire, predicted weather, and available resources. The finance chief keeps track of expenses, handles contracts for resources, and takes care of administrative paperwork. The logistics chief works out the details of getting resources where and when they are needed, as well as making sure everyone is fed and gets adequate rest.

More than 500 people can be working on a large fire at any one time. Rather than having a finite time limit, days are broken into "operational periods" that are outcome driven. Typically these are four-, six-, or twelve-hour shifts, after which rest is mandatory. Even the IMT staff must stand down after fourteen hours to prevent the mistakes or errors of judgment that fatigue can cause. If 500 people are engaged in the fire actively, another 500 may be refueling and recovering.

In addition, the county sheriff will have all hands on deck managing traffic, alerting homeowners to evacuate, and preventing looting. The sheriff may also take charge of holding press conferences and deciding what information to make public, much to the chagrin of many evacuees. The state governor may call out the National Guard to take over some of the policing activities, such as manning roadblocks, to free up sheriff officers for other duties.

With outside troops called in, local firefighters may have a chance to recuperate somewhat, because they may have spent the first thirty-six to forty-eight hours fighting the fire alone. As critical as the big fire may be, there is still a need to handle smaller incidents, such as car accidents and medical emergencies, so they can't just throw everyone at the fire.

TYPES OF FIREFIGHTERS

Many people don't realize that fighting fires is a specialty. Training and equipment differ greatly and affect what a firefighter can or cannot do in the field.

Most people tend to think of urban firefighters as putting out house fires and rescuing kittens from trees. These men and women have a heavy and cumbersome turnout kit. Their protective clothing alone weighs around 45 pounds, and all the extra gear brings the total to over 75 pounds. They are trained to attack a fire directly and are prepared to go inside a burning structure. Importantly, they also have a municipal pressurized water supply, so they can be liberal with water.

By contrast, a wildland firefighter wears Nomex clothing with a lightweight helmet and boots. Their clothing and personal gear weigh less than 20 pounds, which makes them more vulnerable but nimble. They often fight a fire indirectly by building control lines and setting backfires. Water is usually scarce, so tactics are adjusted for maximum conservation.

Wildland firefighters are typically assigned to a truck or a hand crew. An engine crew has three to ten members depending on the size of the vehicle. These are often the first people to arrive on the scene and can be instrumental in keeping a fire small. In addition to attacking wildfires, they also respond to traffic accidents and medical emergencies.

Hand crews consist of twelve to twenty people who carry tools to locations that trucks can't reach. They create fire lines by digging and cutting (or bulldozing if available), setting backfires when the conditions are right, and mopping up the mess after it's all over. One member of the team is assigned as a lookout to keep everyone safe.

There are five levels of training for active firefighters; they carry a "red card" that shows all their certifications. This starts at Type 3 Crew and—with a lot of blood, sweat, and training—works up to the Type 1 Hotshot Crews.

Entry-level certification generally requires contacting your local fire station and joining as a volunteer. Once accepted, you will train as a rookie for about a year, during which time you must pass courses in firefighting technique and fire behavior as well as a fitness test. With a red card in hand, you can be hired as a seasonal firefighter with a starting salary of $10 per hour and possibly no health insurance.

With continued training and experience, a firefighter can work up to Type 2 Crew, then Type 2 Initial Attack. The next level up is Type 1 Crew and then Type 1 Hotshot. A firefighter also can earn many specialty certifications, such as EMT and sawyer. Most of the members of IMTs get their start digging fire lines and rise through the ranks.

Interagency Hotshot Crews are among the elites of the wildland firefighter world, with the most training and high levels of fitness. At present, 112 Hotshot teams deploy on short notice to major hot spots. Considered a shared national resource, the teams often travel far from their home base—even to Canada, Mexico, and Australia—and can be away for weeks at a time.

When a fire burns in a remote area, firefighters can be deployed by helicopter either by setting down or having the helitack crew rappel to the ground. Where even a helicopter isn't practical, smokejumpers may be sent in. All of these specially trained individuals are prepared to be self-sufficient for several days, because they often have to hike out to a road.

Firefighting is a dangerous job and has cost many lives. After the Storm King tragedy of 1994 that claimed fourteen firefighters in Colorado, the Wildland Firefighter Foundation (wffoundation.org) came together to help the families of the fallen and injured firefighters. There's also a forum to thank firefighters for their service. And the foundation maintains the Wildland Firefighters National Monument in Boise, Idaho, which features three large bronze statues and a memorial walk.

FIRE VEHICLES

Due to their large size and low clearance, urban fire trucks are ill-suited for fighting wildland fires on steep, twisty roads. Some don't carry any water, so they are completely dependent on fire hydrants or other external water supplies. In addition, most of these vehicles use their engines to power pumps, so they can be operated only when stationary. When a wildfire is encroaching on a town or city, urban fire trucks are great for putting out house fires because they can move a lot of water in a hurry.

Wildland fire engines are smaller and more rugged, with four-wheel drive and high clearance. A Type 1 Attack Engine is intended for structure fires and has a tank with 500 to 1,000 gallons of water, but these too are stationary when pumping. They carry the big 2$\frac{1}{2}$-inch hoses for dousing fires fast.

There are five classifications of true wildland fire vehicles that can pump water while on the move. Largest are the Type 3 wildland-urban interface trucks that carry 500 to 1,000 gallons of water and at least 1,500 feet of 1$\frac{1}{2}$- and 1-inch hose. For fast attack on fires, the vehicle of choice is often a Type 6 truck carrying 250 to 500 gallons of water and at least 600 feet of hose. Some Type 6 and 7 engines are also outfitted for medical and rescue response.

Not to be confused with engines, support tenders are giant rolling water tanks that carry from 5,000 (Type 1) to 1,000 (Type 3) gallons of water. These shuttle water from reservoirs and cisterns to fire trucks, but they have no direct firefighting capability themselves.

Where terrain permits, bulldozers are very effective at cutting a fire line in a hurry. Dozers frequently work in pairs so they can assist each other. These beasts can weigh from 4 tons (Type 3) to 48 tons (Type 1) and clear paths from 7 to 16 feet wide. The most common are the medium-size Type 2 dozers, like the Caterpillar D7, that weigh around 16 tons. Bulldozing can be a dangerous task because they are prone to rolling over on steep hills and they're slow, which makes escape difficult if a fire suddenly changes direction. In addition, a hand crew usually needs to follow the dozer to finish the control line and burn out areas inside the perimeter.

In relatively flat and non-rocky parts of the country, plows are often used to make fire lines. These can be pulled by dozers or even 4WD vehicles and do a better job at creating a fire line than bulldozing alone.

FIRE ATTACK

The plan of attack on a wildfire will depend on many factors including the size of the fire, the type of fuels burning (grass fires are fought differently than forest fires), topography, proximity of homes and livestock, and weather conditions. All of this has to be evaluated quickly so that a strategy can be determined.

The primary objectives for wildland fires—in order of importance—are to ensure the safety of firefighters and civilians, protect houses and outbuildings, and either contain a fire or conserve resources until help arrives. Based on conditions, a quick decision must be made about whether to go on the offense or defense in fighting the fire.

Structures in the fire zone are classified into one of three categories: those that need little or no immediate protection, those that can be saved with help, and hopeless structures. This triage is based on the work you've done in advance as well as current conditions. If a house is deemed unsavable due to lack of mitigation or because it's already engulfed, firefighters may work on preventing the fire from spreading further.

LCES is a key concept for wildland firefighters: having Lookouts, maintaining Communications, planning Escape routes (always two), and establishing a Safety zone. Without all these elements in place, it's too dangerous to remain in the field. With LCES established, the first action generally is to create one or more anchor points—positions for attacking the fire that cannot be outflanked. This is often at the rear or side of the fire, sometimes right where the fire started.

From an anchor point, crews will start building fire lines to surround the fire. To prevent the spread of surface and ground fire, mineral soil is exposed by hand tools or machinery for a path 1 to 4 feet wide. The goal is to turn a fire line and natural defenses (roads, streams, lakes, rock barriers) into a control line that confines and eventually contains the fire. Care must be taken to prevent burning logs from rolling and falling snags from crossing the control line. The surrounding area must be monitored also for spot fires that can escape.

A crew may also attempt to cool hot spots with a "scratch line" quickly made to slow the advance. This can buy time for construction of a more complete fire line. But it's also a dangerous practice because the firefighters are relatively unprotected.

Sometimes when working big fires, teams will use "coyote tactics," meaning they stay in the field for three or four shifts. They sleep out overnight and eat rations or sandwiches. The teams must be self-sufficient because resupply and rescue can be difficult.

When flames burn fewer than 4 feet high, the fire can be attacked at the head and flanks by using hand tools. Once a fire line is built, other crew members will light "burn out" fires to establish a control line. In fact, with a direct or parallel attack, the control line isn't considered established until it burns out to eliminate fuels.

When the flames rise from 4 to 8 feet, the heat becomes too intense at the head of the fire for a crew with hand tools, and it's even difficult for engine crews to hold back using water. Sometimes engine crews can knock down flames and cool off hot spots enough for hand crews to get in and build their fire lines. Otherwise, an indirect attack is made using "backfires" to create wider buffers. If terrain permits, bulldozers can construct effective fire lines under these conditions.

Backfiring is also used to slow the progress of a fire, change its direction, or even alter the convection column that pulls air into a fire.

While burning out is a standard procedure on a direct attack, backfiring is used for indirect attacks and is a decision made by the IMT. If conditions aren't right for a backfire, things can go wrong in a hurry.

The head of a fire is pretty much out of control when flames reach 8 to 11 feet tall. At that point, spot fires may occur, trees suddenly burn like torches, and the fire gets into the crown of the forest. The only way to attack a fire with flames that high directly is with planes and helicopters.

Once it turns into a crown fire with flames in excess of 11 feet, get out of the way! This is when thousands of acres go up in a flash. Even air attack is ineffective at stopping the advance.

The color of the smoke gives you an idea of what's burning. If it's primarily white smoke, it's most likely forest burning. When you see black smoke, that's probably a house, which contains a multitude of plastic and other petroleum products that emit a lot of carbon.

Aerial Assault

The most effective use of air tankers is at the start of a fire when it's still smaller than 20 acres. It might cost $50,000 for an aerial assault on a small fire that is put out quickly. It may sound expensive, but it's a lot cheaper than the average $40 million it costs to extinguish a major fire.

If the planes can get in early, they buy crucial time for ground crews to get in position to prevent the fire from exploding. While water is the cheapest option for airdrops, retardants and gels are much more effective at stopping a fire (see Chapter 5). Typically, water is used directly on flames, while retardants are used in front of the fire to create a fuelbreak.

Fire retardant like Phos-Chek is primarily used in a defensive roll to slow the progress of a fire. For greatest efficacy, retardant is laid down early so it has a chance to dry before the flames arrive. Fire gel such as FireIce can be used for a direct attack on the flames at the head of a fire. The intent is to put half the gel on the fire and half on the unburned area to keep it from igniting. In Canada they even allow the big Martin Mars seaplane, which holds 7,200 gallons, to drop gel directly on threatened houses. At present, fire gel is underutilized in the United States.

Unfortunately, aerial assault is grounded much of the time because most air tankers currently in operation lack the technology to make drops at night. The tankers also can't fly when surface winds exceed 35 mph—common from around noon until sunset during a firestorm—which is, of course, when the fire is raging at its worst. These combined factors mean that planes may not be in the air for eighteen hours out of twenty-four.

Compounding the problem with air support is the dwindling number of air tankers in the national fleet. In 2002 the US Forest Service contracted forty-four large air tankers capable of dropping 3,000-plus gallons of retardant to fight forest fires. A decade later, only ten big planes are under contract. When those are tied up on fires, the Air Force Reserve can convert eight military C-130s into fire fighters, and five more large air tankers can be borrowed from Canada and Alaska. More contracts are in the works, but it's an overly slow process.

Some states contract firefighting planes and helicopters instead of relying on federal resources. California owns the largest fleet, with twenty-three air tankers, eleven helicopters, and fourteen tactical aircraft. Colorado may share planes with Arizona and Utah.

The issue of withholding the C-130s until all private planes are in use remains controversial. During the first forty-eight hours of the 2012 Waldo Canyon Fire, two of the planes sat on the runway at Peterson Air Force Base, just a few miles away. The policy derives from an interpretation of the 1932 Economy Act, and it may be overturned soon. The following year, during the nearby Black Forest Fire, the planes were cleared to fly in under twenty-four hours.

Most of the antique propeller slurry bombers, such as the Lockheed P-2V, hold around 2,000 gallons of retardant, and they lumber along at 210 mph when loaded; C-130s hold 3,000 gallons but are nearly as slow. Jets like the British Aerospace 146, which holds 3,000 gallons and cruises at nearly 400 mph, are slowly replacing these.

But the Forest Service has been dragging its feet on adopting the DC-10 tankers (only one is currently in operation), which hold nearly 12,000 gallons and can lay down a fire line 50 feet wide and $5/8$ mile long. The 747 Supertanker can drop 20,000 gallons of retardant for 1 mile using a pressurized spraying system but still isn't authorized. The DC-10 can cruise at 440 mph with a full load, and the 747 hauls at nearly 600 mph, so they can get to fires fast, and they can operate at night. Plus, they are cheaper to operate than the smaller planes that require more trips to drop the same amount of material.

While the big bombers can disperse a large swath of retardant in one fell swoop, the little crop planes can drop 800 gallons with much more precision. Called SEATs (Single Engine Air Tankers), they are more maneuverable and can get in closer, making them ideal for direct attacks and filling gaps in fire lines. To be effective, SEATs need to operate within 50 miles of their air base for fast turnarounds.

Normally a small, twin-engine turboprop acts as lead plane for the large air tankers. The small plane may make several passes to determine the best and safest approach for the bigger plane. The pilot then guides the way and emits a line of smoke where the bomber should begin its drop.

Helicopters are also invaluable tools for dropping water, foam, or gel. Because they can pull water out of nearby lakes or even swimming pools, choppers often make round-trips in fewer than five minutes. They cruise at about 120 mph, so they must be based near the fire for refueling.

The puny Type III helicopters can carry only around 120 gallons, so they're used for very small fires. A medium-size Type II helicopter (such as a Bell 205) can deliver about 350 gallons, either in a bucket slung underneath on cables or in the new belly tanks that hang off

Sikorsky S-64 Skycrane attacking a spot fire with 2,650 gallons of water. The snorkle allows them to refill in 45 seconds while hovering over a body of water only 18 inches deep.

the bottom. The bigger Type I choppers (Sikorsky Skycrane, Boeing Chinook, etc.) can drop as much as 3,000 gallons.

Since 1983, following a fatal collision five years earlier, nighttime helicopter operations on wildfires have been prohibited in the United States. This is starting to change, as of 2013, with one test helicopter in Southern California that makes water drops at night. Assuming this trial goes well with all the new technology, including better night-vision goggles, helicopters could become a major advancement in nocturnal firefighting.

Night is the ideal time because decreasing wind and temperature along with increasing humidity naturally make a fire lie down. The colder air is also denser, which gives helicopters more lift, and pilots and spotters can see hot spots much more easily than in the daytime. It will always be a risky operation, however, because the water drops must be made only a few hundred feet above the ground. Often they operate in narrow canyons with a chance of hitting power lines or even trees.

Controlling and directing all of this air traffic requires spotters, usually small propeller planes, which fly high in the sky. Both spotters and lead planes have radio antennae underneath the fuselages for better ground communication. (Normal planes have antennae on top.)

A handful of planes are equipped for night flights over fires with infrared cameras; these work best when the temperature difference is greatest. Spotter planes outfitted with side-looking infrared radar and even drones outfitted with infrared video cameras will become standard tools for monitoring fires and detecting hot spots.

With satellite imagery and mapping software, it's becoming easier for incident managers to understand complex fires and make decisions. During the 2013 Rim Fire, a National Guard MQ-1 Predator drone mapped a wildfire. In the future, it's possible that drones will be used for dropping gel on fires, which could change the nature of firefighting.

The Home Front

What happens in your particular neighborhood will depend on many factors, not the least of which is the speed at which the fire is moving in that direction. With sufficient time and manpower, firefighters will try to defend structures until it becomes too dangerous.

If there's time to prepare, structural protection teams will visit each home to check on whether it can survive. They may do some basic mitigation, such as pulling flammable objects away from the house, detaching propane bottles from grills, and removing cushions from deck furniture. However, homes that have performed little to no mitigation will likely be written off entirely. A building on a steep slope—surrounded by bushes and trees, with limbs hanging over the roof and litter in the gutters—has no chance of survival. The fire department will deploy resources only to structures where they can win the battle.

As the fire approaches, crews will attempt to hold it back with fire lines and direct attack (shoveling dirt, batting with fire swatters, spraying water). The crew may spray down your house and immediate area with fire foam or gel. If you already applied fire gel, they can reactivate it by spraying it with a fine mist of water.

When conditions become severe, firefighters are required to pull back to a safety zone. The entire neighborhood will be evacuated until the danger passes. This is why it's important to create a survivable space, not just a defensible space, for your home.

Structural protection teams will rush back in to save what they can. They triage which houses are savable and which are too far gone. If a home can be saved, they'll extinguish any visible flames and check the area for smoldering embers that could cause problems after they leave and before you return.

CONTAINMENT

Contained does not mean out. When a fire is officially declared contained, that means it's unlikely to spread any more. Within the control line, the fire is still burning, and a chance remains for slopover into unburned areas or a spot fire escaping. It's also possible for an area to re-burn if all of the fuel wasn't consumed when the fire passed through the first time.

With partial containment, the control line surrounds only a percentage of the fire, but the head can still advance. For example, a fire with a perimeter of 20 miles might have control lines along 12 miles, providing 60 percent containment. This number is just a rough estimate of the fire situation at the time.

Frequently, a fire considered 80 percent contained suddenly can turn into 20 percent containment if winds pick up. This means that everyone has to keep their guard up until the fire is contained fully.

In remote areas with rugged terrain, the IMT may decide to allow the fire to keep advancing as long as it's headed toward wilderness. The 2012 Fern Lake Fire in Rocky Mountain National Park, which started in early October and burned 3,500 acres, continued to smolder six months later. Even with intense cold and several feet of snow, there wasn't enough heavy, wet snow to extinguish the fire completely.

MOP-UP

A fire isn't officially "controlled" until it is all the way out. This can take days, weeks, or even months after it's declared contained; sometimes it requires winter snowstorms. The fire is brought under control by extinguishing hot spots and strengthening the fire line so escape is impossible.

Even before a fire is contained fully, crews begin mop-up work. This involves extinguishing any flames and making sure that any remaining fuel cannot burn. It may require burying smoldering material with dirt, dousing embers with water, cutting down burning snags, and turning logs so they can't roll. Handheld infrared digital thermometers are used to locate hot spots—a marked improvement on the old way of sticking your hands in the ashes.

On small fires, the entire area is mopped up so there are no potential fire starters left. On big fires, the inside of the control line may be mopped up for 100 to 500 feet, depending on conditions. This may leave islands of unburned fuel well inside the fire area, but they no longer pose a threat to the surrounding countryside.

AFTER THE FIRE

When you finally are given the go-ahead to return home, hopefully you will have a home to which you can return. Whatever the outcome, you likely to have a lot of work to do.

First, do a quick inspection to verify that nothing is burning, and get a rough damage estimate. Then get in touch with your insurance agent to go over claims, as well as numerous service providers. You also may need to take action to prevent further damage. Then you may have to go about rebuilding and restoring your land.

EXAMINE YOUR PROPERTY

When the authorities allow you to enter the fire zone, expect a hazardous environment. Wear a long-sleeved shirt, pants made of cotton, and heavy-duty footwear suitable for walking in rugged terrain. You may also want an N95 breathing mask and eyewear for protection against smoke and ash.

On your first visit, either go in with your insurance adjustor or don't do anything not related to safety or protecting the property from further damage. Don't start cleaning up or throwing things away until the damage is documented. Take photos and videos with a digital camera or cell phone.

As you drive in, look for downed power lines as well as charred snags and power poles that might topple. Make note of any power poles standing but smoldering at the base because they may continue to burn unless extinguished. When a power line is down, there's no visible way to tell if it's energized; sparks aren't always present. Stay far away from any power lines on the ground. If one falls nearby, shuffle your feet until you're at least 20 yards away to avoid a ground charge.

When you pull up to your house, quickly scan the area for spot fires and hot embers that could present problems later. Stop your car well away from the house in case there's a gas leak.

Assuming that your home is still standing, resist the temptation to run inside. Perform a fast inspection from all sides to make sure that nothing is smoldering. If necessary, get your extension ladder and inspect the roof and gutters for firebrands and burning debris. Don't walk on the roof or decks unless you're sure they're structurally sound.

Before entering, make sure you don't smell gas. If you do, turn off the supply valve and immediately open all doors and windows. It's likely that the electrical power will still be out for the entire neighborhood, but check the breaker box to ensure none of the fuses have flipped.

Once it's safe to go inside, your first priority should be heading up to the attic and down into the crawlspace with a flashlight and carefully inspecting for embers. Even after this first examination, continue to check the attic, gutters, and other vulnerable areas for several days. Many houses have been lost long after the main fire has passed because a fire started in the attic and the fire department was still tied up elsewhere.

Look in the garage and outbuildings, too, but also watch out for animals that may have sought shelter. Use a flashlight to peer under decks and into crawlspaces for any signs of smoke.

After the initial inspection of your house, walk your property to check for hazards such as an ash pit, a hole filled with hot ashes where a tree once stood, into which someone could fall. Another concern is root fires that can smolder for days until the heat reaches the trunk and the tree suddenly goes up in flames. Any heavily scorched tree runs the risk of toppling over unexpectedly, even without wind.

Document damage before cleaning up. Use a still or video camera to create a record for your insurance agent. This can help prove that something like a broken window wasn't a "preexisting condition."

After an evacuation, it's likely that everything in the refrigerator will need to be tossed; this loss easily can exceed $500, so, again, document it. It's possible that even the refrigerator itself will need to be replaced if extensive mold has set in. Be leery of any home-canned foods and other items in the pantry that may have been exposed to high heat, fumes, or water. Likewise, any medications exposed to heat should probably be discarded.

If you don't have one, purchase a vacuum with a HEPA filter (about $60 to $200) to remove fine particulates as you clean the house. A standard vacuum that doesn't have a proper filter throws much of the nastiness up in the air for you to breathe.

If your home got hit by a load of fire repellant, wash it off as soon as possible to prevent staining from the iron oxide used for the red color. Although fire retardant is a fertilizer, it has more ammonia than normal and can cause leaf burn on plants. Hose down your newly red-tinged landscaping as soon as possible.

Total Loss

If your home burned to the ground, your first task, after the initial grieving, will be sifting through the ashes to find anything that remains. This will be a messy, unpleasant chore with lots of hazardous materials around; dress accordingly. You'll want clothes that can take abuse and then get tossed as well as heavy gloves, boots, and possibly goggles and an N95 breathing mask with an exhalation valve.

Also, don't get your hopes up—many homeowners report that everything they salvaged would fit in a shoebox. After you've recovered what you can, the rest of the debris needs to be hauled away to locations designated by the county. This is a job for professionals with heavy equipment.

While contacting your insurance company is, of course, a top priority, many others also need your attention. In particular, your mortgage lender needs information right away. You're still going to have to make payments on the loan, and they'll be first in line for insurance payouts. Work out a system by which money is released for contractors and building supplies.

If it was a large fire that was declared a federal disaster, you will need to file a claim with FEMA as soon as possible. Over the next few weeks, a stream of contractors working for the agency will contact you. And each one will give you different answers so take copious notes.

Your mailing address will change for months or even years, so contact the post office, credit card companies, banks, utilities (electric, gas, phone, television, Internet, newspaper, garbage, and possibly water). You may want a temporary PO box at your local post office and they will be in short supply so get in there early. Also notify government authorities, such as the department of motor vehicles and voter registration office.

Get in touch with the county assessor so your property taxes can be reduced. Taxes are paid on the prior year's assessment, so that nasty bill may still hit, but the following year should be much lower. Make sure that your property isn't reclassified as vacant residential land, because that's often taxed at a higher rate.

Other tax consequences related to your loss may work in your favor. All sorts of deductions and benefits may apply, so it's worth talking to a tax accountant who knows all the rules. If you ran a business out of your home, you may also qualify for special loans.

Make sure that service providers stop charging your accounts if you had set up automatic payments. If possible, put your service on vacation status so it can be restored later without fees. You may want to keep your landline with a voice message telling people your new contact information.

You will likely be racking up a lot of charges on your credit cards, so you may want to increase your credit limit. Let the card companies know in advance of an increase in spending. Otherwise, it may trigger a fraud alert, and your accounts will be frozen when you need them most.

PROTECT YOUR PROPERTY

Read the fine print on insurance contracts, and you'll find that you have an obligation to prevent further damage when possible. This means that if windows are blown out or there's a hole in the roof, you should make a temporary repair (plywood, plastic and tape, whatever) to keep the elements from doing more harm.

In many parts of the country, that fine print also says that your home isn't covered against flooding. If the creek in the backyard turns into a torrent or the slope above your house sends a mudslide down, standard homeowner's insurance may not cover the damage. Even homes far downstream from the fire may be subject to a flash flood if a thunderstorm stalls out in the fire zone.

National companies like Servpro and Sun Rental, have disaster trailers and teams equipped to get important tools to affected parts of the country quickly. Hardware stores such as Home Depot and Lowes can move a lot of product into your region in a hurry. These resources may be able to help you prevent a bad situation from getting worse.

Buy flood insurance if there's even a slight risk of floodwaters or a mudflow reaching your house. Do it now. There's a thirty-day waiting period before the policy kicks in, so in the meantime pray that no big storms come along in that first month.

Erosion Control

After an intense wildfire, trees and brush can leave a waxy, water-repellant layer at the surface of the soil. Unless a physical disturbance breaks this up, the ground won't absorb much water during a rainstorm, creating high runoff. Test for hydrophobic soil by putting a drop of water on the bare ground to see if it beads up on the surface or absorbs; repeat after removing an inch of soil at a time.

Your local forest service will have advice on steps to take. Heed their warnings because the danger is real. Inadequate erosion control can not only cause major land damage, but also threaten lives.

To prevent erosion, particularly in important areas like uphill of buildings and roads, homeowners may need to build defenses. Don't worry that everything is black at first glance. To find out the real harm, inspect the soil to see if any organic matter (duff) remains, which indicates moderate damage, or if it's just black all the way down to mineral soil. The latter is the ground that will have the most problem with heavy rain.

Seeding grasses is important but takes time to become effective. Purchase certified grass seeds locally so they're weed-free and an appropriate mix for your area. Soil should be raked prior to broadcasting the seeds, then raked again and tamped down.

For the Colorado Front Range, one suggested mix includes slender wheatgrass, mountain bromegrass, western wheatgrass, Regreen, and Sandberg bluegrass. Other options are thickspike wheatgrass, steambank wheatgrass, and green needlegrass.

Applying 1 to 2 tons of weed-free straw per acre of burned land will protect the soil from the impact of raindrops and help keep the grass seed in place. A 74-pound straw bale will cover 800 square feet to a depth of about 3 inches. This leaves about 30 percent of the soil visible for good seed and soil protection.

However, straw tends to blow away quickly unless it's crimped. With a square-tip transfer shovel, push the straw 4 inches down into the ground about every 12 inches to help it stay in place. Plastic netting is an alternative but has to be removed at some point and can snag animals.

A better alternative is heavier wood straw (rogueinc.us) made from beetle-killed evergreens and aspen trees by a sophisticated chipping process that creates long strips. Agricultural straw will blow away in a 20 mph wind, while the wood straw stays in place beyond 40 mph wind and doesn't require crimping. Wood straw also lasts about four years, animals won't eat it, it carries no seeds, and it has no dust.

Another option is the unsightly silt fences that consist of 36-inch stakes driven into the ground with 16-inch-tall landscape cloth stretched over wire fencing. The fencing material must be sealed at the bottom to prevent water running underneath. Silt fences are most effective on gentle slopes that won't receive heavy runoff.

Straw wattles are long, flexible tubes that can be wound along a slope and staked in place. These are less visually intrusive, a bit easier to anchor, and will eventually decompose.

Another method of erosion control is contour logging, in which burned trees are felled so that they lie along the contour of a slope. This works best with logs 6 to 10 inches in diameter and 10 to 30 feet long. Beware that trees killed by fire don't fall like live trees when cut; they are much more likely to snap and fall unpredictably. If the roots are damaged, the tree may even fall over on its own with little provocation. After the tree has been dropped (and limbed if necessary), it has to be dragged into position so that the terraces are offset. Then stakes are driven to keep it from rolling, and the log is partially buried and backfilled so water can't run underneath.

Bales of straw sometimes are placed strategically in rows to create check dams so that they can trap sediment running off from a burned slope. However, these must be staked down heavily and carefully arranged. Even after all that, they are effective only for the first couple of storms because the check dams fill with silt.

If you have dirt roads or trails below a slope, it's a good idea to build water bars to channel runoff. A good water bar has a packed-down berm a couple of inches high with a trough at the front nearly as deep. It's angled across the road to catch and direct water that otherwise would run down the road.

If culverts run under your road, you may need to clear out debris both inside and upstream that could wash down and clog the hole. If this dams up, the road could be washed out during a downpour. During the recent epic flood in Boulder (9 inches of rain in 24 hours), a 36-inch culvert clogged and created a mini-Niagara Falls over our road resulting in huge damage.

INSURANCE CLAIMS

Prepare for the battle of your life. Many people are surprised to discover that their agent, the person who sold them the policy, doesn't actually have anything to do with the claim. Instead, you'll be working with a specialist whom you've likely never met before.

Sometimes you get lucky and have a great adjustor and a good insurance provider. But there are so many horror stories of victims getting shortchanged or an endless runaround that you should go in with an abundance of caution. Expect the best and prepare for the worst. Try to start on good footing with your adjustor, even if it pains you.

If your fire claimed hundreds of houses, the major insurance companies will send specially trained large-loss disaster-response teams. For example, State Farm has a Catastrophe Team with a fleet of huge trucks and trailers equipped with satellite communication, generators, and portable offices that can set up almost anywhere. The staff knows how to process disaster claims quickly and get the process moving.

It helps immensely to start a notebook and filing system to manage the project, because you'll be dealing with massive amounts of paperwork. Consider using a three-ring binder with dividers so everything stays organized and in one place. Also create several folders for organizing receipts, correspondence, printouts of important e-mails, and research. If you don't have one, get a printer that doubles as a copier so you don't have to send in original receipts.

The first step is to find an insurance adjustor. In many states, you have the option of working with adjustors provided by the insurance company or hiring your own. Check the National Association of Public Insurance Adjustors (napia.com) for a list in your state. Check references because many "adjustors" travel to disasters from other states . . . and not all of them are honorable. Licensing requirements are vague and vary from state to state.

One reason to hire a public adjustor is continuity. After a big fire with lots of lost houses, it's common for insurance companies to rotate adjustors multiple times. A licensed public adjustor works on your behalf with all of these people in exchange for a portion of your settlement, usually about 20 percent. Their job is to get you the best settlement possible while saving you an immense amount of time.

You will be majorly stressed and perhaps not in the best frame of mind when you start working with your adjustor. Try hard not to antagonize him or her because a friendly relationship with your adjustor will make a months- or years-long process less stressful. Things may seem to move at a glacial pace from your perspective, but a friend on the inside is better than an enemy.

Never pay any fees up front to a public adjustor. When you hire one, he or she becomes a co-payee, so make sure all settlement checks come to you. Negotiate either for a flat rate or a "not-to-exceed" clause. If they don't agree to either, find a different adjustor or work with the one provided by the insurance company.

Whether or not you hire your own adjustor, get a copy of your insurance policy and read it carefully—several times if necessary. Start with the declarations page (the one with your name, amounts of coverage, endorsement codes) to grasp fully what's covered.

When your case is filed, you will receive a claim number and a coverage letter that spells out in detail what your policy covers and what's required of you. Ask your adjustor questions and get clear answers on what it all means. Have them create a timeline for when certain things will or should happen.

Keep meticulous notes of all conversations with anyone working for the insurance company or FEMA; include their name, job title, contact information, and even a supervisor's name. You will deal with many people over the course of a settlement, and they work with a lot of clients. Get anything of importance in writing and print out any significant e-mails so you also have hard copies.

The insurance company should cut you a check as an advance on the settlement so you have spending money during your evacuation. Keep *all* receipts and jot notes on the cryptic ones as reminders. Pretty much everything you buy from the moment you leave your house until you return is reimbursable, and it can really add up. Submit copies of the receipts within thirty days for full reimbursement, and mark the original as paid when paid.

If you lost your house, you're probably wishing you'd followed the advice about creating a detailed inventory in advance. Trying to recreate a list of everything you owned has often been described as "arduous," "gut wrenching," and "hateful." Without documentation, the insurance company will double-check every item claimed and may deny some of it.

Never lie when making a claim for items. If you're caught padding a claim with a Rolex watch you never owned, it's insurance fraud. This is both a felony and can null the entire claim. Huge mistake.

Beware of any adjustor who tries to rush a large settlement so you can "get paid quickly" and asks you to sign a waiver. This will often be a lowball bid and can release the insurance company from any additional liability. A thorough and fair settlement takes time and may be considerably higher.

The biggest negotiation in many cases will be over depreciation of personal property; full-replacement policies eliminate much of this headache (see Chapter 6). Despite what an adjustor may tell you, there's no set amount that an item loses in value over time. If they use a standard depreciation schedule, insist on seeing a copy because you may need to argue over amounts on major items.

If you owned high-quality gear, it often has a longer lifetime than department store products and doesn't depreciate as quickly. You may be able to show that it holds a high resale value by looking at sales histories on eBay.

If, as you complete your inventory, it becomes obvious that you're underinsured, you can try for a quick settlement. With good negotiating tactics, you might get a check for the full limit on the policy. If you're in a real hurry, you might make the headache go away by settling for 90 percent of your limit.

When you receive a check, read both sides of it carefully before depositing. If it has words like "final," "full," or "settlement" anywhere on it, you may not want to endorse it. Make sure you completely understand every word of any document that you sign. Homeowner's policies don't require that you give up legal rights to get paid. Consult an attorney before signing anything that says "release" or "waiver."

If your claim is denied, absurdly low, or dragging along at an unreasonable pace, contact an attorney who specializes in insurance. You may have to pay a contingency fee, but the results may be worth it. You can also contact your state insurance commission for assistance with getting a fair settlement.

One good source of information is United Policyholders (uphelp .org), a nonprofit that advocates for consumers on insurance problems. Their Roadmap to Recovery program has a lot of tips on disaster recovery.

After a major fire, some states will offer disaster unemployment assistance to people who don't qualify for normal unemployment benefits. This could be invaluable to the self-employed or those who can't work due to the destruction.

DAMAGED PROPERTY

When your home is damaged but not destroyed by fire, you enter a nebulous region where your ideas of what's reparable clash with your insurance company's. Start documenting everything with photos the moment you walk in the door.

We were fortunate to have an understanding adjustor who worked on our behalf. Even though the fire never touched our house, it still caused more than $20,000 of damage. We had to evac several times during the repair process when they were cleaning smoke damage and working with nasty chemicals.

Other homeowners report nightmare scenarios in which adjustors denied that an item was damaged or called it preexisting and ineligible. Major disagreements can also erupt on how much repairs should cost or what should be replaced. There can be delaying tactics to withhold payments as long as possible in the hopes that homeowners will capitulate.

Smoke damage is pernicious in that it's difficult to detect, harder to clean, and can have serious health consequences. Insurance should cover the cost of cleaning by a professional service, and I highly recommend this if available. In our case, a crew came in and wiped down every surface in the entire house. Carpets and soft furniture were cleaned professionally, and all the air ducts were vacuumed. Even after all that, we could still smell smoke months later.

Don't let the insurance company go cheap when your contract clearly calls for "like materials and quality." Patching a rug instead of replacing it doesn't cut it. An inferior appliance to what you owned is inadequate. However, this also may be the time to upgrade even though you will have to make up the difference.

When personal property is damaged, you have to document it even more thoroughly than if the house was destroyed. That's because the insurance company will give you only the depreciated value up front, so they need to know what it cost and when it was purchased. Only after you have bought a replacement and submit a receipt will you get a reimbursement for the difference (assuming you had replacement coverage).

When working on your inventory, start with the high-value collections and categories first. This is fairly easy to do if you have inventory software that lets you concentrate on big-ticket items first and not spend time on the small stuff.

If you document a loss of property at least 30 percent greater than your unscheduled and scheduled coverage, the insurance company will likely give you a check for the full amount of the policy. This is actually a better scenario because you can then purchase what you want.

If you haven't exceeded the policy limit, you only get paid if you replace something at full retail. There's no incentive to be thrifty and shop around, and you have to purchase items that you may not actually want anymore.

REBUILDING OR RELOCATING

Among your first big decisions after a total loss is whether to rebuild or to relocate. Many factors come into play here, not the least of which are how much damage was sustained to the landscape and your financial situation.

Most policies don't require that you rebuild to collect on the insurance payout. But incentives help steer you in that direction. For example, if you have extended replacement cost coverage, it might only apply if you rebuild.

You also have the option of just taking the insurance money—what's left after the mortgage is paid off—and relocating or even going on vacation. The big caveat here is that you still own the land and will need to do something with it.

Right after a fire is the worst time to sell land because the value is artificially depressed. If possible, wait a couple of years until the landscape and the neighborhood have begun to recover. You'll get a much higher return.

Most victims who go through it will tell you that the process of major repair or rebuilding a house is like having a full-time job on top of your full-time job. You have to file countless permits; make buying decisions; and schedule meetings with architects, bankers, contractors, and inspectors. You don't get paid for this other job either.

If you decide to rebuild following a major fire in which many homes were lost, get started early to beat the rush. Only so many framers and laborers are available in an area, which can lead to labor delays.

Start by selecting a reputable general contractor, who will serve as your front person on many aspects of the job. Don't necessarily use the contractor your adjustor recommends. In fact, it's probably best to avoid that person because the contractor works for you, not anyone else.

Find someone with good local references and who understands quality workmanship. If you or a friend doesn't know the contractor, verify references carefully. Letters and a website aren't good enough. Also check with the Better Business Bureau.

Look over the contract carefully and make sure you know all the costs before signing. Many people have reported getting wildly inaccurate quotes, which drove the final cost of rebuilding up (never down) more than 20 percent. Plan ahead for cost overruns and push for accurate bids that will be honored. Also establish a payment plan based on achieving specific goals; sometimes this may need to be verified by the insurance adjustor before the insurance company will cut a check.

Unfortunately, fly-by-night scammers are a reality after big disasters. They may come to a victims' aid meeting and pass out cards or come to your door (if you have one) selling their services as repairmen or contractors. Next they promise a "great deal" on a project and give some serious-sounding reason why they're so much cheaper than the other guys. They'll ask for payment in advance with some soulful story of why it's needed. Don't give them the time of day.

Local contractors likely will have worked with architects in the area and have some good recommendations. They also should know their way around the building permit system and can smooth the hassles of bureaucracy.

After a hot fire, concrete used in a home's foundation is often destroyed. This may need to be scraped away, but that will give you a clean start for a new design—assuming that ordinances don't get in the way. Sometimes the county will speed the permit process if you rebuild in the same footprint, but they still require all the other upgrades.

When an entire subdivision on the edge of a city is wiped out, such as Waldo Canyon near Colorado Springs in 2012, more infrastructure can speed the rebuilding effort; utilities can be restored faster, debris is easier to haul away on good roads, workers can move to different job sites the same day. Just one year after that fire claimed 347 homes, nearly two-thirds had been rebuilt.

More rural settings will take longer due to greater distances that delay utilities and increase travel time for work crews. In addition, there may be downed or dying trees on a lot that must be cleared just to reach the construction site.

Because many homes in Colorado and other mountain states lie at higher altitudes, you may also deal with a shorter construction window because of weather. This becomes a major issue if an insurance policy says you have only one year to rebuild—in which case, push hard for an extension. It also means surcharges for delivery of materials and logistical hassles.

Typically insurance companies prefer to pay in full only after a rebuild or major repair is complete. Until the housing market crash, contractors were able to carry the entire cost of construction until the project ended. Nowadays, they simply can't afford to wait long for payment.

To keep the project moving in a timely fashion, you may need to work out a loan with your bank. Even if you get only 60 percent of the costs up front, that's still enough to purchase building supplies and pay subcontractors. The longer it drags out, the more expensive it tends to get.

Whether rebuilding or relocating, you're also replacing everything that you owned or at least a good chunk of it. That's going to mean a lot of receipts that should be kept and organized. The home inventory software that (hopefully) you used before the fire will become even more valuable now. Because you're buying everything, it will be easy to enter it into the program as acquired. This not only lets you start a new inventory, but also gives you a wide range of reports to submit with your claims.

RESTORING LAND

Even if you do nothing, the land will recover on its own eventually. The biggest fires just hit the reset button on an ecosystem. It will come back and become more vibrant with life than before. What you *can* do is speed and shape the process.

Before a fire is fully contained, the Forest Service may send a Burned Area Emergency Response (BAER) team, which consists of about twenty-five specialists including biologists, engineers, and archaeologists. They study the effects of fire on roads and trails, soils and waterways, plants and animals.

After a few weeks, the BAER team creates a report that includes a soil burn severity map that indicates high, moderate, low, and undamaged areas. This recommends restorative actions such as slope stabilization and grass seeding. The prevention of possible flooding is a major action item in the report, so culverts may be highlighted for enlargement.

Following a forest fire, it may take five years for the understory— grasses, bushes, and flowers—to recover. Without planting, it can take trees decades to move back into a fire zone. Additional concerns for ranchers include burned pastures for grazing livestock, miles of fence line possibly destroyed, and melted water systems.

Every region has its own specifics for fire recovery, so check with your local forestry service for recommendations on particular plants and trees. The following discussion focuses on ponderosa pine–Douglas-fir forests because they form a predominant and well-studied feature in the western United States. But many of the concepts apply elsewhere. Aspen forest can regenerate quickly because their roots generate suckers (new stems).

Evaluating Trees

It's not dead yet! A heavily scorched tree still has a chance of survival. Ponderosa pines bigger than a fence post have thick bark and deep roots. On the other hand, thin-skinned trees like the Colorado blue spruce have shallow roots that can be damaged if the duff burns. Overcrowding in unmitigated forests is the bigger factor in tree mortality.

If the roots and bark are mostly intact and the canopy is less than 50 percent scorched, there's a fair chance the tree will survive. Check the buds at the end of the branches to see whether they are still flexible and don't break off easily. Give a questionable tree a few months to see if it survives.

Standing trees killed by fire are waiting to fall over. If there's a chance one will fall on somebody or block a road, cut it down. Remember that dry wood is much more brittle than wet wood and may snap sooner than expected.

The thought might cross your mind that you could sell your dead trees. The reality is that salvage logging is seldom profitable for anyone. This is due to the difficulty of removal and the lower quality of the product damaged by fire. Of course, if you have some nice hardwood trees, they could be quite valuable.

Replanting

If the fire was fast-burning, there's a good chance that many of the bushes, forbs, and grasses will come back on their own through shoots sent up by roots or rhizomes. The best course of action might be no action and letting nature take its course. However, a slow-moving, hot fire means the area may need some extensive TLC. See the "Erosion Control" section earlier in this chapter for more on selecting and planting grass seeds. If the ground was badly scorched, you may need to purchase soil and compost to give seedlings a head start.

It might be time to consider planting aspen trees instead of conifers. They have a fairly high water requirement for the first few years, but once established, aspens are fast-growing deciduous trees that look nice and are relatively fire resistant.

Look out for invasive plants, particularly noxious weeds. They encroach rapidly after a major disturbance and can soon take over an area from the native plants. If you've planted grass that's still under a few inches tall, avoid spraying weeds. Use a swing blade or string trimmer to take out the flowers before they have a chance to germinate.

Consider planting fast-growing bushes and grasses for the wildlife. Birds and animals will have lost food sources and shelter during the fire, so you could be very popular.

The Nebraska Game and Parks Commission is testing an innovative seed-dispersal solution. Their biologists have created a mixture of seeds from twelve species of trees and shrubs, molasses, and livestock minerals molded into dried blocks. The blocks are placed a quarter mile apart so that deer, elk, turkeys, and songbirds will consume them and then do their thing.

MENTAL HEALTH

Everyone relates to the stress of a wildfire differently. For some, the constant reminders can be overwhelming, and they begin to suffer from post-traumatic stress disorder (PTSD). Others will feel a powerful need to talk about the experience, but choose your listeners wisely. You may even develop survivor's guilt that you were spared while your next-door neighbors lost everything.

As you get over the trauma of the fire, it's a good time to rebuild your life for the better. As soon as possible, try to return to normal routines such as dining with friends, going to movies, and working out. Resist the temptation to self-medicate with alcohol or other drugs. It's far better to focus on a healthy lifestyle during times of stress, so make sure you get plenty of quality sleep, eat a nutritious diet, and exercise frequently.

Even though parents may take the brunt of the stress, children also suffer with life as they knew it in ashes. Younger kids may feel deep anxiety about fire returning or losing family members and friends. Teenagers may turn increasingly inward and become even more surly than normal. Parents need to recognize these problems before they become debilitating and help their children even as they help themselves.

It can be difficult for many to accept help from strangers, but your mental health is more important than stubborn pride. After the Fourmile Canyon Fire, 120 residents used free mental health vouchers at local clinics. Following a small fire in the area three years later, there was a spike in people seeking counseling. Check your health insurance policy; it's likely that mental health care is covered. An extensive list of nationwide counseling resources can be found on the family recovery page of the Arizona Firewise website (cals.arizona .edu/firewise/family.html).

Some people see a fire as a chance for a new beginning. With clutter gone, it becomes easier to focus on what's important. The aid you receive from others may surprise you.

Communities often come together after disasters for fund-raiser parties and leaning on one another's shoulders. For example, the residents of the communities affected by the High Park Fire near Fort Collins got together and had a "Stone Soup" party before the holidays in which everyone chipped in what they could for dinner and music. All the kids got presents.

RECOVERY

No matter how bad it looks, the land will recover in time. Ignorant news reporters often blather about devastated or destroyed landscapes. This hyperbole may sell newspapers, but it does nothing to inform the public about the truth. What at first may appear barren will soon teem with life.

The classic example of this is the 1988 Yellowstone fires, which blew up during a slow news cycle in late August. With nothing else to cover, reporters blew the seriousness of the fires way out of proportion and set the nation back a decade in fire science. Those fires are considered a success story today, but the lasting image in the mind of the public is still negative.

Even in the biggest, hottest fires, the entire forest is never completely sterilized. Frequently within 150 to 650 feet of badly burned areas lies relatively undamaged forest that will act as a seed bank. Areas blackened along the perimeter will soon sprout with plants from roots sending up suckers or seeds germinated by the heat.

Soon after the fire, the area will see an influx of insects, such as the fire-chaser beetle and jewel beetle. Using sensors under their legs, the former can detect fires over 80 miles away. When the beetles arrive, they lay their eggs exclusively in burned trees.

With an influx of a food supply, predators are sure to follow, looking for an easy meal. Enter the woodpeckers. One species in particular, the black-backed woodpecker, has adapted well to bug hunting after a fire. Unlike many other often brightly colored woodpeckers, these are camouflaged while on a blackened tree from the next predators up the food chain.

When trees and shrubs burn, a class of chemicals called karrikins is released that remains in the soil. These karrikins bind with a protein in seeds that in turn stimulates germination. Thus without the fire, the seeds remain dormant, and the plants have less competition.

Snowbrush ceanothus is one of those plants you may not see much of until shortly after a fire. The seeds can lay dormant for well over a century until the heat scarifies their hard coating. Once this shrub emerges, it can enhance soil recovery by fixing nitrogen for other plants to use.

Homeowners should be vigilant for invasive weeds and grasses. Often these interlopers hail from other parts of the world and can alter entire ecosystems if allowed to grow unchecked. Work with your local nurseries to reseed native wildflowers and shrubs.

Aspen trees frequently move into burned areas previously occupied by evergreens. While the seeds from lodgepole pine mostly fall within 200 feet of the tree, aspen seeds are known to cover 9 miles. When an established aspen forest burns, it can recover quickly by sprouting from the roots.

Eventually, perhaps in a couple hundred years, the more shade-tolerant evergreen trees will work back into their old territory. With a warming climate, the entire makeup of the region may also shift . . . until the next cooling period.

RECAP

If you made it this far, you have hopefully picked up a few nuggets of wisdom. Becoming Fire Smart means dealing with information overload. I've tried to condense a lot of complex topics down into digestible and actionable items. Certainly my biases and opinions have crept in so don't take this as gospel. Rather, use this book as a jumping point for making your home and family safer.

All of this boils down to doing the critical things first: Clear the immediate area around your home, get up on your roof and clean your gutters, prepare an evacuation plan, and create an inventory. After you've dealt with the majors, then work on the significant improvements such as enhancing the zone around your home, upgrading building materials where possible, and making sure your insurance is adequate.

Even if you do everything right, there are no guarantees that your home will survive a major conflagration. But you will have greatly improved your odds and at least you'll have the peace of mind knowing that you did what you could.

The key takeaway for anyone living in the Red Zone: Preparing for wildfire starts now.

INDEX